RACIALIZING JESUS

D1553874

The racial divide between East and West finds its way into biblical scholarship in a number of ways. It is particularly visible in nineteenth-century thought, where we see the construction of ancient Palestine (i.e. the Orient) and Hellenistic Greece (i.e. the origin of the West). The Hebrew/Hellene divide, along with philosophical and theological preoccupation with the Greeks, emerges out of Europe's anxiety about its own racial origins. Racial thinking helps to give shape to F.C. Baur's seminal narrative of early Christianity. Racialization finds its way into the study of the bible in the twentieth century primarily through the thought of Martin Heidegger and those who followed him.

Racializing Jesus demonstrates that crucial categories of biblical existentialism (i.e. authenticity, temporality, objectification, origins, eschatology, 'the They', parable, and allegory) are racialized, as is the narrative of early Christianity that gets constructed with the help of these categories. Heideggerian biblical scholarship (from Bultmannian demythology to American parable scholarship) contains unmistakeable traces of racial thinking, despite the best intentions of scholars who are genuinely committed to freedom and equality.

Racializing Jesus lays out all these issues for readers, showing the many subtle and complex ways in which racial thinking finds its way into biblical scholarship.

Shawn Kelley is Associate Professor of Religion at Daemen College in Amherst, New York. He is co-chair of the Synoptic Gospels Section of the Society of Biblical Literature.

BIBLICAL LIMITS

Series editors:
David Gunn, *Texas Christian University, USA*
Gary A. Phillips, *Sewanee, The University of the South, USA*

RACIALIZING JESUS

Race, ideology and the formation of modern biblical scholarship

Shawn Kelley

London and New York

First published 2002
by Routledge
11 New Fetter Lane, London EC4P 4EE

Simultaneously published in the USA and Canada
by Routledge
29 West 35th Street, New York, NY 10001

Routledge is an imprint of the Taylor & Francis Group

© 2002 Shawn Kelley

British Library Cataloguing in Publication Data
A catalogue record for this book is available from the British Library

Library of Congress Cataloging in Publication Data
A catalog record for this book has been requested

ISBN 0–415–15402–2 (hbk)
ISBN 0–415–28373–6 (pbk)

FOR MYRIAM

CONTENTS

CONTENTS

PREFACE

Race, racism, and racialized discourse; these are the topics taken up in the pages of this book. I intend to show that the racial values of modern, imperial Europe (and the United States) have found their way into the discipline of modern biblical scholarship. The remainder of the book will be dedicated to making the case for this thesis. It might be helpful, in the preface, to explain how it is that this book came to be written.

This book emerged out of an accident of reading. Early in my teaching I happened to include Elie Wiesel's *Night* and Martin Luther King's speeches in one of my introductory courses. It was my hope that the students would see that biblical themes had consequences beyond the confines of the classroom. While preparing to discuss these books I came to realize that I was unable to answer some rather rudimentary questions that were bound to arise. Why, for example, did so many white, educated Americans object to the civil rights movement? Why did King have to write "The Letter from Birmingham Jail" in the first place? Why did the Nazis think it a good idea to systematically murder the Jews, and how did they get so much support for their genocidal program? As I began to research these topics I discovered quite specific historical links between the two phenomena. The two forms of racism (American antiblack and Nazi antiSemitic) had remarkably similiar intellectual lineages: they had emerged around the same time, had followed many of the same twists and turns, and often revolved around the same ideas and texts. Most especially, both had emerged out of the relatively rarefied world of elite, learned culture and both were part of the modern project of social engineering. I was stunned by this discovery. Rather than growing out of ignorance and political manipulation, racism emerged from the very fabric of high, European culture. As someone who cherished the learned culture of the

West, I was overwhelmed to discover that racism was a product of this same culture. My dismay was heightened by the fact that, as I read about the history of modern racism, I kept coming across the names of biblical scholars (i.e. Bruno Bauer, Ernst Renan) and of philosophers who helped shape the discipline of biblical scholarship (i.e. Herder, Hegel, Heidegger).

Around the same time, I was preparing to defend my dissertation (on Acts 10–11) and was trying to plot the next stage in my career. The last thing I expected to do was to drop my own research and turn to the question of race in biblical scholarship. I was simply unable to stop reading about modern racism. I was simultaneously engrossed by the scholarship I had discovered and appalled at my own ignorance about these important topics. It was also around this time that I became engaged to Myriam Jean-Laurent, a woman from Haiti. Suddenly the question of race and its effects became for me a personal as well as an academic question. My scholarship on Acts could certainly wait a year or so while I educated myself.

As I continued to read, however, it slowly began to dawn on me that what I was reading might well prove relevant to the field of biblical scholarship. As I continued to read on the topic of modern racism, I began to suspect the following: (1) Racism is a modern ideology rather than an irrational hatred that erupts from the depth of the soul. (2) Modern biblical scholarship developed alongside this racial ideology and employed categories culled from this racial ideology. It was, therefore, possible that racism had played a role in the development of modern biblical scholarship. (3) Deconstruction might be able to play a helpful role in recognizing and unmasking the blindspots in modernity, and therefore in modern racism. These three suspicions began to haunt me, and I eventually came to realize that there was no returning to my carefully planned research path. I had an obligation, to myself and to scholarship in general, to produce an argument explaining and defending these three assumptions, or to convince myself that they were misguided.

This book also grows out of an increasing sense of intellectual curiosity. As I began to research this topic I kept coming across brilliant, thoughtful, erudite scholarship on the question of race in scholarly discourse. This scholarship had profoundly shaken a number of academic disciplines: literature, philosophy, art, music, history, law, psychology, anthropology, and even classics. While I remain indebted to all this scholarship, my thinking has been particularly influenced by two areas of inquiry: critical race theory (which gives shape to Chapter 1), and the recent scholarship exploring the relationship between Martin Heidegger and National Socialism (which gives shape to Chapter 4). Part of what I wanted to do with this book was to bring these vibrant debates to my own field of biblical scholarship.

This project, then, does not grow out of my own personal experiences. I am a white man who has lived with all the privileges that come with that status. I have never experienced the sort of subtle but pervasive racism that continues to exist in today's society. This book has instead been inspired by the fascinating books that I have read. I was riveted by the question of racialized scholarship and by the means by which other disciplines were exploring the issue. It is my hope that other biblical scholars will find the topic to be equally engrossing.

This book has been difficult to write, partly because I have discovered so much that has proven to be personally upsetting. As an undergraduate I toyed with majoring in either classics or philosophy. While I would be unduly flattering myself to pretend to be an expert in either field, I have always had warm feelings for both. I will always treasure my father's Liddell and Scott dictionary that he passed along to me when I was learning Greek. It has not been easy to discover that the fascination with all things Greek, a fascination which I share, emerged as a process of European (i.e. white) self-definition. As an undergraduate and graduate student I was fascinated by phenomenological hermeneutics and I was deeply influenced by, and moved by, the writings of Martin Heidegger. My doctoral dissertation, successfully defended a few weeks before I started thinking about this project, relied heavily on Heideggerian ideas, particularly the hermeneutical circle. It was extremely distressing to discover that Heidegger was an antiSemite, a Nazi, and a Hitler enthusiast. It was even more distressing to discover that these political views, which I detested long before I fully understood, had spilled over into his thought, which I so admired. Had they somehow spilled over into my own as well?

ACKNOWLEDGMENTS

Many people have provided me with invaluable assistance in the writing of this book. I have been fortunate enough to present sections of my argument in a number of groups and sections of the Society of Biblical Literature, especially the Ideological Criticism Section and the African-American Theology and Biblical Hermeneutics Group. I have also presented sections of my argument at the Eastern Great Lakes Regional Meetings of the SBL and at the Contemporary Biblical Hermeneutics Task Force of the Catholic Biblical Association. I am grateful to those who invited me to speak.

My colleagues in the Religion department at Daemen College have been extremely supportive. Members of my department (especially Charlie Sabatino, Jim Moran and Sherri Lyons) read sections of the book, recommended helpful texts, provided thoughtful and insightful responses to what I had written, and helped me with the topics outside of the world of New Testament scholarship. I hope that they realize the depths of my gratitude.

I am also grateful to all the students who were willing to struggle with the difficult topics raised in this book. I wish especially to thank one particular group of students. It was my privilege to teach a number of courses in the prisons of upstate New York. Each week these students, in the most trying of circumstances, engaged me in the most serious and thoughtful debate. The fact that so many of these bright prisoners are African-American reminded me that racism cannot be safely relegated to the past. I learned much from them, about the topic of race and about much else, and I wish to express my gratitude.

Much of the writing of the book occurred during a semester-long sabbatical that I received in the spring of 1998. I am grateful to Martin Anisman, President of Daemen College, and Charles Reedy, the then dean of the College (and a New Testament scholar himself) for arranging the sabbatical.

Three people provided me with research assistance: Berit Brogaard-Pederson, Anthony Moulesong, both graduate students in the philosophy department at the University of Buffalo, and Steven Klonowski, a Religion Major at Daemen College. A number of people at Daemen College also offered their support. I would like to thank in particular Dorothy Lutgen, Kitty Mahar, and Darrell Moore.

I have developed a number of dialogue partners along the way. They have asked penetrating questions, honed in on weak points in my argument, suggested thoughtful texts, and listened to my developing ideas. Of those, I would particularly like to thank Dennis Duling and Timo Eskola.

I would also like to express my gratitude to a number of people from Routledge. Richard Stoneman's support made this project possible in the first place, while Catherine Bousfield and Sangeeta Goswami helped me to bring the book to completion. I am particularly grateful to my copy-editor David Sanders, who read my manuscript with care and who made a series of insightful recommendations.

I also owe a special debt of gratitude to Gary Phillips. It was Gary who taught me New Testament scholarship as an undergraduate. Like most New Testament scholars who work in postmodernism, it was Gary who helped me grapple with postmodernist critical theory. Anyone who has worked with him knows of his intellectual rigor and his intellectual generosity. I was delighted, and somewhat relieved, to discover that he was to be my editor for this book. He has proven helpful in innumerable ways. Most especially he has helped me turn thousands of discrete and disconnected ideas into a coherent argument. It was Gary who helped me develop the book proposal and it was Gary who helped me turn my early drafts into the final form of the book. He has read a number of drafts of this book, offered innumerable helpful suggestions, has posed many thoughtful questions, and has helped me maintain my focus throughout. I am especially grateful.

I wish also to thank my parents, Paul and Barbara Kelley. They instilled in me a love of learning, encouraged me to receive a higher education, and supported me, both emotionally and financially, during college and graduate school. They have bought me computers, listened to me talk about my ideas, and encouraged me in times of doubt. My father gave me books and even read a draft of what I have written. I owe more to them than I can ever say.

Most especially I want to thank my family. My two adorable children, Melissa and Alex, have been as understanding as possible when they hear that daddy needs to work on the computer. My beloved wife Myriam has been a constant source of love and support throughout the writing of this book and has helped me maintain some sense of proportion about the whole process. She has also helped me with my French. It is to her that I dedicate this book.

Portions of Chapter 2 are reprinted by permission from *Proceedings: Eastern Great Lakes and Midwest Biblical Societies*. Copyright 1994 by Eastern Great Lakes Biblical Society and Midwest Region of the Society of Biblical Literature.

Portions of Chapter 4 are reprinted by permission from *Semeia* 77, edited by Dana Nolan Fewell and Gary A. Phillips. Copyright 1997 by the Society of Biblical Literature.

Thanks are due to the following publishers for permission to reprint passages from the following works: *The Philosophy of Hegel*, by G.W.F. Hegel, edited by C. J. Friedrich, copyright 1953, 1954 by Random House, Inc. *The Heidegger Controversy: A Critical Reader*, edited by R. Wolin, copyright 1993, MIT Press. *In Parables: The Challenge of the Historical Jesus*, by J.D. Crossan, copyright 1973 by Harper and Row. *Language, Hermeneutic and Word of God*, by R. Funk, copyright 1966 by Harper and Row. *The Classic Slave Narratives*, ed. H.L. Gates Jr., copyright 1987 by Penguin Putnam Inc.

ABBREVIATIONS

BT   Heidegger, M. (1962) *Being and Time*, trans.
J. Macquarrie and E. Robinson, New York: Harper and
Row.

CH   Baur, F.C. (1878) *The Church History of the First Three
Centuries*, 3 vols, trans. Allan Menzies, London: Williams
and Norgate.

DC   Baur, F.C. (1860) *Das Christenthum und die christliche
Kirche der drei ersten Jarhhunderte*, 2nd edn, Tübingen:
Fues.

EF   Bultmann, R. (1960) *Existence and Faith: Shorter Writings
of Rudolf Bultmann*, trans. and ed. Schubert Ogden,
New York: Meridian Books.

Essays   Bultmann, R. (1955) *Essays: Philosophical and Theological*,
trans. J.C.N. Greig, London: SCM Press.

F&U   Bultmann, R. (1969) *Faith and Understanding*, trans.
L.P. Smith, New York: Harper and Row.

HE   Bultmann, R. (1957) *History and Eschatology: The Presence
of Eternity*, New York: Harper and Row.

IP   Crossan, J.D. (1973) *In Parables: The Challenge of the
Historical Jesus*, New York: Harper and Row.

JCM   Bultmann, R. (1958) *Jesus Christ and Mythology*, New
York: Charles Scribner's Sons.

NTM   Bultmann, R. (1984) *New Testament and Mythology and
Other Basic Writings*, trans. and ed. Schubert Ogden,
Philadelphia: Fortress Press.

Paul   Baur, F.C. (1876) *Paul, the Apostle of Jesus Christ,
His Life and Work, and His Epistles and His Doctrine:
A Contribution to a Critical History of Primitive
Christianity*, 2 vols, trans A. Menzies, London: Williams
and Norgate.

Paulus   Baur, F.C. (1866-7) *Paulus, der Apostel Jesu Christi: Sein Leben und Wirken, seine Breife und seine Lehre*, 2nd edn, 2 vols, Leipzig: Fues.

PC   Bultmann, R. (1956) *Primitive Christianity in its Contemporary Setting*, trans R.H. Fuller, New York: Meridian Books.

Theo I   Bultmann, R. (1951) *Theology of the New Testament*, vol. I, trans. K. Grobel, New York: Charles Scribner's Sons.

Theo II   Bultmann, R. (1955) *Theology of the New Testament*, vol. II, trans. K. Grobel, New York: Charles Scribner's Sons.

INTRODUCTION

> Thus the Semitic race is to be recognized almost entirely by
> negative characteristics. It has neither mythology, nor epic, nor
> science, nor philosophy, nor fiction, nor plastic arts, nor civil
> life; in everything there is a complete absence of complexity,
> subtlety or feeling, except for unity.
>
> Ernst Renan

This quotation, unearthed by Martin Bernal (Bernal 346) and found
in the scholarly writings of an eminent biblical scholar, is simultaneously disturbing and revealing. These sentiments are not what one
would expect to find in a serious, scholarly work. The ideas expressed
here seem to reflect the opinions of a crank rather than the reasoned
arguments of a scholar. Renan, of course, was no crank. While this
quote seems to represent the antithesis of modern, Enlightened
rationality, it actually represented the pinnacle of the learned
opinion of the early modern period. Renan was hardly the only great
modern figure enchanted by the noble goals of modernity who also
expressed rank racial prejudices. While modernity's noble ideals
have permeated popular consciousness, the casual racism which coincides with these noble ideals has received far less attention.

A growing number of recent scholars (Appiah, Bauman, Bernal,
Fredrickson, Gates, Gilman, Gilroy, Goldberg, Gould, Stepan, Said,
West, R. Young) have examined the racial views of the pillars of
modernity and have shown that Renan is hardly alone in his ability
to maintain simultaneously the noble ideals of Enlightenment
rationality and the less than noble ideals of white, European superiority and triumphalism. The aforementioned scholars have identified the following disturbing pronouncements, all from lofty
sources.

1

- I am apt to suspect the negroes, and in general all the other species of men (for there are four or five different kinds) to be naturally inferior to whites. There never was a civilized nation of any other complexion than white, nor even any individual eminent either in action or speculation. No ingenious manufactures amongst them, no arts, no sciences. Hume (quoted in Gates 1985: 10)

- Americans (i.e. Indians) and Blacks are lower in their mental capacities than all other races. Kant (quoted in Gilman 1982: 32)

- This fellow was quite black from head to foot, a clear proof that what he said was stupid. Kant (quoted in Gates 1985: 11)

- I advance it therefore as a suspicion only, that the blacks, whether originally a distinct race, or made distinct by time and circumstances, are inferior to whites both in body and mind. Thomas Jefferson (quoted in Fredrickson 1987: 1)

- The natives are idolaters, superstitious, and live most filthily; they are lazy, drunken rascals, without thought for the future, insensitive to any happening, happy or sad, which gives pleasure to or afflicts them; they have no sense of modesty or restraint in the pleasures of love, each sex plunging on the other like a brute from the earliest age. The *Encyclopédie* (quoted in Appiah 22)

- Every Idea thrown into the mind of the Negro is caught up and realized with the whole energy of his will; but this realization involves a wholesale destruction . . . it is manifest that want of self-control distinguishes the character of the Negroes. This condition is capable of no development or Culture, and as we see them at this day, such they have always been. The only essential connection between the Negroes and the Europeans is slavery . . . We may conclude slavery to have been the occasion of the increase in human feeling among the Negroes. Hegel (quoted in Gilroy 41)

- We face a choice between sustaining our *German* intellectual life through a renewed infusion of genuine native teachers and educators, or abandoning it once and for all to the growing Jewish influence – in both the wider and narrower sense. Heidegger (quoted in Ott 378)

These sentiments are not unknown among biblical scholars, as the following quotes from Bruno Bauer reveal.

- Instead of praising the tenacity of the Jewish national spirit and regarding it as an advantage, one should ask what its basis is and where it comes from. Its base is lack of ability to develop with history, it is the reason of the quite unhistorical character of that nation, and this again is due to its oriental nature. Such stationary nations exist in the Orient, because there human liberty and the possibility of progress are still limited. Bruno Bauer (Bauer 12)
- In the Orient, man does not yet know that he is free and gifted with reason. He does not recognize freedom and reason as his real nature. He sees his highest task in the performance of mindless, baseless ceremonies. The oriental man likewise, has as yet, no history, if only that which is a development of general human liberty deserves to be called history. To sit under his vine and his fig tree, is for the oriental the highest boon man can achieve. Bruno Bauer (Bauer 13)

I argue throughout the course of this book that racism is neither accidental nor peripheral to modern thought, that it permeates the perception and reasoning of many seminal modern thinkers and modern institutions. For most modern Europeans, racism was *a morally and empirically justifiable way of thinking*. This was true for thinkers in most academic disciplines, including biblical scholarship, for most of modern history. Repulsion in the face of overt racism is a relatively recent phenomenon.

If this assessment is true, it raises a number of interesting and disturbing questions. How is it possible for racism to appear reasonable, coherent, and rational to the most careful and rigorous thinkers of the modern age? How can racism be reconciled with the modern embrace of autonomy, individuality, and freedom? Why were so many audacious and critical thinkers willing to elevate dubious racial prejudice to the status of certain knowledge? Why was racial thinking accepted by so many readers and thinkers and challenged by so few? What was it about modernity that made this sort of nonchalant racism respectable and intellectually legitimate?

Behind these questions lurks another question specifically directed to biblical scholarship: if racism is embedded deeply within the culture and political practice of modern European countries (as slavery, imperial conquests, and the Shoah imply), and if it is also embedded in the thought of the great intellectuals of the modern era (as I hope to show), is it not reasonable to assume that racist thought has also found its way into the discipline of biblical scholarship? After all, modern biblical scholarship did not emerge in a vacuum. While philosophers, theologians, and scholars have interpreted the Bible since antiquity, the critical study of the Bible took its current shape in the nineteenth and early twentieth centuries, most especially in Germany. It was within this environment that biblical scholarship's central categories were formed and that the contours of the discipline shaped. These formative years, which saw the formation and institutionalization of biblical studies, coincides with the development of a complex racial ideology which infused most aspects of political and intellectual life. Were these disciplinary movements in any way indebted to the racial ideology that was reigning in so much of modern European society? If so, how did this reigning ideology find its way into the discipline of biblical scholarship? How can contemporary critics recognize and come to terms with the traces of racist thought that might remain buried in the discipline? And, finally, how can a critique of racism be performed? On what grounds do I stand as I undertake such a critique? These are the questions which have given rise to this book.

My thesis is that modern biblical scholarship has been influenced by the category of race. The influence of race has been sometimes subtle and sometimes far from subtle.

In the first chapter I grapple with the theoretical problems posed by race. I will begin by distinguishing between the seemingly universal human problems of stereotyping and heterophobia and the specifically modern problem of racism. These terminological distinctions will allow us to begin the difficult process of thinking critically and rigorously about the topic of race. With the help of the category "discourse" I will argue that the permeable category "race" penetrates the major intellectual movements of the modern world and, in the process, gains its legitimacy by being infused into these authoritative movements. In other words, the category of race becomes widespread and legitimized because it becomes so thoroughly intertwined in widely accepted intellectual movements. This argument leads me to one of the central claims of this study. It is my contention that the major (philosophical, aesthetic, historiographical, philological) intellectual movements of the modern world have become 'racialized' (i.e. have become infused with the category of race). Modern biblical scholars carried out their work by engaging the major intellectual movements of their day. By taking up these widely accepted intellectual movements, they imported the category of race into the study of the Bible.

The remainder of the study will trace the process by which

biblical scholarship became racialized. I will focus upon the ways that modern philosophy became racialized and will trace the infusion of (racialized) philosophical ideas into the discipline of biblical scholarship. I will pay attention to three major and influential philosophical movements (Hegelianism, Heideggerianism, and Romanticism) and will explore the ways that these movements became racialized. I will then trace the ways that these philosophical ideas and systems traveled into the discipline of biblical scholarship, paying particular attention to the Tübingen school (which was deeply Hegelian), Bultmann and his students (who were explicitly Heideggerian), and the parable scholarship of Funk and Crossan (who combined Heideggerianism with Romanticism). My argument is that biblical scholarship became, and in important ways remains, racialized because it appropriates and participates in a series of racialized discourses. This has happened *irrespective of, and sometimes in opposition to, the intention* of the biblical scholar in question. I wish to be clear here. Rather than accusing individual philosophers and scholars (especially twentieth-century scholars) of being racists or antiSemites, I am arguing that modern biblical scholarship is trapped by the racialized discourse that it employs. It is this racialized discourse that has led and continues to lead the discipline into unfortunate directions. The problem, for the most part, is one of intellectual resources that permeate the discipline rather than flawed intentions of individual biblical scholars.

In the early nineteenth century, that racialized thinking began to spread throughout European culture and began to fuel the political and intellectual life of imperial Europe. The nineteenth century saw ferocious debates about racial slavery, massive imperial conquests of the Orient and Africa, and the rise of racial antiSemitism. It also saw, within the continent of Europe, the rise of a form of nationalism that took a particularly racialized turn. Chapter 2 examines the ways that these racialized political realities influenced Hegel's philosophy. I explore the way that racialized thinking took hold of his philosophy, particularly his historiography and aesthetics (i.e. his view of art, language, and myth).

As Christian monarchies began to decline in prestige, the social world of Europe needed to be placed on a new foundation, and many nineteenth-century thinkers turned to race and, in the process, racialized the way that they thought of the nation and "the people" (*das Volk*). Each people, defined linguistically, was to live on its own land and have its own unique culture. The development of a healthy people required a double move: the nurturing of an authentic, pure, uncontaminated culture; and the expulsion of that which was alien, foreign, and corrupting. This ideology emerged alongside the development of modern racism and took an explicitly racial form. It was the racially alien (i.e. the Jew, the Oriental, the African, the non-European) who was to be expelled, if an authentic people was to be created. Hegel took over the notion of the people, arguing that art, culture, and myth were ultimately reflections of the spirit of the particular people that produced them.

This idea of a racialized and nationalized people became an essential part of Hegel's narrative of world history. Hegel argued that Spirit (*Geist*) was an active force that shapes and drives history by the force of its own inner logic. Hegel's Spirit develops progressively, moving from lower to higher levels of consciousness. It also develops geographically and racially, as the levels of consciousness are assigned to particular races and particular peoples. For Hegel, Africans have no real consciousness and no culture; Orientals have lower levels of consciousness and a real, albeit backwards and despotic, culture; while Europeans, particularly the Germanic rather than Latinic peoples, are capable of the highest level of consciousness. It is the Germanic Europeans who possess the potential for authentic culture and for real freedom. At the very moment that Europeans are enslaving Africans, slaughtering natives, conquering Orientals, and demonizing the Jews, Hegel develops a narrative of world history which denies humanity to Africans and denies the consciousness of freedom to Jews and Orientals.

Chapter 3 explores the migration of Hegel's racialized views of art and of history into biblical scholarship. This occurs most especially under the influence of F.C. Baur (founder of the Tübingen school), who employs Hegel's views in his own highly influential history of emerging Christianity. While Hegel's narrative of world history culminates in triumphant modern Europe, it also devotes considerable space to the ancient world. In Hegel's narrative, the conflict between a conquering West and a conquered East is projected back upon antiquity. This is particularly visible in the way that Hegel and his contemporaries began to think about the ancient Greeks. For Hegel, and for most nineteenth-century thinkers (particularly within Germany), the Greeks represented something fundamentally new in the history of the world. With the Greeks we have the birth of the West and the triumph of Western individualism and freedom over Oriental despotism and servility. The Greeks come to symbolize freedom, individualism, and intellectual vibrancy, while the Orientals come to symbolize despotism, collectivity, and intellectual ossification. Baur takes over this fundamental antithesis between the Western (free) Greeks and the nonWestern (servile) Orientals and interjects it into the very heart of his analysis of emerging Christianity.

Baur took over Hegel's general narrative of world history, with the Jews standing in for the Orientals. In this way he combined the antiJudaism of Christian theology (where the Jew, the repudiator of Jesus, comes to symbolize the antithesis to all that is good and honorable) with the racialized Orientalism of his day. He interjected this narrative into early Christianity by arguing that the fundamental divide within early Christianity was between the (despotic, fleshly, backwards, Eastern) Jewish Christians and the (free, spiritual, dynamic, Western) Hellenistic Christians. Early Christianity, for Baur, is fueled by a conflict between Hebrew and Hellenist, which means between a slave and a free consciousness. The conflict of earliest Christianity eventually gives way to compromise, as the Western spirit of freedom makes its peace with the despotic spirit of the East and transforms itself into 'early Catholicism'. It becomes the task of radical biblical scholars to strip away the Eastern and Catholic debris that impedes access to the authentic Western core of the New Testament. The chapter concludes by showing how Baur's views quickly become the consensus position, even among those who came to reject the Hegelianism of the Tübingen school.

Chapter 4 makes the transition to the twentieth century by taking up the philosopher who has most profoundly influenced the discipline of biblical scholarship: Martin Heidegger. It is my contention that Heidegger's deeply racialized thought can best be understood in light of his enthusiasm for Hitler and for National Socialism. There has been an explosion of careful and thoughtful scholarship on the nature and significance of Heidegger's political commitments and on the significance of these commitments for his thought. Heideggerian scholarship of the late 1980s establishes that, contrary to his postwar testimony, Heidegger was deeply involved in the National Socialist movement. It also shows that he remained loyal to the regime long after his 1934 resignation from the political post of University Rector. Heideggerian scholarship of the 1990s returns to Heidegger's philosophical texts as it explores the ways that Heidegger's Nazism interjects itself into his philosophy. This recent scholarship is deeply influenced by Jacques Derrida, who is often mistakenly accused of being a pro-Heidegger apologist seeking to whitewash Heidegger's political transgressions and intellectual failings. Derrida argues that Heidegger's thought is deeply divided and contradictory, with metaphysical and authoritarian strains competing with post-metaphysical and liberatory strains. I have become convinced that Derrida's analysis is particularly helpful in identifying those moments when Heidegger's thought turns itself towards racist and fascist ideologies.

I identify four moments where Heidegger's thought opens itself up to racialization. These moments reveal his commitment to his own rather idiosyncratic version of the racialized and aestheticized ideology of organicity; the same ideology which brought racialization and aestheticized nationalism into the thought of Herder, Hegel, and Baur. Taken together, these problematic moments lead me to ask if Heidegger can continue to offer intellectual nourishment to a discipline that seeks to flourish in the multicultural world of the twenty-first century.

The first moment involves his early definition of authenticity, which occurs in his lectures on religion. This initial definition of authenticity takes over and secularizes central tenets of Christian theology and Christian antiJudaism. The second moment involves the definition of authenticity in *Being and Time*, revealed especially in his analysis of "falling" (*das Verfallen*) into "the They" (*das Man*). Here he aestheticizes and universalizes a series of oppositions that he inherits from *völkisch* nationalism (i.e. the pure, German, primordial, rooted, organic world of the peasant versus the impure, Jewified, racially mixed, rootless, inorganic world of the city). These oppositions are central to his analysis of temporality: authentic temporality reflects the values of the rooted peasants and inauthentic temporality reflects the values of the Jewified city. My analysis is buttressed by comparing and contrasting Heidegger's views with those of the father of postwar German fascism: Oswald Spengler.

The third moment involves the place of the German people in his thought. In *Being and Time* Heidegger argues that he is able to provide a proper philosophical foundation to the community (*der Gemeinschaft*) of the German people (*des Volkes*). Following Johannes Fritsche, I argue that Heidegger's argument here directly borrows from, and tries to make the philosophical case for, the emerging National Socialist movement, which sought to provide a biological ground to the community of the German people (*Volksgemeinschaft*). Heidegger does become dissatisfied with the direction of the regime, although this should not be mistaken for opposition or rebellion. After this occurs, Heidegger begins to rethink the ground of this German community. It is this reflection, which seeks to deepen rather than reject National Socialism, that leads to his analysis of poetry and to his radical engagement with antiquity (particularly with the Greeks, who, for him, are racial forefathers to the Germans). His highly influential and deeply racialized linguistic turn is part of his ongoing attempt to elevate fascism beyond the vulgar regime created by Hitler and his cohorts. This leads Derrida to ask if Heidegger's spiritual racism is less disturbing than the vulgar racism of the Hitler regime.

The fourth moment involves the question of his postwar views on the genocide. He is mostly silent on the question of the genocide, which suggests that his thinking is unable to confront some of the most disturbing questions of the age. His few, recently discovered public statements about the genocide only make matters worse. They are so shockingly insensitive to lead the philosopher Emmanuel Levinas to wonder if they do not imply a form of consent to genocide.

In the final two chapters of the book I will ask the following question: To what extent are biblical Heideggerians influenced by the values imbedded in Heidegger's thought? At this point it might be helpful to reiterate the distinction between racist individuals and racialized discourse. The former is a matter of intention while the latter can assert itself irrespective of the individual's intention. I will argue that these Heideggerian values exert a negative influence upon the work of all who take up his perspective without submitting it to rigorous ideological and deconstructive critique. This negative influence occurs in the case of those who do not share Heidegger's fondness for fascism, Germanic superiority and racialization. It even occurs in the case of those who might be repulsed by Heidegger's political and ethical values.

Chapter 5 takes up the most influential biblical scholar of the twentieth century and the figure who did the most to ensure that Heidegger's thought would find its way into biblical scholarship: Rudolf Bultmann. After discussing the relationship between the two men and the general contours of Bultmann's idiosyncratic reading of Heidegger, I turn to the ways in which Heidegger's racialized thinking finds its way into Bultmann's thought. My analysis of Heidegger identified four problematic moments that left his thought open to racialization. My analysis of Bultmann explores the ways that these four moments do and do not find their way into Bultmann's thought. I argue that many of the ideas that Bultmann appropriates from Heidegger are thoroughly racialized. This is especially the case for authenticity, temporality, and "the They"; three of Bultmann's ideas that are deeply Heideggerianized and deeply racialized.

Authenticity is the linchpin of Bultmann's Heideggerianized and racialized thought. Bultmann translates Heideggerian authenticity to the New Testament by means of what I will come to call an "existential morality tale". In this narrative of authentic existence, life consists of three crucial moments: habitual inauthenticity, existential encounter, slothful fall back to inauthenticity. When this tale is historicized, early Christianity comes to have three phases: late Judaism (of the Second Temple period, especially the Pharisees), Hellenistic Christianity (especially of Paul), early Catholicism (especially of Luke–Acts). These three moments are defined with the help of traditional antiJudaism, Heideggerian racialization, and Tübingen's racialized narratives of world history and of early Christianity. Late Judaism is Eastern, despotic, servile, inauthentic, and legalistic. It seeks security and boasts of its relationship to God, even if its experience of God is in the past rather than in the present. Pauline Christianity is Western, free, authentic, and open to radical insecurity. In it God is experienced authentically, in the present. Early Catholicism, especially in Luke–Acts, trades in the radical insecurity of eschatological urgency for the security of salvation history. As a result it turns Jesus into a figure from the past, obscuring the power of the gospel. It is the task of the radical critic to see through the debris of centuries of misreading and to restore the primordial, Hellenistic core of the gospel. It is this critical reading of the gospel which will make possible true freedom in the modern age.

If Bultmann takes over Heidegger's thinking, he parts ways with him on the question of National Socialism. Heidegger enthusiastically joined the Nazi party and did all he could to see to it that their ideas took hold throughout the universities and the nation. Bultmann, who joined the Confessing Church, was one of the rare German intellectuals who did not publicly support the regime. At the same time, his critique of Nazism was shaped by his racialized and Heideggerianized intellectual resources, which saw the elimination of the alien as an essential act in bringing about freedom. The question becomes: can Bultmann articulate a critique of Nazism that is free from the racialized framework of his intellectual resources? Does his discourse, which is deeply indebted to racialization, stand in the way of his honorable intentions to criticize Hitler's radically racist regime?

Chapter 6 takes up American parable scholarship of the 1960s and 1970s, particularly as carried out by Robert Funk and J.D. Crossan. This scholarship seeks to show that American scholars can intervene in the debates that were then raging inside Germany. The particular debate that was taken up involved the work of Bultmann's students (the "New Hermeneutic"). The New Hermeneutic sought to improve upon Bultmann's demythologizing program by appropriating the later Heidegger's views on language and poetry. In the process, American parable scholarship became deeply intertwined with the very views that are most closely linked with Heidegger's National Socialism. The question that I pose is this: What happens when Heidegger's particularly Germanic ideas (i.e. his *völkisch* nationalism, aestheticized racialization, Greco-Germanic identification, and racial antiSemitism) get translated to the American context?

It is Funk's classic study of the parables (*Language, Hermeneutic and Word of God*) that renders accessible the theoretical reflections of the New Hermeneutic. It is a work which is very much in dialogue with the demythologizing program of Bultmann, and it goes a long way towards infusing Bultmann's ideas into the fabric of American biblical scholarship. Funk takes over, without modification, many of Bultmann's racialized ideas: his existential anthropology, as well as his views on authenticity, temporality, and "the They". Funk also modifies Bultmann's position by raising, with the help of the later Heidegger, the question of language. For Funk, it is objectified and degraded language (rather than objectifying wordviews) that brings about inauthenticity, as the parables become the primary example of authentic religious language. It is this Heideggerianized (and Bultmannized) theoretical framework which provides the seminal parable scholarship of Funk and Crossan with its fundamental, and fundamentally racialized, presuppositions and interpretive framework.

Crossan takes over Funk's framework and makes two major additions, both of which are relevant to the question of the racialization of biblical scholarship. First, he analyzes poetic experience, poetic writing, and poetic reception with the help of a thoroughly Romantic aesthetic. While the development of an aesthetic does fill in a void in Funk's position, Crossan's Romanticism further chains biblical scholarship to the aestheticized and racialized ideology of organicity. We should remember that this is the very ideology, and the very set of aesthetic values, which permeate the thought of Herder, Hegel, and Heidegger. Second, Crossan categorizes the parables around Heidegger's (racialized) temporal care structure. For Crossan there are three modes of the Kingdom's temporality, and they match the threefold movement of Heidegger's temporality and Bultmann's existential morality tale. The Advent parables offer an existential encounter that shatters the inauthentic world of conventionality; the Reversal parables call us out of that world, revealing the radical insecurity of existence; and the Action parables make possible the decision to live authentically, without the security of ethics and programs.

Taken together, Funk and Crossan translate the existential core of the New Testament from Bultmann's Pauline kerygma to the authentic word of the parables. In so doing, they also ensure that Jesus' teachings will be understood through the eyes of Heidegger's racialized thinking. American parable scholarship will take over wholesale Heidegger's racialized narrative of origin and fall, as well as his racialized categories (i.e. "authenticity", "the They", "temporality"). Even as Crossan challenges the religious and racial chauvinism of New Testament scholarship, the intellectual resources that permeate his parable scholarship remain deeply indebted to the category of race.

In the Conclusion, I ask about the possibility of escaping from the problem of racialization. Throughout the book I argue that the problem is one of discourse rather than intention. My central argument is that the biblical scholars discussed throughout the book (especially the twentieth-century ones) are trapped by their intellectual resources. Part of the task of the Conclusion, then, will be to identify those aspects of mainstream biblical scholarship that are most problematic. I do so by distinguishing that which can be discarded (i.e. those arguments and perspectives that the discipline should learn to do without) from that which can be profitably reconfigured (i.e. those topics that are essential to the study of the Bible, but which have been defined in a problematic manner).

This gesture (i.e. discarding, redefining) will go a long way towards addressing the problem of racialization within the discipline. It is my contention that racialized resources have prevented many biblical scholars from creating the sort of liberatory critical practice that they explicitly endorse. If the problem is one of resources, then the solution comes in finding a new ground for future biblical scholarship. Much current biblical scholarship offers a promising start towards developing a new, nonracialized ground for New Testament studies. The last two decades have witnessed a variety of new methodologies, new historical perspectives, and new forms of ideological critique. This new scholarship has gone a long way towards challenging the theoretical and exegetical framework of traditional scholarship. My argument implicitly poses the following question to these new methodologies and movements: Are these innovations sufficient to make it possible for biblical scholarship to free itself from racialization? I wrap up the book by reflecting upon this question.

1

RACIALIZED DISCOURSE

Modernity, race, and reason

> The problem of the twentieth century is the problem of the
> color line – the relation of the darker to the lighter races of
> men in Asia and Africa, in America and the islands of the sea.
> W.E.B. DuBois, *The Souls of Black Folk*

Recent biblical scholarship has been quite successful in exploring
antiJewish or sexist sentiments within the New Testament and
within modern scholarship. Few contemporary scholars continue to
hold that the Jews are guilty of deicide (see Brown 383–397; Crossan
1995: 147–159) or that all the innovative leaders of the primitive
Church were male. This is all for the good, and my own research
would not have been possible without the pioneering work of people
like Krister Stendahl, Rosemary Reuther, E.P. Sanders, and
Elisabeth Schüssler Fiorenza. My own work is deeply indebted to
theirs. Yet purging offensive material and correcting mistaken ideas
represent only part of the process of settling accounts with a troubled past. If we wish to reckon with the post-Auschwitz, post-Civil
Rights moral and religious imperative, we need to pay as much
attention to modern racism as we do to Christian hostility to the
religion of Judaism and male oppression of women. We need to
identify those forces which made racial atrocities both conceivable
and possible. This is an important part in the discipline's unfinished
attempt to come to terms with the Holocaust and American racism.
Many contemporary biblical scholars wish to engage the ethical
issues raised by Auschwitz, by the end of colonial occupation, and
by the dissolving of Jim Crow racism. This book intends to engage,
in a systematic and rigorous manner, the relationship between
modern racism and modern biblical scholarship. This particular
chapter analyzes, in general and theoretical terms, the interrelation

14

between race, ideology, and modernity. This analysis makes the case for the existence of a relationship between modern biblical scholarship and modern racialized discourse and sets the stage for my argument that the scholarly study of the Bible and of antiquity is intertwined with the racialized and often bloody encounter between Europe and the rest of the world.

Human history is replete with examples of petty hatred, bloody conquest, and economic exploitation. Ruthless exploitation seems to be ubiquitous enough to be considered virtually universal. Given this, racism seems to be yet another symptom of human cruelty and misery that, like poverty, will always be with us. Allow me to begin with an assertion that runs contrary to this common-sense conclusion. It is my contention that, rather than being a universal human temptation, racism is a particularly modern phenomenon. In order to demonstrate this claim, it is important to distinguish between heterophobia, stereotype, and racism (see Bauman 1989: 62–82; Fredrickson 1988: 189–193, 206–215; 1987: 1–3; Goldberg 90–147).

Heterophobia is generic fear of the other. Bauman defines it as "that diffuse (and sentimental rather than practical) unease, discomfort, or anxiety that people normally experience whenever they are confronted with such 'human ingredients' of their situation as they do not understand, cannot communicate with easily and cannot expect to behave in a routine, familiar way" (1989: 64). This unease is, according to Bauman, a manifestation of anxiety arising out of finding oneself in a situation that can be neither controlled nor influenced (ibid.). "Heterophobia may appear as either a realistic or irrealistic objectification of such anxiety – but it is likely that the anxiety in question always seeks an object on which to anchor, and that consequently heterophobia is a fairly common phenomenon at all times" (ibid.). In modern society, this anchor is often a racial, ethnic, or national "other", although the otherness could also be found almost anywhere.

By *stereotype* I mean preconceptions about a particular group which are then applied to members of that group. Stereotypes can be applied to ethnic groups, to racial groups, to a particular physical type, to an occupation, to religious affiliation, to a nation, or even to a smaller local region. Stereotypes are usually thought of as negative, but they need not be so (e.g. a particular group can be viewed as hardworking and loyal). Stereotypes can be exaggerations based on common observations, but often have little to do with the actual behavior of the group in question. Furthermore, while stereotypes can be idiosyncratic, more often than not they are widely held and are manifested throughout different levels of society. Most homophobes and antiSemites, for example, have had little actual experience with homosexuals or Jews. It is highly unlikely that one would conclude, based on observing Jewish behavior, that they are parasites dedicated to the destruction of the world economy. These and other stereotypes remain widespread and fairly stable for long periods of time, despite the best efforts of Jewish or homosexual civil rights groups. Such widely held, elaborate, inaccurate, and speculative stereotypes are hardly the product of direct observation or of ignorance. They must originate elsewhere in the culture at large rather than in the agitated mind of the cruel or the ignorant. Given this, then, we can follow George Fredrickson in arguing that stereotypes tell us little about those defined by the stereotype but tell us a great deal about those doing the defining (see Fredrickson 1988: 207). So, for example, contemporary homophobia tells us little about the lived experience of homosexuals, but tells us a great deal about the sexual anxieties of homophobes and of the culture at large.

Fredrickson also points out that widely held stereotypes are often irresolvably contradictory. For example, pro-slavery literature often defined black men both as loyal, contented children and as bloodthirsty savages wanting to murder their masters and rape their mistresses (1988: 208). In the same way, Nazi intellectuals defined Jews both as capitalists and as anticapitalist socialists (see Katz 82–93). These competing stereotypes were applied to the same population, but were trotted out in response to varying social factors. So, for example, the image of the slave as bloodthirsty savage appeared in the immediate aftermath of a revolt, while the image of the contented child appeared in the aftermath of abolitionist criticisms of the cruelty of slave-owners.

Modern *racism* is related to heterophobia and stereotyping, both of which played an important role in the origins and function of modern racism. At the same time, racism should not be collapsed into the other two terms. Racism emerged in the early modern period, became systematized in the early nineteenth century and spread throughout the intellectual and political worlds of nineteenth- and twentieth-century Europe (and its colonies) and America (and its colonies). Racism covers a dizzying array of topics, beliefs, social arrangements, and political practices. Despite this diversity, nineteenth- and early twentieth-century racisms did share a relatively stable structure that permeated the thought of virtually all their adherents. Virtually all modern racists assume that all of humanity can be classified as one of a few races; that this racial classification defines physical structure, intellectual ability, moral acumen, and cultural content; that racial identity is stable, unchanging and of fundamental significance for all members of the race; and that racial identity establishes natural and proper social status. As a result, racism also establishes a social hierarchy which is strictly enforced through a variety of means: from violence to legislation and the courts. It is legitimated by intellectual elites, and it permeates both elite and popular culture. As a result, it is widely accepted by the general population, particularly by those parts of the population who benefit from the social hierarchy.

Despite these structural similarities, modern occurrences of racism do vary significantly from each other. Racists agree that the races can be classified and that the classification reveals something essential about the group in question, yet there is significant disagreement on the content of the classification and on the proper borders between groups. Racism did establish social hierarchies, but the hierarchies varied over time and from place to place. The social practices and the intellectual support varied along with the form of racism that was dominant. This diversity makes it difficult to define the term "racism". Definitions which start with a particular topic (such as antiblack racism) have difficulty explaining other topics (e.g. radical antiSemitism), and definitions which start with a particular practice (such as genocide) have difficulty explaining other practices (e.g. slavery). The challenge, then, is to develop a way of thinking about racism which is concrete enough to recognize its existence and potency but which is also flexible enough to account for its diversity in beliefs and in practices.

David Goldberg has offered the most rigorous attempt at addressing the theoretical and definitional problems that arise in coming to terms with the category of race. He makes the persuasive argument for thinking of race with the help of Foucault's category of a "field of discourse" (see Foucault 1972: 21–76; Goldberg 41–60). It is the field of discourse that establishes the objects (i.e. antiblack racism, racial antiSemitism) and that establishes the rules of expression (i.e. what is said about slaves or about Jews). What is said in the name of race takes a variety of forms and is expressed in a variety of modes (academic, legal, cultural, political, for example), but it is governed by and functions within a larger field of discourse (Goldberg 52–56). While the objects and the rules of expression change over time, the field of discourse that renders them possible remains stable.

17

The fact that "race" is fluid and that it functions within a larger discourse leads us to one of its most enigmatic aspects: its permeability. Goldberg argues that "*race* is chameleonic and parasitic in character: It insinuates itself into and appropriates as its own mode more legitimate forms of social and scientific expression" (Goldberg 107). The category of race does not so much exist alongside other foundational aspects of modernity, as it penetrates these foundational aspects and gains its legitimacy from them. Having penetrated the foundation of modernity, it permeates and infuses itself into modern forms of knowledge and modern culture. The discourse of modernity makes possible the category of race, and the category itself renders modern discourse racialized. For these reasons, this book will employ the term *racialized discourse* to signify the discursive field out of which racism emerges and the discursive statements that have been infused with the category of race. My argument will be that we can best come to terms with the functioning of race in the modern world by examining the way that race has infused itself into modern categories and terms. This study will explore the ways in which the thought and ideas employed by biblical scholars have become racialized.

Let us return to the question of the relationship between heterophobia, stereotypes, and racism. It may well be the case that heterophobia and stereotyping are universal human phenomena, that humans are naturally afraid of those with whom they are unfamiliar and that humans tend to approach the unfamiliar with the help of stereotypes. It may well be the case that the process of natural selection produces heterophobia and that the human mind necessarily appeals to stereotypes. It is also possible that heterophobia, the generic fear of the other, is exaggerated and inflamed by racial classification and by racial hostility. A number of theorists argue that racial stereotypes both predate systematic racism and later come to permeate racist societies and racialized ideologies (especially Anderson 51–61; Fredrickson 1988: 191–194; Gilman 1982; Hood 26–43; Said 1979: 55–73). Racial stereotyping, and the prejudices produced by this stereotyping, do play an important role in the practical functioning of systematic racism. There is a complex relationship between genuine racism, on the one hand, and heterophobia and stereotyping, on the other hand.

At the same time, we should not reduce racism to another example of fearing or exploiting the stranger. Heterophobia may be an unfortunate but inevitable human reaction to the unknown. It may also necessarily attach itself to unfamiliar groups and individuals. But it is not necessarily the case that it manifests itself in the face of people with different skin color, instead of, say, different hair color, different height or people who speak different languages. In the same way, stereotyping may be inevitable, but it need not be based on skin color. Many societies held nonracial stereotypes about Africans and Jews. Stereotyping and heterophobia may predate racism, but they do not necessarily produce racism. There is no necessary relationship between stereotypes and racism, no inevitable progression from heterophobia and stereotyping to racism.

Furthermore, if we collapse these three terms together, we lose sight of what is most particular, most distinctive, most enduring, and most pernicious about racism. Failure to distinguish between stereotyping and racism ends up denying racism's power, misdiagnosing its place in modernity, and trivializing its negative effects. As I will demonstrate in the next section, much public discussion of race and racism fails to distinguish between these terms and, therefore, fails to come to grips with genuine power that racialized discourse has exerted and continues to exert in popular culture and in the elevated world of scholarship and elite culture. With this in mind, let us distinguish the approach taken in this study from some other common methods of addressing the problem of racism.

Current theories on race

> The truth is that there are no races: there is nothing in the world that can do all we ask race to do for us . . . Talk of "race" is particularly distressing for those of us who take culture seriously. For, where race works . . . it works as an attempt at metonym for culture, and it does so only at the price of biologizing what *is* culture, ideology.
>
> Kwame Anthony Appiah, *In My Father's House*

One possible way to approach the problem of racism is to accept "race" as a legitimate, biological category and to accept racial differentiation as an intellectually sound practice. This perspective posits the existence of a few large groupings of human society, and further assumes that these racial groupings tell us something essential about the members within this grouping. While this perspective reigned throughout most of the modern era, it has fallen out of favor within the past thirty years, for both political and scientific reasons. The political reasons are well known. The centuries-long abuse of nonwhites by the Euro-American imperial powers, punctuated by the Nazi genocide, did much to delegitimize the category of race. The post-war civil rights and decolonization movements completed the process of challenging the legitimacy of the category of race. The political contamination of the category coincided with, and helped influence, changes in the scientific approach to race (see especially Barkan 228–340). A recent issue of the journal *Discover*, which was dedicated to race, synthesized the current scientific consensus on the question. The editor of the journal, Paul Hoffman, argues that race is less than helpful in explaining human diversity.

> What is clear is that the genetic differences between the so-called races are minute. On average there's .2 percent difference in genetic material between any two randomly chosen people on Earth. Of that diversity, 85 percent will be found within any local group of people – say between you and your neighbor. More than half (9 percent) of the remaining 15 percent will be represented by differences between the ethnic and linguistic groups within a given race (for example, between Italians and French). Only 6 percent represents differences between races (for example, between Europeans and Asians). And remember – that's 6 percent of .2 percent. In other words, race accounts for only a minuscule .012 percent difference in our genetic material.
>
> (Hoffman ed. 4)

As James Shreeve explains in the same issue, there are morphological differences (i.e. teeth, hair, skin color, body shape) between various groups, but they function independently of each other (Shreeve 58). As Jared Diamond argues, scientists could classify people by antimalaria genes, lactasse, fingerprint patterns, or skin color. Each method would produce radically different configurations completely disconnected from geography. Biologically, there is no more reason to group Swedes with other Europeans than with Africans, or with American Indians, Italians, and New Guineans; it all depends upon which biological criteria become essential to the classification system (Diamond 83–89).

The furor created by the reactionary book *The Bell Curve* has done little to relegitimate this problematic category. A category which had for centuries been accepted by most modern intellectuals in the human, the social, and the natural sciences has, for the most part, fallen out of favor in all of them. Race tells us virtually nothing important about the biological reality of either individuals or larger groups.

There are some who wish to retain the category of race but who also wish to reject the hierarchical structure associated with European racism. This is certainly a minority position in the contemporary academic landscape, but it continues to find a hearing among some racially defined liberation movements. The question yet to be answered here is as follows: is it possible to rehabilitate the concept of race without implicitly accepting the intellectual and political flaws inherent in nineteenth-century racism? Or, does the category of race necessarily commit us to intellectually and politically dangerous positions *despite the best intentions of the interpreter?*

A second, antithetical way to approach the problem is to deny the reality of race entirely, rejecting it as an irrational prejudice that is intellectually groundless (Goldberg 5–6). This is the position of contemporary liberal humanism, which rejects race as a particular which has been falsely elevated to the status of human universal. A particularly lucid example of this position is offered by Luc Ferry and Alain Renaut, who argue, in their criticism of Martin Heidegger's philosophy, that "racism can never be a humanism" (Ferry and Renaut 4–5). They conclude that "it is only through abstract universality that we can get away from all the particularisms whose absolutization in the form of a *false universal* leads to the plan of exclusion and even extermination" (Ferry and Renaut 5, italics theirs). This view tends to see the modern examples of racism (i.e. imperial conquest, slavery, and the holocaust) as irrational, depraved outbursts of violence. As such they are antithetical to civilization and can only be rooted out by the modern, rational, civilizing process. From this perspective, the problem is an excess of irrational barbarism and a paucity of humanism and civilized tolerance. This view does not deny that modern societies have often failed to live up to the noble ideals of enlightened humanism, but it does deny that this failure invalidates the ideals themselves. What is required is the completion of the modern, Enlightenment project, with human rights applied to white women and to nonwhite women and men.

While this position is certainly more attractive than the first, and while it seems like a logical outgrowth of the rejection of the first, it is not without its problems. In the first place, the very act of declaring race philosophically irrelevant has the unfortunate effect of expunging race from the current dialogue, making it very difficult to explore the degree to which racism has permeated and continues to permeate the modern intellectual and political world. Furthermore, it does not allow for the possibility that modern, humanist ideals and educational practices were influenced by modern racism, nor does it allow for the possibility that these ideals and practices might have significantly *contributed to* the origins of and legitimacy of racial ideology. It is my contention that racism was carried out *in the name of* humanism, reason, and enlightenment. Goldberg explains this process in the following way:

> Now it can be shown that just as ideals of rationality are gender constructed as predominantly male, so, too, are they racially constructed as exclusively white. Historically, various sorts of racially defined non-Europeans, and more recently "non-Westerners", have been excluded on racial grounds from membership (or at least full membership) in the human species. In large measure, the grounds for these exclusions have been Reason itself, or more precisely, the claimed absence of Reason on the part of the excluded.
>
> (Goldberg 118)

Racism, as distinguished from heterophobia and stereotyping, grows out of modern modes of rationality.

Furthermore, the humanist, color-blind position has a hard time reconciling itself with the actual values of most of the major figures of traditional humanism. It may be the case that humanism should reject racism, but it is also the case that most of those who defined humanism in its formative years held racist views. If we expunge Kant, Jefferson, Hume, and the Enlightenment's *Encyclopédie* from the category "humanism", then we have redefined the term "humanism" out of meaningful existence.

While race may not reflect biological reality, it does have a very potent historical, political, and social reality. Race may be rejected by modern science (and rightly so), but it has played an extremely important role in the development of modern thought and in the construction of modern society. The humanist (i.e. "color-blind") perspective, alluring as it is, does not provide a way of recognizing and engaging this complex history of racial discourse and oppressive practice. It does not provide a way to explain the historical preoccupation with race in European and American society. It does not provide a way of explaining the horrendous social and political practices carried out in the name of race and in the name of reason. While it sees race and racism as a philosophical error, it is unable to explain how it emerged, how it found its way into modern thought, and why it remained so potent for so long. This position is certainly morally praiseworthy, but it has the unexpected effect of preventing contemporary Euro-American thought from settling accounts with its racist past.

The most interesting variation on the humanist analysis of race has come from African-American intellectuals and activists. A number of intellectuals and activists, both famous (Frederick Douglass, W.E.B. DuBois, Martin Luther King) and less famous (Benjamin Banneker, George Moses Horton, Frances Ellen Walker Harper) have confronted and criticized the practice of racism from the perspective of the more noble ideals of modern Europe. The most common, and persuasive, tactic is to contrast the ideals of the Bible (usually as interpreted through the lens of the abolition movement and the black church) and the Declaration of Independence with the casual yet brutal racist practices of slavery and legalized segregation. For these thinkers, there is a tragic contradiction between thought and practice, an appalling hypocrisy that threatens to delegitimize the noble ideals of Christian freedom, as defined by the abolition movement and black churches. Frederick Douglass, to cite one particularly eloquent example, deplores racialized slavery as "mere bombast, fraud, deception, impiety, and hypocrisy – a thin veil to cover up crimes which would disgrace a nation of savages" (Douglass 1993: 160). He indicts racialized slavery, "in the name of humanity", "in the name of liberty", and "in the name of the Constitution and the Bible" (158). While there is much justification in the charge that religious slaveholders were hypocrites, this potent political accusation does little to help us identify racism's origins and enduring power. Whatever the genuine success of the humanist position, it is unable to shed a great deal of light on the nature of modern racism.

Racialized discourse: race as a social construct

Race remains a particularly vexing category. It seems to have no intellectual grounding or legitimacy, yet it has negatively impacted the lives of millions of people for hundreds of years. It is now accepted by very few serious intellectuals, yet for most of the modern era it was accepted by virtually all serious intellectuals in virtually all academic and religious disciplines. We have thus reached a bewildering paradox: if we accept the reality of race then we may be on the slippery slope towards legitimizing racism, yet if we deny its reality we become powerless to confront it. If we wish to get anywhere in our discussion we need to find a way to recognize the historical centrality of race without falsely elevating race as a biological category. We need to take race seriously without giving in to racial thinking. We need, in short, to look at race as a social and intellectual *construct*. Following the work of Michel Foucault, I shall attempt to define race's emergence as a category, its dissemination throughout various academic disciplines and political institutions, and its permutations and variations. Foucault explains the procedure well:

> The analysis of the discursive field is oriented in a quite different way (from traditional history of ideas); we must grasp the statement in the exact specificity of its occurrence; determine its conditions of existence, fix at least its limits, establish its correlations with other statements that may be connected to it and show what other forms of statement it excludes.
>
> (1972: 28)

This study will establish race as a social construct by analyzing the interconnection of race and modernity.

In undertaking this analysis of race as a construct, I will be relying heavily on the critical perspective pioneered by Edward Said. Said is as opposed to racism and imperialism as a Frederick Douglass or a Martin Luther King, Jr., but he combines his political commitment with enough theoretical sophistication to allow him to trace the precise ways that racism permeates high European culture. Said is widely read in postmodern and poststructuralist theory and is deeply engaged in the issues raised from within these theoretical perspectives. He helped identify a way in which postmodernism could be intellectually sophisticated and politically engaged, challenging the prevailing leftist complaint about the a-political nature of postmodernism.[1]

Said developed his theoretical framework in the essays collected in the volume *The World, the Text, and the Critic*, especially in "Criticism Between Culture and System", and applied the theory in the magnificent volume *Orientalism*.[2] Shortly after the publication of *Orientalism*, there appeared Sander Gilman's widely read volume entitled *Essays on the Image of the Black in Germany*. Gilman confirmed Said's thesis about the dissemination of racist thought into the very fabric of high European culture. These theorists further verified the analysis which had already been produced on American racism (Winthrop Jordan, George Fredrickson) and on European antiSemitism (George Mosse, Leon Poliakov), adding theoretical sophistication to the rigorous historical documentation that was already available. An outpouring of insightful scholarship followed quickly, demonstrating the extent to which racism permeated modern Christianity (Cornel West), modern science (Elazar Barkan, Stephen Gould, Nancy Stepan), and modern feminism (bell hooks). Other scholars sought to show that racism provided the context out of which Afrocentrism's Africa was constructed (Anthony Appiah), against which African-American literature was produced (Henry Louis Gates, Jr.), against which Freud and Kafka wrote (Sander Gilman) and, most provocatively, against which the discipline of classics was constructed (Martin Bernal). David Goldberg recently published a fine study clarifying the theoretical issues raised by post-modern racial analysis. Virtually every academic discipline has had the opportunity to re-examine its fundamental working assumptions in light of the recent critical analysis of modern racism. Unfortunately, biblical scholarship and theology are exceptions to this rule. This study seeks to fill in this void.

Despite the diversity of topics, this recent scholarship shares one major conclusion: modern acts of racial exclusion and violence were consistent with the fundamental principles and beliefs of modernity and were an essential outgrowth of modernity. It was during the modern era that racism was transformed from a common prejudice into an authoritative ideology, and even into scientific knowledge. It was also during this time that racism prepared the way for and then rationalized European colonial conquest. At the start of the nineteenth century, Europe had colonized 35 per cent of the non-European world, yet by the beginning of the First World War, after a century in which racism spread into the academic disciplines, Europe had colonized 85 per cent of the world (Said 1979: 39–41). The same century also witnessed an increase in the most brutal mistreatment of the African slaves and former slaves and the rise of racial antiSemitism to complement the loathsome antiJudaism of Christian history. The nineteenth century was a time of vast social engineering, fueled by the widely held category of race. We should also note that this is the formative period of modern biblical scholarship, when its categories were developed, when seminal theories were proposed and debated, and when methods were developed and institutionalized. Is it possible that biblical scholarship could exist untouched by the ideological context during which it was conceived?

The history of the category of "race"

> It will be necessary not only to rethink the fundamental bases
> of "Western Civilization" but also to recognize the penetra-
> tion of racism and "continental chauvinism" into all our
> historiography, or philosophy of writing history.
>
> Martin Bernal, *The Black Athena*

The category of race existed in neither the ancient nor the medieval world.[3] While the ancient and medieval world managed its fair share of hatred and exclusion, this hatred and exclusion was either cultural (against the "barbarian") or religious (against the Jew or Muslim) rather than racial (against the "Oriental" or "Savage", see Appiah 47–50; Bauman 1989: 31–83; Goldberg 18–24). Frank Snowden, Jr., has conducted extensive research into the material and symbolic place of dark-skinned Africans ("Ethiopians") in the Greco-Roman empire and concludes that prejudice based on skin color did not exist. He argues that dark-skinned Africans were present in later antiquity in large numbers and in diverse roles (Snowden 1970: 183; 1983: 63–103; see also Bailey 1991: 170–183 and, for a dissenting view, Hood 32–43). Their presence ensured that they were common figures in the cultural world of the time. It is significant, therefore, that they were treated "without rancor", even during times of mili-tary conflict (Snowden 1983: 56). Ethiopians might have become an easily recognizable type, yet the stereotypes were mostly positive. Ethiopians were seen as good, brave, pious, wise, and as lovers of freedom and justice (ibid.). More importantly, the classical period attaches no stigma to color and there is no evidence in antiquity of a well-developed theory of race. There may have been stereotypes employed about dark-skinned Africans, but the stereotypes were in no way *racial*. Ethiopians were another ethnic group, but were not fundamentally different from those with lighter skin, and whatever differences were recognized had nothing to do with skin color.

In the Middle Ages, dark-skinned Africans were largely absent from the European continent and negative stereotyping became more common. Within the economy of Christian theology, darkness became associated with madness and/or evil (Fredrickson 1988: 191–193; Gilman 1982: 14–16). Such distasteful stereotyping may have foreshadowed and contributed to later racism, but it neither produced nor can it be directly identified with modern racism. These stereotypes produced no political or economic exploitation and inspired no oppressive legal hierarchies. The negative characteristics were not seen as permanent and unchanging, were not systematically developed, and were not consistently distributed throughout the intellectual and cultural world. Within Christian Europe, non-Europeans were identified as infidels rather than as dark-skinned.

The English word race was first used in 1508, but was not applied to human beings until 1580 (Goldberg 63). Racism emerged in the late fifteenth century, in reaction to the voyages to the New World. These were voyages of discovery of seemingly unconquered land filled with inestimable wealth, natural resources, and exotic and antagonistic creatures (Goldberg 44; Shreeve 60). The voyagers assumed that there were clear links between the dark skin color of these creatures and their seeming savage nature. The conquest of the continent, combined with the African slave trade, facilitated the development of modern racism (see Bernal 201–204), every bit as much as it facilitated the emergence of capitalism. This process was furthered by the form of slavery that began to emerge in the New World. New World slavery was economically lucrative in a way that European serfdom was not, and, as a result, New World slavery was better integrated into the emerging capitalist system than economic serfdom (Fogel 22).

This new economic structure led to the creation of new internal social arrangements. It also led to the creation of a new intellectual order which would make sense of the emerging material and social order. This new economic, social, and intellectual order is what is commonly called *modernity*. Goldberg defines modernity as follows:

> By modernity I will mean . . . that general period emerging from the sixteenth century in the historical formation of what only relatively recently has come to be called "the West". This general self-understanding becomes self-conscious in the seventeenth century, reaching intellectual and material maturity in the Enlightenment, and solidifies as Western world hegemony the following century.
>
> (Goldberg 3)

Most especially, the modern world is marked by the unique social and political structures of European societies. The dissolving absolutist feudal system, and the theological perspective that supported it, were replaced by capitalism and European imperial conquest. For Europeans, it meant a new set of economic practices, and, therefore, a change in the legal and political structure of society. As capitalism and democracy replaced absolutism and feudalism, philosophy developed a new intellectual foundation to support this new economic and political structure. The central aspect of this new foundation was the conception of the autonomous, competitive, self-interested subject and the embrace of reason. The rational, transcendental subject will separate himself (and here I do mean a gendered "him") from the world and will examine and master the world (Foucault 1973: 217–387; Goldberg 3–4). The subject will classify the world, employing the new physical sciences, and will be able to dominate nature and society by using the tools of science and reason. Zygmunt Bauman explains modernity in the following way:

> There would be as much order in the world as we manage to put into it. The practice stemming from a conviction that order can be only man-made, that it is bound to remain an artificial imposition on the unruly natural state of things and humans, that for this reason it will forever remain vulnerable and in need of constant supervision and policing, is the main (and, indeed, unique) distinguishing mark of modernity.
>
> (Bauman 1992: xv)

In modernity the philosophy of the autonomous subject lays the groundwork for an era of rational social planning and engineering.

For the non-European, socially engineered modernity meant slavery, social dislocation, and the appropriation of natural resources. The conquest of the non-European, dark-skinned, world presented an intellectual and moral problem to the emerging philosophy of European democratic society. The question would be how to envision the bloody imperial conquests in a way that would be consistent with the emerging secular sense of rationality and morality (see Bernal 201–204; Goldberg 24–6). The answer to this question will be helped by the emergence of the category of race, which will explain the nature of both the conqueror and the conquered. As the new intellectual world crystallizes, the foundational figures of modernity will not only employ significant philosophical and cultural categories to understand race, they will racialize their philosophical and cultural categories. In other words, race infused itself into the central intellectual categories of the nineteenth century, the very categories that informed biblical scholarship at its foundations. It will be the task of this book to demonstrate that the foundational categories of modern biblical scholarship were thoroughly racialized.

Racializing modern knowledge: science and the humanities

> There emerged a complex Orient suitable for study in the academy, for display in the museum, for reconstruction in the colonial office, for theoretical illustration in anthropological, biological, linguistic, racial, and historical theses about mankind and the universe, for instances of economic and sociological theories of development, revolution, cultural personality, national or religious character. Additionally, the imaginative examination of things Oriental was based more or less exclusively upon a sovereign Western consciousness out of whose unchallenged centrality an Oriental world emerged.
>
> Said, *Orientalism*

Systematic racism emerged from, and was supported by, the central concepts and categories of modernity. This leads Goldberg to argue that the contradiction between the humanist ideal and the imperial practice, which we noted above, is only apparent. He begins by observing the co-emergence of rationality and race in defining the subject, and argues that, from the beginning of modernity, the two concepts were intertwined. According to the very logic of the Enlightenment, women, "savages" and "Semites", were a-rational. These conclusions were supported by science, the handmaiden to the new rationalist philosophy.

The concept of race provided the framework to cluster all of humanity into a few large groups. Agreement was never reached on the number of races, but the most common view was that there were roughly three large clusters: the Westerners (i.e. Europeans or Aryans), the Easterners (i.e. Semites and/or Orientals, who were also often separated into two distinct races), and the rest (i.e. savages). The concept of race also provided the framework for understanding the individuals within these large groups. The external markers (skin color, physical characteristics, language) signified the internal nature and abilities of each race.

One of the defining features of the modern world was the increasing acceptance of the authority of science as a way of viewing and explaining the world, upon secular philosophy. The discourse of science, particularly biology, becomes one of the preconditions for modern racism. The first step towards the development of racism was the scientific discussions about the natural world of animals and plants. The principal aim was to observe animals on the basis of their physical characteristics, and then group them according to families (see Appiah 38–9; Foucault 1973: 125–162; Goldberg 48–52; Said 1979: 116–120). This classification system was soon applied to humans, inevitably inviting the category of race. This led to the racialization of the scientific discipline of biology. Racial classification first appeared in 1684 and the first authoritative racial classification was posited in 1735 by Linnaeus, the preeminent naturalist of his time (Bernal 219; Goldberg 206; Said 1979: 119). This authoritative classification was amplified in 1776 by the German anatomist Johann Friedrich Blumenbach (see Gould 1994) and in 1808 by the British scientist James Cowles Prichard (Stepan xii–xiv, 9–12). We should not be surprised to find that racial classification assumed racial ranking, with those doing the ranking (white Europeans) placing themselves at the apex of the biological ladder. The supposedly objective ranking system nicely mirrored the political position of imperial Europe (see Gould 1994).

Racism may have its roots in science and nineteenth-century biology may have been thoroughly racist (see Barkan 15–227; Gould 1981: 30–145), but racist thought quickly spread beyond the walls of biology. Race will become particularly important in the study of culture and of history, the two categories that will be central for foundational biblical scholars. Indeed, as Anthony Appiah argues, race *is* the biologizing of culture (Appiah 45). The spread of race beyond the walls of biology will lead to the racialization of the humanistic disciplines that study culture: history, philosophy, and literature. Nonscientific racism will emerge in the writings of Hegel, and anti-scientific racism will emerge in the writings of Heidegger, the two philosophers who most influenced the development of biblical scholarship. In the next chapter we will take the opportunity to see what role race played in early biblical scholarship.

While racial blueprints varied from intellectual to intellectual, there was agreement on the general contours of the racial caste system. A brief overview is in order. Europeans were fully civilized, the adults of the racial hierarchy; Orientals and/or Semites (including the Jews)[4] were semi-civilized, the teenagers of the caste system; while the savages were incapable of civilization and were the children of the hierarchy. The racial hierarchical system defined the intellectual ability, moral sensibility, and cultural configuration of each racial group. Savages, for example, were thought to be sexually, intellectually, culturally, and morally primitive. African or indigeneous people, and their descendants, are essentially and naturally primitive and are destined to stay that way forever. They are not now, nor can they ever be, civilized. The situation for the

Orientals is not so bleak. They were able to create a society, albeit a backward one. If savages were thought to be without society and culture, Orientals were thought to be politically despotic and culturally atrophied. Jews were simultaneously enemies of the gospel and an alien (i.e. Oriental) presence in the heart of Europe. As a result they came to represent that which corrupted and destroyed from within. It is only Europeans who are advanced enough to create societies that are free and cultures that are sophisticated and vibrant.

These racial definitions also determined the (seemingly) natural political arrangements and the (seeming) historical destiny of each group and inform the colonial practices of the conquering Europeans. Civilized Europeans are capable of freedom and, therefore, require an appropriate form of government. Semicivilized Orientals and uncivilizable savages, on the other hand, are by nature servile and incapable of self-determination and freedom. Self-government would go against their very nature and, therefore, should never be contemplated by the Euro-American imperial powers. Since Orientals are capable of limited civilization in a way that savages are not, imperial power towards the two should and will vary. Orientals should be ruled firmly, of course, but within the context of colonial occupation. Savages, on the other hand, are unfit even for benign colonial occupation and would inevitably die out were it not for the Christian charity of their white rulers. As for the particular problem posed by the presence of Jews in Europe, who knows how that problem can be solved? Imperial conquest, chattel slavery and antiSemitic policies can, therefore, be defended as politically necessary and morally justifiable. Rather than being acts of unscrupulous exploitation they affirm and reflect the natural order, as established by rigorous scientific standards.

Conclusion

Race as a critical and cultural concept is a social construct, an idea that emerged out of the intellectual, cultural, and political world of European modernity. Racial thinking tends to assume that there exist essential and fundamental differences between the races. Racial thinking also tends to assume, either explicitly or implicitly, a racial hierarchy. In this racial hierarchy Europeans are on top, Orientals and Semites are in the middle, and 'savages' (the Africans and the indigenous populations) are on the bottom. Racial thinking argues that this hierarchy is natural, rational, and just; that the rank of a particular race reflects its unchanging essence. Orientals (to choose one example) are conquered because they are by nature supine and culturally backward, which renders them incapable of achieving political freedom. Racial thinking provides Europeans with the following comforting thought: it is the servile consciousness of the East and the a-rationality of the savages, rather than the brutality of the West, that produce slavery and imperial conquest.

Race becomes a widely disseminated category that infuses itself into the intellectual movements of the modern era. In more technical language, the major intellectual movements of the modern era, including those appropriated by biblical scholarship, became racialized. I will spend the rest of the study tracing, as specifically and concretely as possible, the racialization of the discourse of biblical scholarship. I will begin with Hegel and his biblical heirs, before turning to Heidegger and his followers within the discipline.

My concrete analysis will begin with Hegel, the seminal nineteenth-century thinker who deeply influenced modern philosophy, modern political thought (by way of Marx), and modern biblical scholarship (by way of the Tübingen school). My analysis will demonstrate that the category of race helps Hegel structure his narrative of world history, his views on art and literature, and his philosophy of religion – the three aspects of his thought that directly find their way into biblical scholarship. Hegel's thought is one of the ways that racialization finds its way into biblical scholarship, which makes him an appropriate starting point for our analysis.

2

THE HEGELIAN SYNTHESIS

Early modernity, race, and culture

The ideological shrillness of the polemics that surround the
advent of literary theory in our time cannot entirely conceal
that these debates, however ephemeral and *ad hominem* they
may be, are the external symptoms of tensions that originate
at the furthest remove from the stage of public debate.

Paul de Man, "Sign and Symbol in Hegel's *Aesthetics*"

Our age, whether through logic or epistemology, whether
through Marx or through Nietzsche, is attempting to flee Hegel
. . . But to truly escape Hegel involves an exact appreciation of
the price we have to pay to detach ourselves from him. It
assumes that we are aware of the extent to which Hegel, insid-
iously perhaps, is close to us; it implies a knowledge, in that
which permits us to think against Hegel, of that which remains
Hegelian. We have to determine the extent to which our anti-
Hegelianism is possibly one of his tricks directed against us, at
the end of which he stands, motionless, waiting for us.

Michel Foucault, "The Discourse on Language"

This chapter will trace the infusion of racialized discourse into the
grand philosophical system of Hegel while the next chapter will
follow the movement from Hegel into the historical reconstructions
of the Tübingen school. Hegel's racial thinking finds itself expressed
most clearly in his analysis of the world of culture (myth, art, history,
religion). We will explore Hegel's views on these topics and position them within his overall system. By locating his analysis of
culture in his larger project, we will be in a better position to determine the extent to which his racialized vision of culture and history
permeates his entire system. We will then be in a position to learn
how his racialized system finds its way into biblical scholarship.

We will begin by locating Hegel's writings within the rising tide of European nationalism that emerged in the early part of the nineteenth century. This will provide us with a context for examining Hegel's analysis of culture, an analysis which is itself indebted to the pioneering philosophical-cultural analysis of Johann Gottfried Herder. It is Hegel's analysis of culture, developed in dialogue with emerging nineteenth-century nationalism and racism, that turns his thought towards racialization.

Aesthetic and racial nationalism

Is a metaphysics of race more or less serious than a naturalism or biologism of race?

Derrida, *Of Spirit*

By the early part of the nineteenth century the supremacy of reason was no longer taken for granted (see Beiser 1987; 1992). Reason's authority was particularly under attack in German thought (Beiser 1992: 1–3, 363–365). A number of factors helped bring about the decline in reason's prestige, from the excesses of the French Revolution to the widening influence of market capitalism and consumerism. The Revolutionary Terror brought about the reconsideration of the French Revolution and of the Enlightenment presuppositions behind the Revolution, while the spread of consumer capitalism demonstrated that reason was being put to ignoble and debasing ends (see Schulte-Sasse 99). Intellectuals were disturbed to discover that even book sales were driven by the marketplace rather than by aesthetic quality, as the Enlightenment hope for a progressively educated public was beginning to prove illusory (Berghahn 62–72). Reason, which had been the driving force of the Enlightenment, seemed to be bringing fragmentation, social division, atomism, racial degeneration, economic competition, and poor reading habits.

The cosmopolitan rationality of the Enlightenment was particularly under siege in the German-speaking principalities (see Schama 101–109). The great principle of modernity was the development of the nation-state, and Germany, which consisted of a series of disparate principalities, was not yet a nation-state. On top of that, by the turn of the nineteenth century, Napoleon's army had conquered these disparate principalities. Inside Germany, the French Revolution produced conquest, humiliation, and defeat. How can the devastating military defeat be explained? How can the defeated German principalities arise from the ashes and claim their rightful place in modern Europe? The remainder of this chapter will explore the way that these questions, and the historical-political setting that produced them, helped to shape Hegel's thought. It might prove helpful to pause here, before undertaking a detailed reading of Hegel's thought, and give a general summary of some of the common ways that these questions were being answered in Hegel's day.

Since it was the Enlightenment that produced the French Revolution, and the French Revolution that produced Napoleon's humiliating defeat, then the Enlightenment itself must be the source of the problem. Early nineteenth-century intellectuals, especially in Germany, increasingly concluded that it was Enlightenment rationality that produced alienation, social unrest and state-sponsored violence. The fundamental problem faced by the defeated German principalities becomes one of self-definition: how could these disparate German principalities unite into a modern state that would avoid the excesses of revolutionary France and the atomism of British capitalism? As Enlightenment cosmopolitanism increasingly gave way to nationalism, German intellectuals sought to discern the proper foundation for the emerging German people. Inspired by Fichte's 1807 *Addresses to the German People*, German intellectuals called for a spiritual revolution that would revive a culture which they deemed to be moribund. It is this spiritual revolution that would *create* the German people. The authentic German people, then, would be in a position to form a new German state, a state which had yet to exist anywhere but in the imagination of the intellectuals.

The task of creating an authentic, German state raises once again the question of identity. How can the borders of German identity be established? Should German identity be defined around the geographical borders of a new German state? Or should German identity be defined around the linguistic borders of the German-speaking peoples? Nineteenth- (and later twentieth-) century intellectuals adamantly insisted upon the latter. A people should be defined in terms of linguistic groupings (which were assumed to be natural) rather than in terms of state borders (which were assumed to be arbitrary and unnatural). For a clear statement of this view we can briefly turn to Herder, whose position strongly influenced later German thought.

One of Herder's central tenets, which will be picked up both by Hegel and by later folklore theorists, is that the myth and culture of a particular *Volk* (people) emerge naturally from the racial spirit of that *Volk* (see Beiser 1992: 202–209; Schama 102–103).

> For every nation is one people (*Denn jenes Volk it Volk*),
> having its own national form (*National-Bildung*), as well as
> its own language: the climate, it is true, stamps on each its
> mark . . . but not sufficient to destroy the original national
> character (*das ursprüngliche Stammgebilde der Nation*).
>
> (Herder 1968: 7 (1989: 255–256))

His philosophical-historical method is to discern the spiritual nature
of a particular people as revealed in its culture, literature, mythology, political institutions, and religious practices. We should note
the way that Herder's views, here, emphasize the role of aesthetic
and cultural purity. Each single people has its own, authentic culture
which stems from its own land and its own way of life. Alien
thoughts and alien ways of life would contaminate an otherwise pure
people and an otherwise pure culture.

This explicit connection between a nation, its land and its culture,
which will be increasingly influential throughout the nineteenth
century, is thoroughly racialized.

> That striking national character (*die sonderbaren National-
> charaktere*), which, deeply imprinted on the most ancient
> people, is unequivocally displayed in all their operations on
> earth . . . The ancient character of nations arose from the
> family features, the climate, the way of life and education,
> the early actions and employments, that were peculiar to
> them. The manner of the fathers took deep root, and became
> the internal prototype of the race (*Geschlechts*).
>
> (Herder 1968: 159–160 (1989: 508))

For Herder, this racial spirit of a people (*Volk*) creates its culture
and its myths, which are an "expression of the particular mode in
which they viewed nature" (1968: 47).

Throughout the nineteenth century, race, nationalism, and
culture will become thoroughly entangled with each other, as
nationalism and aesthetics will both become racialized. As Appiah
explains:

> Race, nation, literatue: these terms are bound together in
> the recent intellectual history of the West . . . Many of those
> works that are central to the recent history of our under-
> standing of what *literatue* is are also thematically pre-
> occupied with racial issues. . . . The reason for this is not far

to seek: it lies in the dual connection made in eighteenth and nineteenth century Euro-American thought between, on the one hand, race and nationality, and, on the other, nationality and literature. In short, the nation is the key middle term in understanding the relations between the concept of *race* and the idea of literature.

(Appiah 48)

"Literature", "race" and "nation" belong together because "from the start they were made for each other" (Appiah 59).

This racialized and aestheticized ideology shapes the way that German intellectuals conceive of the question of true German identity. For these intellectuals, the German-speaking populations of Europe formed a single *people* (*Volk*), even if they lived in a number of different political *states*. A key link would be forged between the people, the culture, and the land. There was much debate throughout the nineteenth century as to whether it was anatomy or culture which gave the unified people their ground. In the later part of the nineteenth century, racialized science would locate the source of this unity in the blood. Healthy blood produces healthy individuals and a healthy people (*Volk*), which is destined to live on its own land and to create a dynamic, unique culture. In the early part of the nineteenth century, German philosophers located the source of this unity elsewhere: in the realm of spirit (*Geist*). It was assumed that there was something profound, something ineffable, that held each people together. Herder, for example, implies that the source of this unity could be climate, or language, or reason itself, or even human nature. On the one hand, he is careful to separate his views from the emerging biological racism. "Some for instance have thought fit, to employ the term of *races* (*Rassen*) for four or five divisions . . . but I see no reason for this appellation" (1968: 7 (1989: 255)). On the other hand, he does not escape the racial categories and racial thinking that also find their way into this biological racism. In a move that will reverberate throughout the work of those influenced by him (Hegel, Heidegger), he is opposed to *biological* racism, not racialization itself.

According to this view, each distinct people (the French, the Germans, the Anglo-Saxons) shared an ineffable essence, a fundamental national character which should forge an identity and a specific culture (see Sluga 106, 115–119). According to Fichte, whose *Addresses to the German People* helped to set this argument in motion, it was primordiality (*Ursprünglichkeit*) that formed the spiritual essence of the German people. The Germans were a primordial people (*Urvolk*) because they were living in their ancient home, speaking their original language, and capable of primordial thinking (Sluga 37, 102; see also Schama 101–103). According to Fichte, instrumental rationality and Enlightenment cosmopolitanism have combined to render the German people supine and unable to defend themselves against its conquering enemies. Authentic German primordiality can only be revived by exorcizing alien thought from German life. Only then can Napoleon's army be defeated and modern Germany be created.

The essential first step to reviving a defeated Germany, then, is the creation of an authentic culture, one which is truly in tune with the primordial core of the German spirit (see Schama 101–120). It will be art, largely defined, that will be able to overcome the tyranny of instrumental reason. It will be art, and art alone, that can elevate consciousness in a society degraded by instrumentality and plunder. Genuine art alone was capable of elevating the human consciousness, even if that consciousness had been debased by alien thought, instrumental reason, abstraction, and greed. Art makes possible an *unalienated* consciousness, a consciousness now in a position to offer a critique of fallen society (Beiser 1992: 222–227; Schulte-Sasse 117–118). This newly elevated and authentic consciousness can reestablish the severed relation between the self, others, and the world. Art makes possible an *organic* relationship between self and language, self and others, self and world. As the self is reunited with the world, genuine art and a properly rooted national culture can bring social cohesion, organicity, and harmony (Beiser 1992: 5, 222–239; Schulte-Sasse 114–129; Sluga 34–41, 76, 101–104). It is art which makes possible a better world.

It is important to recognize the way in which Fichte's influential argument aestheticizes the growing nationalism of his era. For Fichte and those influenced by him, the new German state will be built around the aesthetic values of the *organic, harmonious, unique, originary*, and *primordial*. This emphasis on social organicity links aestheticism to nationalism and nationalism to aestheticism. Categories drawn from the world of art become essential to the emerging political positions of the philosophers, and political arguments continually slide into the analysis of the world of art (see Schama 93–120).

Social organicity is the essential link between literature, race, and nation. It is the defining feature of the aesthetic ideology which will become so important for the development of modern, philosophical racism (see Lacoue-Labarthe and Nancy; Norris 1988: 28–64). Aestheticized racialized nationalism is constructed around the principles of cultural purity (which animates a harmonious and organic people) and around the alien (which must be excluded lest it corrupt the people from within). An organic, harmonious people must be in touch with its own, unique culture and must exclude all that is alien from its culture and its land. Modernity's problems can be traced to its failure to cultivate purified national culture and to the practice of sexual and cultural miscegenation. Throughout the modern period, nationalism and aesthetics will both become racialized. Race, then, would become the primary means of producing the authentic social unity which had, until this point, been missing.

Hegel and the nature of reason

(Spirit) does not flounder about in the external play of accidents. On the contrary, it is absolutely determined and firm against them. It uses them for its own purposes and dominates them.

Hegel, *Reason in History*

The necessity of *logical* continuity is the decision or interpretative milieu of all Hegelian interpretations . . . Hegel has bet against play, against chance.

Derrida, "From Restricted to General Economy:
A Hegelianism without Reserve"
(in *Writing and Difference*)

For Hegel, the socio-political crisis of his day is the result of a deeper and more fundamental philosophical failure. Despite its genuine achievements, the Enlightenment had turned sour because it had misunderstood the true nature of reason. The great thinkers of the Enlightenment had misconstrued that which it most cherished. To properly resolve the social problems of his day, it would be essential to confront the most important philosophical issue of the Enlightenment era: reason (see Guyer; Gillespie 24–56, 65–68). Through the course of this confrontation, Hegelian reason turns itself towards racialization.

For Hegel, reason is not an instrument, a human faculty, or an abstract principle by which philosophy operates. It is instead the Absolute, Spirit (*Geist*), and, as such, is creative, active, and dynamic. *Geist* reveals itself in phenomenal reality and in history.

(Reason) is both *substance and infinite power*, in itself the infinite material of all natural and spiritual life as well as the *infinite form*, the actualization of itself as content . . . That this *Idea* or *Reason* is the True, the Eternal, the Absolute Power and that it and nothing but it, its glory and majesty, manifests itself in the world – this, as we said before, has been proved in philosophy and is being presupposed here as proved.

(Hegel 1953a: 11; see also Beiser 1993: 15; Gillespie 63–79)

Since reason reveals itself in the world, it is reason itself which reconnects the self to the world and which will heal the social problems plaguing the modern world.

At this point, Hegel makes an assumption that radically separates him from Enlightenment thinkers. For Hegel, reason is the self-revealing force propelling history and infusing itself into culture (art, religion, philosophy, socio-political institutions). "Reason is the law of the world and . . . therefore, in world history, things have come about rationally" (Hegel 1953a: 11; see also Forster 138–139; Gillespie 47–63; Inwood 27–28, 244, 274–277). It is not enough, for Hegel, to claim that history can be judged according to the standards of reason, or that reason can play a role in the interpretation of history, or that history can provide fodder for philosophical reflection. As Gillespie explains:

This is the fundamental impetus of Hegel's philosophizing, to reveal the ground and unity of the antinomous or dialectical, to establish a ground for the twofold of nature and spirit, to reconcile the political and spiritual diremption in a rational political order grounded in the perfect knowledge of man, his institutions, and his world, in the knowledge of the phenomenological ground of history.

(Gillespie 55)

History is guided by reason, by spirit.

Reason/spirit itself requires a philosophical method appropriate to the task at hand, a method capable of recognizing the dynamic self-revelation of reason. Hegel needs a method that would be true to the nature of reason and that would reconnect self to world and thought to being. Hence the famous dialectic method, which means significantly more than the synthesis of two antithetical theses (see

Beiser 1993a: 18–20; Forster; Gillespie 47–55, 61–73; Pippin 65). Hegel argues that reason works its way through these antinomies and seeming paradoxes to reach a higher unity. Each category is self-contradictory and incomplete, but each necessarily contains some degree of truth. Two competing and self-contradictory categories, residing on one level of consciousness, necessarily give way to a truer category on the next level. This new category contains what is essential from the previous, lower categories but discards what is false about each. Thus the new category both destroys or annuls the lower term and, at the same time, preserves it. This new category, however, will also prove to be self-contradictory and will necessarily give way to another, higher category. There is not only lateral movement (i.e. from one category to another category) but there is vertical movement as well (i.e. from a lower level to a higher level). Reason works its way through error and contradiction, continually getting closer and closer to the truth, to the absolute. With the final revelation of the absolute, reason reigns supreme and history comes to an end. History is in a state of constant motion, but it is always moving towards a higher goal.

If reason reveals itself in the phenomenal world of history and culture, and if history is guided by reason itself, and if history has a teleological destiny (the self-manifestation of the absolute), then Hegel must incorporate culture and history into his own philosophical system. It is not enough for him to assert that history is grounded in reason and guided by reason; he must demonstrate this assertion through extensive analysis of history, of art, and of religion. He must show their interrelationship and their dependence upon the absolute (through speculative philosophy), but must do so historically as well as theoretically. Thus his philosophical argument demands that he turn the empirical events of world history into a coherent narrative, a narrative which reveals the hidden hand of reason and the hidden progress towards the self-revelation of the absolute. It is through this narrative of the reasoned progression of history that Hegel opens his thought up to racialization.

Hegel ventures into the philosophy of history and into the histories of philosophy, of religion, and of art because his overall system demands these excursions. The very structure of the *Phenomenology of Spirit* reveals the interconnection between his philosophical argumentation (Chapters 1–4, Chapter 8) and his concrete cultural and historical analysis (Chapters 5–7). This suggests that he applied his system of thought to his understanding of history, and, at the same time, that he employed his understanding of history in the construction of his system. We will follow the circular relationship between his historical analysis and philosophical system throughout the remainder of this chapter.

Despite his constant protestations to the contrary, Hegel will necessarily overschematize and will necessarily impose order upon the events rather than discern that order from the events themselves. This order imposed upon the phenomenal world will provide racialized discourse with its opportunity to enter into Hegel's thought, as race provides Hegel's system with its structure. For Hegel, the temptation to overschematize and the temptation to racialize will go hand in hand. Hegel posits an intimate relationship between spirit's progressive development (i.e. from lower to higher levels of consciousness) and its geographical movement (i.e. from East to West), infusing his work with a double teleology. Central to his historical analysis is the category of the people (*Volk*), a category which, as we saw above, is infused both with aestheticized nationalism and with racialization. Each people embodies a different level of consciousness, and spirit moves dialectically from the lower races/peoples, with their lower levels of consciousness, through to higher races/peoples, with their higher levels of consciousness. The end of history is not only the self-revelation of the absolute, it is the self-revelation of the absolute to Europeans, to those capable of philosophical self-consciousness and, therefore, capable of freedom. *Race will prove to be essential, rather than peripheral*, to Hegel's history of the world and, consequently, to his entire project.

Hegel and the problem of history

> Whether we know it, or like it, or not, most of us are Hegelians and quite orthodox ones at that. We are Hegelian when we reflect on literary history in terms of an articulation between the Hellenic and the Christian Era or between the Hebraic and Hellenic world. We are Hegelian when we try to systematize the relationship between the various art forms or genres according to different modes of representation or when we try to conceive of historical periodization as a development, progressive or regressive, of a collective or individual consciousness.
>
> Paul de Man, "Sign and Symbol in Hegel's *Aesthetics*"

The racialization of Hegel's thought occurs most clearly during the encounter between modern philosophy and antiquity. Let us dwell for a moment on the nature of this encounter. Antiquity looms large in the modern consciousness. The ancient world proved indispensable when modernity undertook the difficult task of constructing a self-understanding consistent with the emerging material reality of modern Europe. Those influential figures who helped define modernity were in constant dialogue with the ancient world, making the recovery of antiquity central to the project of modernity. The more that the authority of traditional Christianity came into question, the more important became the process of imitating antiquity. As Lacoue-Labarthe argues: "no modern can in fact be constituted without inventing its relation to the ancient. Indeed the modern consists wholly in such an invention" (Lacoue-Labarthe 58; see also Lacoue-Labarthe and Nancy 296–303). This dialogue with antiquity is certainly visible in those exuberant movements that helped construct a normative understanding of the modern world (the Enlightenment, Romanticism, Idealism). It is equally visible in those later, more pessimistic figures who explored the dark underside of modernity's discontents (Freud, Nietzsche, Heidegger, even Joyce). The view of antiquity, the content of the historical reconstruction, the figures to be revered, the lessons to be learned; all of this changed with each new movement or influential figure. It was the centrality of antiquity to the construction of modernity that remained constant. Not only will modern thinkers look to antiquity for inspiration, models, ideals, and literary forms; modern thinkers will also define, reconstruct, perhaps even construct antiquity based on modern needs. Antiquity serves as a model for modernity, in part, because it is created in an image that allows it to so serve. The scholarly, literary, and philosophical reconstruction of antiquity inevitably became entangled with modern self-understanding. As modern self-understanding became increasingly racialized, so did the modern reconstruction of antiquity.

The Enlightenment's classical revival was the third such revival, following on the heels of the scholastic rediscovery of Aristotle and upon the Renaissance romance with ancient Rome (see Gay 240–265). The Enlightenment reconstruction of antiquity was part of a political battle against the tyranny of the Church and Crown. Since the Enlightenment thinkers (the *philosophes*) saw this tyranny supported by mythology, their political assault led to battle against the forces of superstition and myth, on behalf of, and by means of, criticism and reason. The mythical/rational confrontation was the axis around which the ancient world was reconstructed. This self-consciously political battle on behalf of reason was greatly assisted by the construction of a useful Greco-Roman past and the adoption of dignified Greco-Roman ancestors (see Gay 31–126).

The Enlightenment narrative of antiquity is the first step towards the construction of "the West". The Enlightenment gave secular European culture a heritage: it began with Greece and Rome and proceeded, despite the dark days of the Catholic Middle Ages, to modern, Christian, enlightened Europe. There is one fundamental way in which the shape of the Enlightenment narrative may seem dissonant to modern ears. While the *philosophes* praised the Greeks for introducing critical thinking and philosophy into world history, they, like those classical revivals which preceded them, drew their intellectual sustenance mostly from Rome, particularly from Cicero (see Pfeiffer 99, 176; Gay 94–109; Turner xi, 1–5). It is Rome where rationality, freedom, and mature political power all came together. This view is articulated most eloquently in Gibbon's *Decline and Fall of the Roman Empire*:

> It is not alone by the rapidity, or extent of conquest, that we should estimate the greatness of Rome ... The firm edifice of Roman power was raised and preserved by the wisdom of the ages. The obedient provinces of Trajan and the Antonines were united by laws and adorned by arts. They might occasionally suffer from the partial abuse of delegated authority; but the general principle of government was wise, simple, and beneficent.
>
> (Gibbon 28–29)

For most Enlightenment figures, Greece is important as a stepping stone to Roman enlightenment and rationality.

This conventional appraisal of Greece and Rome will be reconfigured by early nineteenth-century intellectuals, who will assert the now-familiar superiority of the authentic Greeks over the derivative, bloodthirsty Romans. The major figures in this reconfiguration will be the German thinkers Herder, Winckelmann, Goethe, and Humboldt (see Bernal 209–223). The attraction to all things Greek was particularly strong in nineteenth-century Germany, which was in the process of developing a sense of authentic identity. The wars of liberation, the emerging sense of German nationalism, the growing dissatisfaction with Kantian reason and the Enlightenment itself, the vexing problem of German self-definition, all these forces played a role in the German redefinition of the Greeks. If the modern nation-state was constructed by means of a dialogue with, and an imitation of, antiquity, then the German imitation of antiquity was particularly problematic. As Lacoue-Labarthe and Nancy argue:

"The drama of Germany was also that it suffered an imitation *twice removed*, and saw itself obliged to imitate the imitation of antiquity that France did not cease to export for at least two centuries. Germany, in other words, was not only missing an identity but also lacked the ownership of its means of identification" (Lacoue-Labarthe and Nancy 299). The collection of disparate German-speaking principalities lacked an identity and, because the dominant models for imitating antiquity were foreign, lacked the means of creating that identity. Germany would need to recreate antiquity so as to be able to create an authentic German identity. German-speaking intellectuals will lead the way in reconceiving the nature of the Greeks and in redefining the relationship between the Greeks and the Romans. This is because this reconfiguration of antiquity is an essential part of the process of creating an identity for the German people.

As a result of the Napoleonic victory, the Prussian government authorized Wilhelm von Humboldt to introduce a series of reforms of the university system (see Bernal 282–288; Iggers 52). At the center of these reforms was the introduction of the new *Altertumswissenschaft* (the science of antiquity). The new emphasis would follow Herder in advancing the study of Greek rather than that of Latin. As Martin Bernal has argued, these educational reforms, and the increasing devotion to all things Greek, were infused with a very specific political and social ideology (Bernal 282–288; see also Lacoue-Labarthe and Nancy). Like Hegel's philosophical system, the study of the ancient Greeks was designed to overcome the atomism of the modern world and to heal the antinomies created by instrumental reason. The Greeks were suddenly seen as infused with an organic, harmonious attachment to their land, their language, and their culture. During the height of the Enlightenment, Gibbon had criticized the Greeks for their failure to intermingle and had praised the Romans for their cosmopolitanism (see Gibbon 33–39). A few short decades later, German thinkers would make the opposite case. The Greeks were now seen as racially and culturally pure while the Romans were seen as derivative and degenerate. The construction of ancient Greece as *organic* had its roots in the post-Enlightenment critique of contemporary society as *fragmented* and *alienated*. This construction of the organic Greeks permeated nineteenth-century German philosophy, culture, and educational system. The organic Greeks were seen as an antidote to a fragmented modern Germany, and the study of the Greeks would open the doors to a truly spiritual revolution, a revolution of consciousness rather than a revolution of mere politics, an authentic Germanic revolution that would surpass the revolution of the instrumental, inorganic, Latinic-Romanized French. Contact with the harmonious, culturally pure, organic Greeks would make possible the construction of a harmonious, culturally pure, organic Germany. There is an intimate relationship between the Greek revival and German nationalism.

Ancient Greece becomes the mythical birthplace of the West, the primordial origin of the unique and profound destiny of the West. Greece represents the end of the rule of the despotic Orient and the birth of the West. Greece becomes a repository of modern desires and longings rather than a particular, historical culture. These desires also take on a particular structure: *organic, harmonious, unique, originary, primordial*. Greek minds invented these aesthetic values, and Greek culture is the unique embodiment of these same values. The ominous presence of race lurks in the background, waiting for an appropriate opportunity to present itself, as the academic study of ancient Greece becomes thoroughly racialized. This moment occurs when the reclaimed Greece tethers itself to the aesthetic ideology which I identified above: an aesthetic ideology which is intimately connected to the construction of modern nationalism and to the emergence of racialized *völkisch* nationalism (and racialized antiSemitism). The connection to racialized nationalism is strengthened when the Greeks are claimed as unique forerunners to the Germans, linking the cultural revival of Germany to racialized *völkisch* nationalism (see Lacoue-Labarthe and Nancy 301). Humboldt is quite specific on this point:

> Our study of Greek history is therefore a matter quite different from our other historical studies. For us the Greeks step out of the circle of history. Even if their destinies belong to the general chain of events, yet in this respect they matter least to us. We fail entirely to recognize our relationship to them if we dare to apply the standards to them which we apply to the rest of world history. Knowledge of the Greeks is not merely pleasant, useful or necessary to us – no, in the Greeks alone we find the ideal of that which we should like to be and produce. If every part of history enriched us with its human wisdom and human experience, then from the Greeks we take something more than earthly – almost godlike.
>
> (quoted in Bernal 287)

The study of antiquity serves ends that are not only overtly political, these ends are also increasingly nationalistic and racialized (see also Turner 8–9).

With the infusion of racialization and nationalism into the study of antiquity, we are finally ready for arrival of the myth of the West, which takes the following narrative form: The West began in Greece, which created civilization, moved through the dark days of Rome and the Middle Ages, which nearly destroyed civilization, to modern Europe, which, through its encounter with the Greeks, returned to its authentic roots and revived a decayed civilization. This myth of the West is the mirror image of the project of Orientalism, and is as ideologically and politically motivated as is the myth of a servile Orient or an infantile savage. These three myths (the dynamic West, the servile and static East, the infantile savage) are fundamentally interrelated and form the matrix out of which the biblical world is reconstructed. Antiquity becomes part of a larger narrative, the story of Western triumph over inferior civilizations with lower levels of consciousness and lower capabilities for freedom.

I have been sketching, in general terms, the contours of the racialized aesthetic ideology and the process by which it found its way into the study of antiquity. It is now time to give a detailed analysis of this racialized narrative and of the role it plays in the thought of Hegel.

Hegel's narrative of world history

> Why does a philosopher so hard on narrative . . . – he always
> opposes it to the concept – why does he incite us to use a kind
> of conceptual narration?
>
> Derrida, *Glas*

Hegel combines transcendental philosophy and historicism as he constructs his own grand philosophical synthesis. The speculative and the historical parts of his thought are intended to form a coherent totality which allows the speculative and the historical to nurture each other. He will not only take over and affirm the racialized myth of the West in his historical lectures (*Lectures on the History of Philosophy*, *Lectures on the Philosophy of History*)[1] and in his historically grounded philosophical lectures (*Lectures on Aesthetics*), he will weave it into the very structure of his system (*Phenomenology of Spirit*, *Philosophy of Right*). This weaving together of the transcendental speculative and the racialized historical will be made possible by the dialectic method which, as we saw above, is rooted in the nature of reason itself.

We have seen Hegel reject the notion of an isolated, atomic human subject, arguing instead that the individual and the world are mutually self-forming (see also Pippin 78; Redding 106–110). His particular means of escaping the isolated subject is to situate him/her in the cumulative development of spirit (see Gillespie 61–73). He is able to do so, in part, because of his previous redefinition of reason (as *Geist*, which reconciles the individual/nature and subject/object). He is also able to do so because of his Herderian conviction that each people has its own unique spirit (Heiman 112–115). He goes beyond earlier philosophies of culture (Herder), however, in that he situates each people (i.e. each spiritual moment) in the grand, teleological sweep of history and in the progressive development of consciousness (Walsh 182–183).

History is propelled by spirit/reason so as to fulfill its destiny. "(World history) is the description of the spirit as it works out the knowledge of that which it is in itself . . . World History is the progress in the consciousness of freedom" (Hegel 1953d: 11–12). History passes through despotism and error as it ascends towards freedom, religion and absolute knowledge. Consciousness also passes through intellectual despotism (the master/slave and priest/penitent relations) as it travels that same dialectical path towards freedom. Consciousness and history go through the same stages of development, in the same order (see Beiser 1993b; Gillespie 87–96; Wicks 348–377). Hegel will move back and forth between the grand sweep of history and the development of human consciousness, so that, in the end, the two meld into one. *To the extent that history is racialized, so too is consciousness.*

Consciousness goes through three progressive stages of development: natural consciousness, spirit, and reconciliation in religion and absolute knowledge.

> The first stage is the immediate one where, as already noted, the spirit is embodied in naturalness, in which it is only in unfree isolation (one is free). The second stage is that in which the spirit emerges into a consciousness of its freedom. But this first emergence is imperfect and partial (some are free); it emerges from the immediate naturalness, is related to it and hence is still affected by it as an aspect. The third stage is the rising from this particular freedom into the pure and general freedom (man is free *qua* man); that is, the spirit

rises to the self-confidence and self-consciousness of the
essence of freedom.

(Hegel 1953d: 23)

These three stages of consciousness also mirror the progressive movement from despotic tyranny (one is free) to imperfect freedom (some
are free) to universal freedom (all are free).
History goes through the same three stages of development.
World history, guided by the spirit, is the movement from despotic
tyranny to imperfect freedom to universal freedom. Each stage of
freedom is defined primarily by the level of consciousness manifested
in the culture. The higher the level of consciousness, the greater the
freedom; and, conversely, the greater the degree of despotism, the
lower the level of consciousness. Hegel explicitly racializes this
process, outlining world history in three distinct, racial, progressively advancing phases: the nonWestern Orient, where natural
consciousness leads to despotism and cultural atrophy (one is free);
the Greco-Roman infancy of the West, where spirit produces imperfect freedom (some are free); and the Germanic/European, where
nature and spirit are reconciled in religion, absolute knowledge, and
true freedom (man *qua* man is free).

The Orientals do not know that the spirit (*Geist*) is free (*frei*)
in itself, or that man is free in himself. Because they do not
know it, they are not free. They only know that "one" is free;
therefore such freedom is only arbitrariness, ferocity, obtuse-
ness of passion or – by contrast – mildness and gentle-
ness, which itself is merely accident or arbitrament. This
"one" is therefore a despot, not a free man, not a man. The
consciousness of freedom (*das Bewußtsein der Freiheit*) arose
among the Greeks, and therefore they were free; but they,
like the Romans, knew only that a few are free, and not man
as such . . . Therefore the Greeks not only had slaves to
whom their lives and their beautiful freedom was tied, but
their freedom was itself only an accidental or contingent,
undeveloped, passing and limited flower, involving a harsh
servitude of the human and humanitarian sentiments. Only
the Germanic (*die germanischen Nationen*)[2] nations have in and
through Christianity achieved the consciousness that man
qua man is free, and that freedom of the spirit (*die Freiheit
des Geistes*) constitutes his very nature.

(Hegel 1953d: 11–12 (1837: 21–22))

As the sun moves from east to west, so too the spirit moves simultaneously westward and upward, endowing world history with its course and its *telos*. Reason moves to Europe and then through European history, until it reaches its final resting place in nineteenth-century philosophy. This racialized portrait of world history is neither innocuous nor careless. Hegel repeats this position, in various forms, throughout his lectures on philosophy, on history, on art, and on religion. He describes it, and the value judgments that go along with it, as "the natural division of world history and the manner in which we shall treat it" (Hegel 1953a: 24).

Hegel's Africa

Historical movements in it (Africa) . . . belong to the Asiatic or European World . . . Egypt . . . does not belong to the African Spirit. What we properly understand by Africa, is the Unhistorical, Undeveloped Spirit, still involved in the conditions of mere nature, and which had to be presented here only as on the threshold of the World's History.
Hegel, *Lectures on the History of Philosophy*

Just at this point of my progress, Mr. Auld found out what was going on, and at once forbade Mrs. Auld to instruct me further, telling her, among other things, that it was unlawful, as well as unsafe, to teach a slave to read . . . "It would forever unfit him to be a slave. He would at once become unmanageable, and of no value to his master" . . . I now understood what had been to me a most perplexing difficulty – to wit, the white man's power to enslave the black man. It was a grand achievement and I prized it highly. From that moment, I understood the pathway from slavery to freedom.
Frederick Douglass, *Narrative of the Life of Frederick Douglass*

My master had power and law on his side; I had a determined will. There is might in each.
Linda Brent (aka Harriet Jacobs), *Incidents in the Life of a Slave Girl*

For Hegel, history is the threefold, circular process of spirit immersing itself in, separating itself from, and reconciling itself with nature. His threefold division of history begins in the Oriental world, which is immersed in nature; moves to the Greco-Roman world where the infant West separates itself from nature;

and culminates in modern Europe, where nature and spirit are reconciled. Hegelian world history originates in the Orient and climaxes in Europe, with the reign of reason and the end of history.

Race plays a doubly important role in the construction of this grand narrative. It both guides the plot, with its movement from Eastern despotism to Western freedom, and it provides the criterion by which much of humanity is excluded from the story. Hegel's narrative has no place in it for the indigenous populations of Africa and elsewhere. There is more to this omission than Hegel's preoccupation with tripartite divisions and trinitarian formulations. His own racial convictions, which reflect the values of his day, preclude him from including the African in his narrative of the development of consciousness, rationality, and history. This is no mere oversight on his part, no accidental omission of a continent that only later became consequential. Hegel chose to expel Africa from his narrative of the development of reason, and he did so because he, like virtually all of his contemporaries except Herder, did not credit Africans fully with humanity, rationality, civilization, or history. The Orient may represent an early stage in the process of civilization, but Africa and its descendants reside outside of civilization entirely.

Hegel's Africa is infantile. It is infantile in its religion, its culture, its ethical values, its political structure, and its art. As Gilman demonstrates, this entire analysis revolves around the (alleged)

> special nature of the Black's perception of the world. In his perception of history, religion, the individual, and the state the Black understands the world in a specific way. His manner of ordering the world places the Black in the lowest category of the historical development of the mind (*Geist*).
> (Gilman 1982: 98)

The unreflective nature of the African is revealed most especially in the fetish; a category which owes its existence to the racial fantasies of imperial Europe.[3] The fetish, which shares the characteristics of magic, stands in the place of true religion.

> Their religion has something child-like about it. The higher sensation which they feel, they do not preserve. It passes quickly through their head. They transfer this higher sensation to the first best stone. They make this into their fetish and cast this fetish aside if it does not help them.
> (quoted in Gilman 1982: 94)

The relationship between the individual and the stone is purely arbitrary, which leads to the inability to develop abstractions or consciousness. From this lack of consciousness flows a dearth of imagination and culture, and, therefore, a society, if it can be called that, which is bestial and chaotic. They lack even the elemental level of consciousness and culture necessary to create the sort of despotic culture which will emerge in the East. All of this points to an indifference to human life, which explains the ease with which they allow themselves to be enslaved and slaughtered. Hegel's Africa, in short, has no family feelings, no ethical law, no constitution, no state, and no history. History begins elsewhere.

Hegel's Orient

In the brightness of the East the individual disappears.

Hegel, *History of Philosophy*

The years leading up to Hegel's writings witnessed a major transformation of the relationship between Europe and the Orient. The crucial turning point in this relationship was Napoleon's invasion of Egypt in 1798, which revealed to Europe the full extent of Oriental texts, languages, and civilization (Said 1979: 76–77). According to Said, Napoleon's invasion may have been a military failure, but it was an ideological triumph. "Quite literally, the occupation gave birth to the entire modern experience of the Orient as interpreted from within the universe of discourse founded by Napoleon in Egypt" (Said 1979: 87). There followed in Napoleon's wake a multitude of Western scholars, bureaucrats, administrators, travelers, adventurers, all seeking to understand and civilize the Orient. These Western travelers shaped the way that Westerners thought about, and related to, the people from the East. "Henceforth in order to get at the Orient he (the Orientalist scholar) must pass through the learned grids and codes provided by the Orientalist" (Said 1979: 67). Said eloquently explains the process:

> To formulate the Orient, to give it shape, identity, definition with full recognition of its place in memory, its importance to imperial strategy, and its "natural" role as an appendage to Europe; to dignify all the knowledge collected during colonial occupation with the title "contribution to modern learning" when the natives had neither been consulted nor treated as anything except as pretexts for a

text whose usefulness was not to the natives; to feel oneself as a European in command, almost at will, of Oriental history, time, and geography; to institute new areas of specialization; to divide, deploy, schematize, tabulate, index and record everything in sight (and out of sight); to make out of every observable detail a generalization and out of every generalization an immutable law about the Oriental nature, temperament, mentality, custom, or type; and, above all, to transmute living reality into the stuff of texts, to possess (or think one possesses) actuality mainly because nothing in the Orient seems able to resist one's powers: these are the features of Orientalist projection.

(Said 1979: 86)

This project was, to use another of Foucault's terms, thoroughly disciplined. This disciplinary conquest was carried out, in part, by means of learned societies, periodicals, traditions, vocabulary, and rhetoric (Foucault 1979: 135–228; Said 1979: 67). By the early part of the nineteenth century, the Orientalist project was transformed into a rigorous academic discipline. It is to this rigorous academic discipline that Hegel turned, when he developed his analysis of the East.

What is distinctive about Hegel's Orient is the place it occupies in his larger narrative of the historical ascent of consciousness. The Orient occupies the first stage in world history and, therefore, it parallels the first stage in the development of consciousness. Hegel's first stage of consciousness is that of the natural consciousness, of unreflective consciousness as it naturally appears. At this stage, spirit is sunk in nature, and the subject lives in a state of empirical immediacy with the natural world. At this first stage of consciousness, there is no recognition of spirit and all that spirit entails (culture, art, religion, freedom). This lack of recognition of spirit helps explain the particulars of the Oriental world. Being sunk in nature means being unable to elevate oneself beyond the particular to the universal. Empirical particularism becomes the principle around which Hegel constructs his Orient.

The inability to elevate towards the infinite defines Oriental art and culture. For Hegel, art expresses universal human desire in concrete terms (Wicks 351). Because the Oriental spirit (which is unable to recognize spirit as spirit) loses itself, Oriental art has "neither the character of freedom nor that of beauty" (Hegel 1953c: 344). Oriental art, which Hegel limits to architecture, is indirect, indeterminate, and distant from art's true purpose of expressing human subjectivity (Wicks 353–356).

> Here the idea seeks its true expression in art without finding it; because being still abstract and indefinite, it cannot create an external manifestation which conforms to its real essence. It finds itself in the presence of the phenomena of nature and of the events of human life, as if confronted by a foreign world. Thus it exhausts itself in useless efforts to produce a complete expression of conceptions vague and ill-defined; it perverts and falsifies the forms of the real world which it seizes in arbitrary relations. Instead of combining and identifying, of blending totally the form and the idea, it arrives only at a superficial and abstract agreement between them.
>
> (Hegel 1953c: 334)

This necessarily leads to a hardening and petrifying of Oriental culture, art, myth, literature, and religion. Oriental culture is necessarily, and racially, *atrophied* and *static*. Oriental writers who lack "free imagination" (Hegel 1953c: 344) take their inspiration in the annihilation of personality.

Spirit sunk in nature defines two essential aspects of Oriental religion. Spirit sunk in nature means the absence of spirit as spirit, or at least the absence of the recognition of spirit as spirit. This absence (of spirit or of recognition of spirit) leads to the absence of inwardness and of subjectivity. It follows that Oriental religions will be sternly moralistic and lacking in introspective spirituality and authentic worship.

> Morality is the subject of positive legislation in the East; but although their moral prescriptions (the substance of their ethics) may be perfect, what should be internal subjective sentiment is made a matter of external arrangement. There is no want of a will to command moral actions, but there is lacking the kind of will to perform them which would result from their being commanded from within ... The spirit has not yet turned inward ... The external and the internal, law and moral sense, are not yet distinguished and still form an undivided unity ... We obey because what we are required to do is confirmed by an internal sanction, while in the East the law is regarded as

inherently valid without requiring a subjective confirmation. In such law men do not recognize their own will, but one which is entirely foreign to them.

(Hegel 1953d: 43–44)

Since moral law is essential to the development of reason and to the realization of freedom, Oriental religion plays a very important role in the movement of world history. In this sense, Oriental religion is far more significant for Hegel's narrative of world history than Oriental art and culture or anything from Africa. At the same time, this first step is hardly complete or even adequate on its own. The recognition of the moral law has yet to lead, in Hegel's Orient, to a fully developed sense of morality. "Conscience does not exist (for the Oriental), nor does morality" (Hegel 1963: 98). Other important aspects of absolute religion (spirituality, introspection, art) are missing. Most especially, Oriental religion has no way of closing the gap between the infinite and the finite. Indeed, Hegel's Orient is premised on the absolute nature of that gap. Oriental religion is simultaneously important, incomplete, and thoroughly lacking in essential elements. Not to worry. The process of dialectic shall work its magic and the West shall incorporate and transform Oriental moral law and discard the rest.

The Oriental world resides at the lowest level of the development of consciousness. According to *The Phenomenology of Spirit*, this level of consciousness has encountered but not yet passed through the master/slave relationship (see Hegel 1977: 234–240). In this relationship, the master lives for himself and the slave lives for the master. Neither has a properly developed consciousness. The slave's consciousness is inadequate because he does not exist for himself and because he accepts his servile status. The slave makes his master into an essential reality and lives in a state of mortal terror of the master, whom he accepts as an alien, external reality. The master's consciousness is also inadequate because his existence is mediated through the slave, through whom he relates to the world and on whom he depends for recognition. Both are mutually dependent upon each other and both are trapped in a life and death struggle. Within this framework there can be no true love, no concrete ethical world, no freedom, no true sense of family, and no aesthetic creativity. It is a hostile world whose internal contradictions render it unstable, despite its authoritarian social structure.

Hegel is insistent that Oriental society is organized around this master/slave relationship:

Finitude of the will characterizes the orientals, because with them the will has not yet grasped itself as universal, for thought is not yet free for itself. Hence there can but be the relation of lord and slave, and in this despotic sphere constitutes the ruling category.

(Hegel 1963: 96)

This relationship provides the organizing principle of Oriental society (and Oriental religion, with God as master who must be feared and obeyed), which renders Oriental society as necessarily and inevitably despotic. Fortunately for humanity, *Geist* will push these contradictions to their limit and, in the process, will propel history upward and Westward.

Hegel's Judaism

> (For Hegel) the Christian thesis, the axial thesis that replaces the Jewish thesis by opposing it, overturns mastery. In substituting love for mastery, for the Jewish relations of violence and slavery, Jesus founded the family.
>
> Derrida, *Glas*

Hegel's analysis of the Jews and Judaism is informed, in part, by the traditional antiJudaism of Christian theology. According to this pervasive theological position, Israel had been assigned the task of preparing the way for the coming of Jesus. Jews rebelled against this divine role by misunderstanding their own scriptures, by lapsing into externality and legalism, and by rejecting and killing Jesus. This act of deicide was thought to reveal the essence of the Jewish people and to establish their identity and their place in the cosmos. They are forever Christ-killers and must forever bear this responsibility. Frank Manuel summarizes the traditional view as follows:

> For this crime of deicide they were condemned to be dispersed and to suffer ignominy among the nations of the earth. After the written laws of the Jews had been superseded by the teachings of Christ, the Jews continued to serve a Christian purpose: they were a living witness to the crucifixion and their books an irrefutable proof of the power of the Holy Spirit, since the prophecies of the Old Testament had been manifestly fulfilled. The Jews were not to be annihilated because they were of the same nation as Christ;

their holy books could not be denied because they affirmed the reality of Christ's existence. The Jews were not to be wiped out . . . though it was foreordained that the Jewish people as a whole would remain obstinate and hard-necked – some believed until the end of the days.

(Manuel 1992: 156)

Jesus' blood is on them and their children (see Matthew 27:24–25). The charge of genocide allowed Christians to convince themselves that Judaism was, in its essence, the negative image of Christianity. Susannah Heschel explains it this way:

Judaism was not simply a religion with its own defined boundaries, but also denoted "Jewishness", dangerous tendencies that might affect any religion, including Christianity. As Jewishness, Judaism represented a set of qualities associated with everything Christian theologians wished to reject and repudiate: false religiosity, immorality, legalism, hypocrisy, physicality, seductiveness, dishonesty, to name a few.

(Heschel 1998: 75)

Judaism, defined as Jewishness, was seen as antithetical to, and corrupting of, all that is good and wholesome. This negative view of Judaism is one of the horizons out of which Hegel writes his world history.

For Hegel, the decisive moment in world history is the transition from Eastern despotism to Western freedom. The Jews, who exist on the (spiritual/phenomenological) border between East and West, are the transitional people in that they bring monotheism into the world. They are able to do so because it is through Judaism that spirit first separates itself from nature, which makes it possible for spirit to be recognized as spirit.

This conception (of monotheism) forms the break between the East and the West; spirit descends into itself and recognizes the spiritual as the abstract fundamental principle. Nature, which is the primary and fundamental thing in the East is now reduced to the condition of a mere creature, and spirit now occupies the first place. God is known as the creator of all men, as he is of all nature; he is known as absolute activity generally. But this great principle of the Jews . . . is an exclusive unity.

(Hegel 1953d: 50)

Hegel's Jews play a fundamentally important yet necessarily limited role in his narrative. Their positive contribution is monotheism, and that alone. The spiritual principle which makes possible monotheism (the separation of spirit from nature) also animates the Jewish people. For the Jews, this separation of spirit and nature is absolute and incontrovertible. It also produces a series of unpleasant consequences for virtually every aspect of Jewish life. The absolute separation of spirit and nature becomes the axis around which Hegel spins his own particular version of antiJewish hostility. Throughout the first part of *Glas*, Derrida exhaustively identifies the antiJewish animus which permeates Hegel's system (Derrida 1990: 10–55; see also Caputo 1997: 230–243). Most especially, Judaism is animated by the principle of separation – separation of spirit from nature, separation of Jews from everyone else, separation of father from children. For Hegel's Jews, separation is so absolute that it is closer to hostility, which becomes a secondary spiritual Jewish principle.

Separation without the possibility of mediation, then, defines Hegel's Jews, who are constantly at war with nature, with each other, with the world, with their own circumcised bodies (see Derrida 1990: 41–46), and with God. The separation from God, the inability to close the infinite/finite gap (i.e. the rejection of the Trinity), produces devastating spiritual results. Hegel's Jewish God remains absolute, stern, and distant, and Hegel's Jewish faith remains incapable of subjectivity and of internalizing its admirable spiritual principles. It remains caught in the master/slave dyad. "The concrete individual does not become free, because the absolute itself is not comprehended as concrete spirit . . . The subject therefore remains closely bound to the observance of ceremonies and the law . . . The subject has no freedom for himself . . . The subject, or individual, person, never achieves the consciousness of independence" (Hegel 1953d: 52). Unable to achieve spiritual freedom or cultural creativity, Hegel's Judaism remains external, legalistic, ritualistic, and ceremonial. "The honor rendered to God, the subjective side of religion, was still very limited and unspiritual in character, however spiritual the objective conception of Him may have been" (Hegel 1953d: 53). Judaism occupies a lower level of ethical consciousness than Western Christianity.

Judaism's spiritual principle may be the precondition for the West, but the Jewish people remain fundamentally mired in the despotism and cultural atrophy of the East. Jewish monotheism and morality must be dialectically purged of its Jewish particularism and its Oriental despotism before it can become the foundation

for Western culture and freedom. *Geist* will be able to simultaneously purge the Jewish principle of its particularism and appropriate this principle as it marches forward. The Jewish people, on
the other hand, are not so pliable. Their bad habits and disagree-
able temperament cannot be purged, even by *Geist*. They remain as
stubborn for Hegel (in resisting *Geist*) as they had been for Kant (in
resisting universal, enlightened rationality) and for Augustine (in
resisting the gospel). Having made their contribution to world
history, they should at least have the good grace to step aside and
let something better emerge.[4]

Hegel's Greece

> Philosophy proper commences in the West. It is in the West
> that this freedom of self-consciousness first comes forth . . . and
> hence we never can be slaves.
>
> Hegel, *History of Philosophy*

In Hegel's Judaism, spirit, having separated itself from nature, is
recognized as spirit. Hegel's Greece takes off from that starting point
and builds an entire world around the spirit and subjectivity. Spirit
is finally ready to bequeath to the Greeks culture, art, beauty, and
freedom. The West is born.

The crucial first step came when the Greeks defeated the Persians
at the battle of Marathon (490 BCE, see Arnott 28) and with them
the spiritual principle of the East.

> (These victories) were the salvation of culture and of spirit-
> ual vigor, and they rendered the Asiatic principle powerless
> . . . World history hung trembling in the balance. Oriental
> despotism, a world united under one lord and sovereign, on
> the one side, stood facing separate states, insignificant in
> extent and resources but animated by fierce individuality.
> Never in history was the superiority of spiritual power over
> material bulk made so gloriously manifest.
>
> (Hegel 1953d: 67)

With this victory, the Greeks ensured that the world would be ruled
by reason, culture, and freedom. World history is ready for the emergence of the glory that was Greece.

Geist, in the form of consciousness and freedom, animates Greek
religion and culture, making the Greeks the first truly spiritual
people.

The Greeks worshipped God as spiritual . . . The essence of the Greek gods is the spiritual itself, and the natural is only the point of departure . . . This transformation of the natural into the spiritual is the Greek spirit itself. The epigrams of the Greeks exhibit such advances from the sensuous to the spiritual.

(Hegel 1953d: 56–57)

Greek religion is nothing but the concrete embodiment of the Greek spirit. The Greeks tell their "lively and most attractive stories" of the gods, which were "continuously gushing forth from the living spirit of the Greeks" (Hegel 1953d: 57–58).

Similar assertions about elevated consciousness and freedom will dominate Hegel's discussion of Greek art. If Oriental art consists of "superficial and abstract agreement" between the form and the idea (Hegel 1953c: 334), Greek art is the stage of perfect harmony between form and idea (see Shklar 73–74).

Here art has attained its perfection, in so far as there is reached a perfect harmony between the idea as spiritual individuality, and the form as sensuous and corporeal reality. All hostility has disappeared, in order to give place to a perfect harmony.

(Hegel 1953c: 335)

Hegel consciously contrasts the perfection of Greek art with its inferior competitors from the East. The connection between form and idea is arbitrary in the East and perfect in the West. Western art "is truly sprung from the creative activity of the spirit"; it has "found its origin in the inmost and most personal thought of the poet", and reveals a faculty of "free creation"; causing the Western artist to take "a position altogether different from that which he had in the Orient" (Hegel 1953c: 343).

Those in the East lack an elevated consciousness and therefore understand neither freedom nor individuality. The inspiration of Eastern artists is found in "the annihilation of personality" (Hegel 1953c: 344). It is in the West, and only in the West, that the individual can appear. The Greeks, as the first Westerners, were the first to discover individuality. This informed their culture with an "exhilarating sense of personality" which revealed itself in the "boundless impulse of individuals to display themselves, and to find enjoyment in doing so" (Hegel 1953d: 54). The master/slave dyad has been broken, and with it socio-political despotism and cultural atrophy. The Eastern world has been surpassed, and freedom, art, beauty, consciousness, spirit can all flourish.

This is not to imply that spirit fully revealed itself to Hegel's ancient Greeks. The ancient Greeks may have been the first to taste freedom and individuality, but they were not to oversee spirit's final self-revelation. Their grasp on the true, spiritual nature of freedom was too tenuous and immature (see Hegel 1953d: 61). As a result, freedom for Hegel's Greeks is as incomplete as it is philosophically immature. Hegel both shared and challenged the general Hellenomania that marked his era. His Greeks were simply one moment in the development of the West. They may have been more glorious than most, but they, like everyone else, were marked by internal contradictions that were in the process of being dialectically surpassed.

Hegel was no partisan of rampant subjectivity. For him, freedom and consciousness occurred when the subjective and the objective were freely united. Hegel's Greeks had not reached that elevated status. They were excessive in their freedom and one-sided in their subjectivity. Their ethical world was exclusively aesthetic and was not rooted in the objective law. The spirit of the Greeks, weakened by excessive individualism and subjectivity, eventually dissipated. *Geist*, having been set free, needed to be disciplined by an austere master. It needed a firm hand to curb its aesthetic excesses and its overwrought subjectivity. It needed the grandeur that was Rome.

Hegel's Rome

> Teutonic (*Germanische*) strength of mind has required to pass through the hard discipline of the church and law which came to us from Rome, and to be kept in check; it is this way that the European character first obtained its pliability and capacity for freedom.
>
> Hegel, *History of Philosophy* (*Werke XIII*)

By Hegel's day, Roman cultural inferiority to Greece was generally accepted. Hegel's innovation was in finding a necessary and important place for Rome in his historical schema. Hegel's system is built on the principle of the synthesis of subjectivity and objectivity. In his view, the Oriental world was completely lacking in subjectivity, but the Greeks were excessively subjective. Spirit needed to reintroduce the objective reality to counter the purely inner world of the Greeks; and spirit needed to provide an anchor to the feathery spirit of the Greeks. With the decline in the sense of objective fate, the individual needed an irresistible power before which it must bend. "The Roman world is such a power, chosen for the very purpose of casting the ethical individual into bonds, as also of collecting all deities and spirits into the pantheon of world dominion in order to mold them into abstract generality" (Hegel 1953d: 80; see also Walsh 182). In choosing Rome for this thankless and gory task, spirit prepared the way for its final self-revelation. Having worked its way Westward, *Geist* is now ready to work its way upward. The lengthy rule of Rome, first as a pagan empire and then as a Roman Catholic empire, will prepare modern, Christian Europe for the emergence of absolute knowledge (in the form of philosophy) and absolute religion (in the form of Christianity). Consciousness, having united the subjective and the objective, will finally be free and history will come to an end.

Conclusion

During the half-century preceding the formation of the Tübingen school, racial thinking became widely accepted. Most learned people were convinced that Africans were a-rational and savage, that Orientals were backward and despotic, that Jews represented an alien and corrupting presence in Western society, and that Europeans alone were capable of freedom, self-governance, and authentic culture. During this time, the categories and ideas that would prove to be fundamental for the study of culture and religion became fraught with racial significance. The racialization of culture, insti-gated by Herder, accelerated during the post-Enlightenment, aesthetic revolt against instrumental reason, alienation, and social fragmentation. In the process, traditional Christian theological themes, including theological antiJudaism, are translated into a new idiom – an idiom that is at home with Europe's increasingly secular, racialized, and nationalistic culture.

If Herder and his heirs provide the general framework for the Tübingen school's historical criticism, Hegel provided the detailed construction of the shape and flow of world history and the detailed view of where different people are located in the flow of world history. According to Hegel, the socio-political hierarchy that permeated nineteenth-century Europe and its colonies was grounded in and reflected the structure of reason itself. It was inevitable that reason, having skipped over the continent of Africa, would begin to reveal itself in the Orient before moving inevitably upward and Westward. This triumphant historical system will be one of the instruments through which ideological racism will find its way into the discipline of critical biblical scholarship. We are now in a position to see how all of this finds its way into biblical scholarship.

3

JESUS AND THE MYTH
OF THE WEST

Tübingen and the construction of
early Christianity

The Tübingen school is the first instance of the systematic and dispassionate application of thoroughly and self-consciously modern, secular categories and frameworks to the New Testament. The Tübingen school was instrumental in the transformation of biblical scholarship into an institutionalized, modern academic project. It is also through Tübingen that Hegel's highly racialized world history and phenomenology entered into biblical scholarship. It is this combination of a self-consciously modern, critical stance, combined with institutional success (rather than individual genius), that makes Tübingen an appropriate starting point for our analysis of the racialization of biblical scholarship. We will attend to the work of Baur and his heirs because he is representative of a position that, through its intellectual vigor *and* its location within the emerging university setting, dominated the conversation in the field that it helped to create. While Baur was not the first critic to read the Bible in light of modern critical questions, his modern, racially informed, Hegelian reading of the New Testament was the modern perspective that became institutionalized in the secular academy. To see how this all came about it might be helpful to summarize my analysis of Hegel's history.

Hegel's portrait of world history is neither natural nor inevitable but is, instead, *constructed*. This construction of the world is infused with ideologically motivated conclusions and perceptions. The most fundamental of these ideologically motivated perceptions is the claim that myth, art, freedom, even culture itself, reveal the fundamental nature of a particular *Volk* at a particular point in its history; that each *Volk* can be reduced to a single spiritual-philosophical principle. This spiritual-philosophical principle is infused with the category of race, ensuring that Hegel's history is, to a significant degree, racialized.

Behind the plethora of detail assembled by Herder and Hegel resides a fundamental dichotomy that informs their grand histories. This is the racial dichotomy between the Occident and the Orient. According to this view, the deficient nature of the East reveals itself in the static nature of its culture, art, myth, and language. This static culture reveals peoples incapable of achieving freedom. The superlative nature of the West reveals itself in the dynamic nature of its culture, art, myth, and language. The dynamic culture reveals peoples capable of achieving freedom, peoples who rightly rule the world. According to the Tübingen school, the New Testament is populated with several groups of peoples: the Jews, the Greeks, the Christians, and the Romans. The nature of each people, and the location ascribed to them within the flow of history, will be ascertained with the help of Hegel's racialized world history.

1   Judaism will be seen as an Oriental religion which, while it may have contributed to the development of world history by introducing monotheism, resides in the distant past. In Hegelian terms, Judaism represents one-sided objectivity without a concurrent inwardness. Monotheism and empty religious ritualism exhaust its contribution to world history. Monotheism, its only positive contribution, has been taken up by Christians who understand its true nature better than do the Jews. Their continued existence is, indeed, a mystery, and all they are still capable of doing is corrupting the spirit of their host continent and races.

2   Greece will be seen as the true founder of philosophy, art, and culture. Everything about the Greeks, from their language to their philosophy, pulsates with the spirit of freedom. Hegel is more critical of the Greeks than are most of his contemporaries, in that he finds their subjectivity and freedom equally one-sided. Despite this, the Greeks remain for Hegel the racial and cultural forefathers to the Germanic nations of Europe who, because of the Reformation and because of their racial make-up, also pulsate with the spirit of freedom. Authentic modern thought must be in dialogue with the spirit of the Greeks.

3   Christianity is seen as the spiritual liberation of the individual consciousness. According to Hegel, Christianity brings with it the absolute accord of the objective and the subjective through the incarnation and Trinity (where the infinite and finite

perfectly meet). This true meaning of Christianity was lost to all but a few in the early Church. *Geist* has been slowly revealing the true essence of Christianity through Martin Luther, through the Enlightenment, through modern art and literature and, eventually, through Hegel's philosophy.

4 The Romans will be seen as lacking the gaiety and levity of the Greeks, and they played, ultimately, an ambiguous role in the development of world history. While they passed on the culture of the Greeks to Europe they also set the stage for the Catholic perversion of the Christian spirit of freedom. Wherever the true essence of Christian freedom is being corrupted, the spirit of Roman Catholicism can be found. Authentic modern thought must struggle against the spirit of Rome. The true task of great thinkers is to peel away the inauthentic, Roman–Latin–Catholic or Jewish–Oriental coating and discover the pristine, Greco-Hellenistic–Protestant core which animates that which is authentic in the ancient world.

5 Africa will not be seen at all. Hegel's seminal historical reconstruction of the flow of world history forcibly excludes Africa from the realm of the human. Hegelian biblical scholarship, and all of those influenced by Hegelian biblical scholarship, will implicitly deny the possibility of an African spirit and will effectively erase Africans from the biblical world. It is one of the crucial tasks of African-American biblical scholars to recover what has been rendered invisible and to see the Africans who do appear in the text (see Bailey 1991; 1995; Copher 153–164; Felder 1993: 8–48; Kelley 214–216; Martin 1989; B. Sanders; Waters).

Tübingen, Hegel, and tendency criticism

The Tübingen school emerged with the publication of Ferdinand Christian Baur's prescient article on the Corinthian conflict (Baur 1831). By the early 1840s Baur had developed a committed group of followers: Eduard Zeller, Albert Schwegler, Karl Christian Planck, Karl Griesinger, and Johannes Fallati. For the next several years the members of the school turned out their most important works as they consistently applied Baur's method to the New Testament. By the later part of the decade, their fortunes began to turn and they spent the next two decades defending themselves from external and internal criticism. The vehemence of Tübingen's critics, combined with the fervor of younger revisionists, indicates that the

Tübingen school had succeeded in establishing the scholarly agenda for the future. It was during the course of the rancorous debate occasioned by Tübingen that Hegel's racially informed historical and aesthetic framework found its way into the center of the emerging field of biblical scholarship.

Baur was the instrument through which biblical scholarship took up Hegel's philosophical system and the aesthetic, political, and racial values that were assumed by – and promoted by – that system (on Baur and Hegel, see Harris 25–27; Hodgson 1968: 21–27). Baur's analysis is hardly positivistic, or even strictly empirical. He makes no pretense to approaching the biblical text without presuppositions. There is an elaborate and nuanced portrait of the entire sweep of history which is consciously imposed upon the text. From Baur's perspective this imposition is not an act of exegetical violence but is the only way of reading that does not lead to fragmentation and incoherence. It is from the Baurian–Hegelian perspective the only method that follows the dictates of reason itself. Any other way of reading is, strictly speaking, unreasonable.

Baur acknowledges that he stands in a new age in the self-revelation of spirit. "Spirit (*Geist*), at rest in itself in the assurance of its own self-consciousness, stands for the first time on a vantage-ground, from which it can look back upon the paths along which it has passed" (*Paul* I. 1–2 (*Paulus* I. 3–4)). From the vantage point of this new historical moment, Baur can do what earlier, unhistorical and fragmented criticism had been unable to do: properly situate early Christianity within the advancement of world history, and detect within early Christianity the spiritual forces and conflicts that propel it forward toward maturity.

This project will require an appropriate methodology, a methodology designed to carry out the specific tasks that Baur has defined as essential. In his seminal 1831 article, Baur named this methodology "tendency criticism", which consists of the following theoretically informed moves. Having accepted Hegel's history of the world, he begins by situating the New Testament in that history. Then he posits, once again on the basis of this history, the overall history of primitive Christianity. From this overall history of primitive Christianity he is able to discern the tendency of each smaller component of that history. Based on this reconstruction of the tendency of each subperiod he situates each writing in the New Testament, and, then, assigns to each a tendency (see *CH* I. 1–2; Hodgson 1966: 197). These various theological tendencies do not emerge from the author's idiosyncratic, subjective, point of view.

They emerge from the spirit of the subperiod in which they were written (Hodgson 1966: 208). "What is so deeply rooted in the inmost being of an individual or of a people (*Volkes*) as to be almost an innate and natural characteristic (*Eigenschaft*), must always exhibit itself outwardly in the occurrence of the same behavior; it is an *invincible tendency*" (*Paulus* I. 57).[1]

For Baur the New Testament documents disclose their location in the trajectory of early Christian history. They are less concerned with imparting reliable historical information about the events narrated than they are with reflecting their spiritual tendencies, in reflecting the spirit which produced them. While considerable scholarly attention has been paid to Baur's historical skepticism (see Baird 258–278; Gasque 21–95; Hill 1–17; Kümmel 1972: 127–143), less attention has been paid to the ideological implications of his methodology and historical analysis.

Baur establishes the practice of situating the New Testament within its larger historical context. This has been an essential component of biblical scholarship throughout the modern era and remains so for current scholarship. The infusion of a racialized ideology into Hegel's historiography, however, raises the question of the intertwining of ideology and historiography. For the remainder of this chapter, we shall focus on the infusion of racialization into the writings of this biblical Hegelian.

The historical context

> The particularism peculiar to the ancient world is to be seen especially in the existence of these two forms of Spirit, religion and philosophy . . . The antithesis between religion and philosophy is also the antithesis between East and West.
>
> Baur, "Introduction to Lectures on the History of Christian Dogma"

Baur, like generations of biblical scholars who followed him, situated the New Testament in its historical context. Baur's historical context, however, was Hegel's narrative of world history. As I briefly summarize the sweep of Baur's history, we shall keep in mind the general consensus that a people should be reduced to a single spiritual principle that supports their entire cultural output. We shall also keep in mind the Hegelian framework of the place of these various people in the progress of world history. As we saw in the previous chapter, for Hegel, world history is guided by spirit, which unfolds itself according to its own inner nature. Baur's research is provoked by the question "why . . . Christianity entered into the world at this particular time and at no other?" (*CH* I. 12). According to Baur, Christianity arose at this particular moment because spirit had prepared the world for this moment of self-revelation. This preparation involved both the appearance of, and dissipation of, the older spiritual forces – the spirit of Judaism and the spirit of the Greece. Christianity emerges out of the conflict between East and West.

Christianity could only appear after the emergence of, and dissipation of, Judaism, which represents spirit revealed in religion and which tends towards exclusivity, nationalism, and particularism. Eastern Judaism never knows spirit as immanent the way that (Western) philosophy does and, as a result, is spiritually one-sided and servile.

> (Christianity) does not, like Judaism, attach itself to outward (*äusserlichen*) rites and ordinances, nor identify itself with the positive authority of a purely traditional religion. To speak broadly, it is a more spiritual (*geistigere*) form of the religious consciousness than these are, and stands above them.
>
> (*CH* I. 6 (*DC* 6))

Once a purified form of monotheism has been taken over by Christianity, all that will remain of the Jewish spirit will be worldly ambition and empty rituals. This combination of ambition and spiritual emptiness exhausts the Jewish spirit and informs the Jewish tendency. Those New Testament writings that reveal Jewish, Oriental tendencies do so because they are informed by the Jewish, Oriental spirit.

Christianity could also only emerge after the dissipation of Greek paganism, which represents spirit discovered in philosophy and which tends towards "freedom of the conscious self" (*Freiheit des Selbstbewusstseins*) (*CH* I. 14 (*DC* 10)). This spiritual love of freedom exhausts the Greek spirit and informs the Greek tendency. Those New Testament writings that reveal the Greek, Western tendency do so because they are informed by the Greek, Western spirit. The Jews bequeathed to the world monotheism tainted by nationalism and particularity, while the Greeks bestowed upon the world a boundless love of freedom, tainted by excessive subjectivity. The dissolution of these two religions prepared the way for the next stage in the development of world history, which was helped along by the emergence of Rome.

> We may say that the time had come when the human spirit was to make this momentous advance. As the barriers and divisions between different peoples (*Völker*) and nationalities were dissolved . . . the whole spiritual consciousness (*geistige Bewusststein*) was proportionately enlarged, and found itself led more and more to disregard the distinctions and exclusiveness which separated men from each other, and to lay hold of what was universal (*Allgemeinen*). The general tendency of the age (was) towards an all-embracing unity. . . . But this universalism was the very goal to which the history of the world had been tending for centuries.
>
> (*DC* 3)[2]

This dissolving of national particularity and movement towards universalism is essential to the Roman spirit and informs the Roman (Catholic) tendency. Those New Testament writings that reveal the Roman, Catholic tendency do so because they are informed by the Roman, Catholic spirit.

The world of the New Testament

I have argued that modern philosophy, particularly that philosophy influenced by Herder and Hegel, posits a fundamental relationship between culture and a particular, monolithic people. The Hellenistic time period, with its constant transgressing of ethnic and cultural boundaries, posed a distinct problem to this position. Baur will prove to be quite resourceful in finding, in this environment, support for his intuition that culture is the product of monolithic peoples, guided by a particular spiritual principle.

Jesus

As Baur sets out to reconstruct emerging Christianity, he will inherit the potent tradition of theological antiJudaism. As a result, Baur will incorporate into his historical reconstruction a series of antiJewish stereotypes, symbols, and myths. At the same time, as Susannah Heschel so astutely argues, theological antiJudaism increased among many nineteenth- and early twentieth-century biblical scholars (see Heschel 1998: 9–13, 63–68, 226–228). This increase in theological antiJudaism was a response to tensions within the project of modern, liberal German theology. The problem arose when theologians sought to interject the conclusions of historical criticism into the framework of Christian dogmatics. While historical criticism sought to situate the Bible in its historical setting, dogmatics insisted on the uniqueness and superiority of Christianity. It is this combination of historical and a-historical analysis which sets the stage for an increase in theological antiJudaism.

The method of historical criticism ensured that the teachings and life of Jesus would be situated within its historical context, which meant within Palestinian Judaism. The more research was done on first-century Judaism, the clearer it became that Jesus could be seen as an essentially Jewish figure whose teachings were in line with those of other Jewish sages of the time. This realization clashed with the central dogmatic claims about the uniqueness of Jesus and of Christianity. This clash created an identity crisis for nineteenth-century German theologians. Historical criticism had discovered an "ordinary" Jesus while dogmatics and German political identity insisted upon the primordiality and superiority of Christianity. How could a religion of unparalleled spiritual depths be founded by a man who was an ordinary practitioner of an inferior religion?[3]

A variety of solutions were offered to the problem of Jesus' Jewishness, from rejecting the principles of historical criticism to positing that Jesus himself was racially Aryan rather than racially Jewish (see Bergen 1999; Heschel 1999; Heschel 1998: 11–12). Liberal theologians, however, found their own solution. They sketched a picture of Palestinian and Pharisaic Judaism that was as negative and as bleak as possible, thereby sharpening the contrast between Jesus and his opponents. Jesus may have taught within the context of Palestinian Judaism, but he was hardly indebted to the spiritual traditions of Judaism and he was certainly not infected by the corrupt and degenerate spirit of "Jewishness". He was, instead, radically opposed to the ideas and religiosity of his Jewish colleagues. The negative picture of "late Judaism" became an essential strategy for taking Jesus out of his Jewish, historical context and elevating Jesus above the Jewish world of first-century Palestine. By separating Jesus from his religious and cultural context, historical critics could continue to hold onto the a-historical and theological view that Jesus was unique. Jesus was uniquely spiritual because he stood in absolute opposition to his shallow, hypocritical, unspiritual, literal, Jewish opponents.

Jesus takes the best from the Jewish and the Greek world and is able to unite the spirituality of the Greeks with the objective knowledge of the Jews. In this process of uniting these antitheses, he purges both of their excesses. The Greeks' exuberant embrace of freedom often led to an excessive subjectivity, while the Christian is able, through his or her knowledge of the objective nature of God, to reject everything that is subjective, arbitrary, or idiosyncratic. "Above the plurality of separate subjects . . . there comes to stand the objective universal (*die Objectivität des Allgemeinen*), where everything particular and subjective is done away" (*CH* I. 33 (*DC* 31)). The Jewish spirit presents Christianity with the opposite tendency. Instead of heading towards flighty subjectivity, it tends towards spiritual severity and formality. Instead of an excessive subjectivity, there is an almost complete lack of spirituality and inwardness. Thus Christianity needed to develop a new principle, one which will be essentially different from that of Judaism.

Baur's Jesus spiritualizes, and therefore elevates, Judaism in a rather familiar manner. He turns morality inward, elevating inner disposition over Jewish legalism. This makes one's moral consciousness the core of the original Christian doctrine and is its unchangeable and substantial foundation. Jesus' teaching about the importance of moral consciousness *Westernizes* the Oriental aspects of the Jewish law. In other words, the *content* of Jesus' teachings combines Oriental ideas with a Western disposition. Judaism also needs to contribute the *form* that Jesus' life and teaching would take. Christianity also took over, from Judaism, the Messianic idea. But once again, it needed to spiritualize, universalize (and Westernize) this form. The Jewish Messianic expectations were external and nationalistic (*CH* I. 37–42).

> It was in the Messianic idea that the spiritual (*geistige*) contents of Christianity were clothed on with the concrete form in which it could enter on the path of historical development. The consciousness of Jesus was thus taken up by the national consciousness, and enabled to spread and become the general consciousness of the world (*allgemeinen Welt Bewusstsein*).
>
> (*CH* I. 38–39 (*DC* 36))

If Christianity had kept its earliest belief (with Jesus as a political or heavenly Messiah residing at the right hand of God), it would not have fulfilled its destiny. To succeed, Christianity needed to purge itself of all Jewish, Oriental elements.

The struggles within Christianity: an overview

The fact that Jesus purged his native religion of its Oriental elements did not immediately lead to a Western religion. His followers were not as quick to renounce their nationalist and worldly (i.e. Eastern) ambitions for a purely spiritual (i.e. Western) consciousness. The earliest followers of Jesus waged war against each other for the soul of Christianity, and the text of the New Testament bore witness to the intensity of that struggle.

According to Baur, there were three different spiritual forces (Jewish/Hebrew, Greek/Hellenistic, and Roman) confronting each other. This confrontation occurs, at least in part, in stages. During the earliest stage of Christian history, the two antithetical perspectives (the Oriental/Hebrew and the Western/Hellenistic) confront each other. These two perspectives are represented both by spiritual tendencies (ritualism and worldly ambition as opposed to spiritual freedom) and by New Testament characters (James, the apostles, and the Judaizers as opposed to Stephen and Paul). Their mutual antagonism flows necessarily from their antithetical spiritual tendencies. Gradually, however, rancor gives way to concession, paving the way for the universalism of the Roman perspective. From this compromise grows the (Roman) Catholic Church. This later stage also has its own tendency (conciliation and universalism). If the antagonism is inherent in the spiritual nature of each perspective, the eventual reconciliation is also equally predetermined. Spirit has been preparing the way for Christianity, which is the absolute and universal religion destined for world domination. Such an important role in world history can be derailed neither by interreligious sniping nor by any misguided spiritual allegiances.

The writings of the New Testament can, indeed must, be divided according to their place in this schema of confrontation and eventual reconciliation. Having recognized the competing principles, "our further task is now to place under this point of view those canonical writings which stand nearest to the apostolic age, and to inquire what relation they bear to the one side or the other of this process of reconciliation; whether their conciliatory tendency bears a more Pauline or Judaistic character" (*CH* I. 114). It is to that further task that we shall now turn.

Conquering the spirit of the East: the Hellenists and the Hebrews

According to Baur, the Christian community, from its earliest days, was divided into two antithetical parties, each representing a competing spiritual force. These two parties split Jesus into *form* and *content*, with the Hebrews latching onto the mere form of Jesus' life while the Hellenists grasped the deeper significance of the content of Jesus' teaching. The Hebrews, guided by the unalterable spirit of the Orient, remained loyal to their worldly ambitions and were content to revel in the cramping influence of the *fleshly form* of the Jewish national Messiah. This made them incapable of embracing the universalism and spirituality of their Hellenistic opponents, who recognized that moral universalism represented the true *spiritual content* of Jesus' teaching.

The conflict simmered until the days of Stephen, who introduced "the new ideas of the Christian consciousness" (*Paul* I. 59). Stephen's role is to "(call) attention to the great difference between the Ideal and the Real, and at the same time to the difference between a spiritual (*geistigen*) and sensuous (*sinnlichen*) worship of God".[4] We should note the slippery use of the term "sensuous". In Hegel's thought the term means the material form that is draped over the philosophical content of an idea. In Christian theology, the term implies the usually Jewish sins of the flesh. The two meanings seem to meld together in Baur's description of the Jews. This is visible in his claim that Stephen opposed "external, sensuous, ceremonial worship (*der äusserliche sinnliche Ceremoniendienst*) of the Jews" and the "external and sensuous turn of thought which lies at the root of the Temple worship". This outward and ceremonial religion is a perversion of true worship. Stephen contrasts the grace of God with the "grossness of the people's perversity; ingratitude and disobedience, with that overwhelming bias towards the sensuous (*sinnlichen*)" which is their "truest and most characteristic nature".[5]

Stephen's speech provoked an inevitable response from his Jewish audience. "The people would have been false to their inmost nature if they had not sacrificed him (Stephen) to their own want of comprehension of a spiritual worship of God, and their consequent hatred of him" (*Paul* I. 50). The murder of Stephen, which is consistent with similar murders from Jewish history, was a refutation of the lofty ideas the Jews entertained regarding the special relationship between God and their race. The root cause of the murder must be

THE MYTH OF THE WEST

sought "not only in the character of the people, but in the nature of the Old Testament religious institutions themselves, in the essential nature of the law, and the impossibility, subjective, if not also objective, of attaining salvation by the law" (*Paul* I. 60).

The murder of Stephen led to a major persecution, but one which was limited to *the Hellenists* who resided in Jerusalem, and, to *Hellenism itself*. The Jewish Christians, including the apostles, were spared.[6] This persecution made inevitable the split between the Hebrews and the Hellenists, leaving the Jerusalem church entirely Hebraic and opposed to the development of Hellenistic Christianity.

The conflict was set for the rest of the first century. The heir to Stephen's insight into the true (Hellenistic, Western) nature of Christianity is Paul, who provides the internal *spiritual* meaning to the external *form* of the crucifixion. In the process he became a trenchant opponent of the "very principle of Judaism" (*CH* I. 46), which is the principle of particularism. In its place he introduces the spirit of Christian universalism. The rest of the apostolic period will consist of struggles between the Oriental, Judaizing, unspiritual, despotic or servile apostles who will confront the Western, Greek, spiritual, free Paul. This will provide the context for reading Paul's letters, which consist of his struggles against the Judaizers, the Jerusalem church and their minions, and the hapless Petrine compromises with these Judaizers.

Paul and the Christian principle

If Jesus' teaching and career constituted Christianity in all its truth and splendor, it did so with enough obscurity to allow his immediate followers to misunderstand him. Paul, however, is another story. For Baur, the Western, Hellenistic, Paul was the first writer to properly elucidate the principle at the root of Christianity.

> (Paul was) the first to lay down expressly and distinctly the principle of Christian universalism (*christlichen Universalismus*) as a thing essentially opposed to Jewish particularism (*jüdischen Particularismus*). From the first he set this Christianity principle before him as the sole standard and rule of his apostolic activity.
>
> (*CH* I. 47 (*DC* 44))

If we wish to understand the essence of Christianity, then we must turn to Paul's theology. Paul, properly understood, becomes, and will remain for a long time, the standard for reading and evaluating the New Testament.

Purging Christianity: Paul and the spirit of the East

> The absolute importance which the person of Christ has for the apostle is the absoluteness of the Christian principle itself; the apostle feels that in his conception of the person of Christ he stands on a platform where he is infinitely above Judaism, where he has passed far beyond all that is merely relative, limited, and finite in the Jewish religion, and has risen to the absolute religion.
>
> Baur, *Paul*

For Baur, Christianity, despite its origins in the East, is a Western religion. Consequently, his task is to define the essence of Christianity by purging it of anything that smacks of Judaism or the Orient, of nationalism, legalism, and particularism.

> His mission as Apostle to the Gentiles was not fulfilled till the absolute importance which Judaism claimed, a claim in which Jewish Christianity sympathized with it, had been wrested from it, both in principle and in all the consequences involved, and Judaism shown to be of merely relative value . . . In the Epistle to the Romans his task is to remove the last remnants of Jewish particularism.
>
> (*Paul* I. 308–309)

This inferiority, particularism, and a-spirituality explain the hostility to Paul exhibited by his Jewish–Christian opponents. "The chief reason why their Judaistic position was so narrow was just their natural incapacity to raise themselves from a lower state of religious consciousness to a higher, and freer (*höher und freiern*) one" (*Paul* I. 253 (*Paulus* I. 283)).

The most obvious failing of Judaism, and of the Jewish Christians (according to Baur) involved their materialistic understanding of the nature of Jesus' messiahship. Paul recognized that Jesus brought a revolution in consciousness rather than a change in worldly conditions.

> For the apostle Paul, on the contrary, the death of the Messiah was in itself simply inconceivable, except by such a revolution in his Messianic consciousness as could not but

produce the greatest effect in his whole view of Christianity. Everything that was national and Jewish (*Nationaljüdische*) in the Messianic idea ... was at once removed from the consciousness of our apostle by the death of Jesus. With this death everything that the Messiah might have been as a Jewish Messiah disappeared; through his death, Jesus, as the Messiah, had died to Judaism, had been removed beyond his national connexion with it, and placed in a freer, more universal, and purely spiritual sphere, where the absolute importance which Judaism had claimed till then was at once obliterated ... From the moment when the full meaning of the death of Jesus burst upon him, he had renounced all the limitations of his Jewish stand-point, and of the Jewish Messianic ideas ... The apostle therefore saw in the death of Christ the purification of the Messianic idea from all the sensuous elements which cleaved to it in Judaism, and its elevation to the truly spiritual consciousness (*wahrhaft geistige Bewusstsein*) where Christ comes to be recognised as ... the absolute principle of the spiritual life.

(*Paul* II. 125–126 (*Paulus* II. 135–136))

Lurking behind Baur's historical reconstruction is one of the central claims of Orientalism: freedom can only be found in the West because Orientals are spiritually and racially incapable of being free. Paul's theology is ultimately a rejection of, and purging of, the servile spirit of the East from the Western religion of Christianity. "This new period (of Christianity) was that of spiritual freedom (*geistigen Freiheit*), in which the unfree servile (*unfreie knechtische*) condition had reached its term, and humanity ... had grown into a free and independent man" (*Paul* II. 203 (*Paulus* II. 222)).

We have here the progress from servitude (*Knechtschaft*) to freedom (*Freiheit*), from nonage to majority, from the age of childhood to the age of maturity, from the flesh (*Fleische*) to the spirit (*Geist*). The state left behind is one in which the divine spirit is so little apprehended, that those dwelling in it are without any higher guiding principle ... The state now reached is a truly spiritual consciousness charged with its own proper contents and at one with itself. It is only in Christianity that man can feel himself lifted up into the region of the spirit and of the spiritual life: is only here that his relation to God is that of spirit to spirit.

Christianity is essentially the religion of the spirit, and where the spirit is there is liberty (*Freiheit*) and light.

(Paul II. 212 (*Paulus* II. 232))

The reconciliation between East and West: Roman Catholicism

Christianity, destined by spirit to world domination, could not remain in a state of perpetual and acrimonious division. It was inevitable that the state of spiritual warfare would be replaced, at a later time, by spiritual reconciliation. This reconciliation, which was not accidental, was foreordained by spirit itself and was built into the nature of the opposing forces.

This process of reconciliation covers virtually all of the New Testament outside of the authentic Pauline letters (see Baird 266–267). It is made possible by concessions on both sides. According to Baur, once the Jewish Christians began to see the Hellenists as their allies they were willing to compromise on circumcision, but did not want the dignity of their Jewish sensibility challenged. The crucial moment in the compromise came when Jewish Christians insisted on claiming credit for the mission to the Gentiles. This compromise, crediting Peter with Pauline universalism, is essential to Roman Catholicism, and it shows how indebted Roman Catholicism is to Judaism.

> (This) proves the energy of Jewish Christianity. It left no expedient untried; it would use any means in order to maintain its claim of superiority against Paulinism, and not to suffer the supremacy over the Gentile world to pass to other hands ... We could not estimate too highly the influence of Jewish Christianity on the formation of the Christian Church. It is indeed in the renewal of its youth, when it developed into Jewish Christianity, that Judaism appears before us in the full splendour of its historical significance.
>
> (*CH* I. 112)

In other words, Catholicism is the attempt to tame, and to reSemitize, the Pauline message of universalism. This becomes especially visible in the theocracy and aristocracy of the Catholic Church. These aspects of Catholicism, which were the conditions for world conquest, come directly from Judaism. Paul gave the Church its *inward, noble, spirit*, but it was Judaism that gave the Church its *external, worldly, sensuous form*.

The reconciliation will always remain unstable. While Christianity will rarely return to the open warfare of Paul's day, Paul's theology will remain a constant reminder of what is essential about Christianity. Whenever the Eastern–Jewish or the Latinic–Catholic tendencies get too powerful, the Hellenistic–Pauline tendency, which will become the principle of Protestantism, will be ready to respond (see *CH* I. 113). The rather shaky compromise between the Pauline spirit of universalism and the Jewish form of external power is essential to the (Roman) Catholic spirit and informs the (Roman) Catholic tendency. Those New Testament writings that reveal this (Roman, Catholic) tendency do so because they are informed by this (Roman, Catholic) spirit. Most of the non-Pauline writings strike Baur as Catholic, but the tendency will be most especially represented by Acts of the Apostles. While Catholicism served a positive role in the gradual development of Christianity, it eventually hardened into "a form so antithetical to the self-consciousness of Spirit as to cause Spirit in its innermost being to rise up against it" (Baur 1968b: 303).

Conclusion to Baur

Before discussing the reception of Baur's thought, let us summarize its essential points. For Baur, both the historical and the cultural are informed by the specific views that he inherits from Herder and Hegel. Most especially, he takes over Herder's position that each people represents, and is animated by, a single spiritual principle. Following Hegel, he assumes that these spiritual principles (and, therefore, the people who are represented by these principles) are ordered by spirit into a narrative of progressive development. It is in this context that he situates early Christian history and writings.

There are three major spiritual principles/peoples who prepare the way for Christianity. The Oriental Jews lack spiritual inwardness and, therefore, their morality is rooted in fear and compulsion and their worship is the embodiment of empty ceremonialism. In a single moment of brilliance, they do provide the world with monotheism, which will form a significant aspect of the objective content of Christianity, but even this is tinged with nationalism, particularism, externality, and sensuality. The Western Greeks are the spiritual antithesis to the Oriental Jews. They are marked by spiritual freedom and subjectivity that is fitting for the Western free nature.

Unfortunately, their giddy freedom lacks an objective foundation in monotheism and, therefore, their subjectivity can degenerate into arbitrariness. The Romans serve to dissolve the particularism of both the Jews and the Greeks and represent universalism. They prepare the way for Christianity's uniting of the objective and the subjective into an absolute religion.

Jesus provides the Christian principle, which should have ensured the sort of revolution of consciousness that was finally achieved in German philosophy. Jesus takes over, and purifies, the essential spirit of Judaism and Greece. From Judaism he takes the content (monotheism purified of its nationalism and particularism) and the outer form (Messianism purged of the nationalism and sensuous materialism). From the Greeks he takes the inner spirit (freedom purified of its arbitrariness). He creates, in the process, the absolute religion which is appropriate for the whole world, or, at least, for certain white, European gentlemen of the nineteenth century.

Jesus' immediate followers battle each other for the proper definition of Christianity, each following their inexorable spiritual natures. The Hebrews (the apostles) cling to the fleshly form of Jesus, misunderstanding the essential Christian principle and hoping for a worldly kingdom. The Hellenists (Stephen and Paul) follow Jesus according to the spirit, adhering to Jesus' authentic spirit of a revolution of consciousness. The Hellenistic spirit is most clearly articulated in Paul's epistles, which have purged all traces of the Orient and of Judaism from the gospel.

The antithesis between the two cannot last forever, and eventually a reconciliation is reached. This reconciliation, which is found most especially in Acts of the Apostles, is Catholicism. The compromise consists of a tepid universalism (which is a concession to the Western/Hellenistic spirit), a Church hierarchy (which is a concession to the Eastern/Jewish spirit) and an agreement on the legality of the Gentile mission (which credits the Eastern spirit with the achievements of the West). This compromise will remain the principle of Catholicism. All is not lost. Whenever Eastern externality, sensuousness, materiality, or worldly ambition threaten to overwhelm the true spirit of Western freedom inherent in the gospel, authentic Christians will revolt and will return to the true source of the faith (i.e. Paul). This will revitalize the Christian faith and will liberate from spiritual bondage the Christian people of Europe.

The emerging consensus

Baur's reconstruction of early Christian history was highly controversial. His work was criticized by scholars from within and from
outside of Christianity. The Jewish scholar Abraham Geiger criticized Baur for ignoring Jewish scholarship, for misreading Jewish
texts, and for relying upon antiJewish stereotypes (see Heschel 1998:
112–119). Despite Geiger's protestations, Christian biblical scholars
continued to make the same errors and to repeat the same ill-
informed antiJewish stereotypes (see Heschel 1998: 186–222; E.P.
Sanders 1977; 1985). Within Christianity, other issues came to the
fore. Baur's students applied his method and perspective with vigor;
the orthodox disputed his skepticism and his claims about deep divisions in the earliest community; moderates were taken aback by
speculation and Hegelianism; and radicals were disappointed that
he had not gone far enough in demolishing the foundation of the
Christian faith. In the debate that followed, Baur's position was challenged, defended, expanded, and refined. Throughout the course of
this ensuing debate, the general contours of his reconstruction
became institutionalized in the discipline.

While I lack the space to undertake an analysis of the complex
debate that emerged in the wake of Baur's reconstruction and its
importance for institutionalizing racialized thinking into the discipline, it is important to emphasize the degree to which the Tübingen
school set the scholarly agenda for much of the remainder of the
century. The reception of Baur's position throughout the course of
the nineteenth century has received a great deal of critical attention.
Two of the more thoughtful and thorough studies of this topic are
offered by Werner Kümmel, who is mostly sympathetic to the goals
of Tübingen, and W. Ward Gasque, who is far from sympathetic
(Gasque 32–106; Kümmel 1972: 162–184). Even though Kümmel
and Gasque offer strikingly different critical responses to the merits
of the Tübingen perspective, both agree about the tremendous influence this perspective exerted on the emerging discipline of biblical
scholarship (see Gasque 99–100; Kümmel 1972: 172). Both agree
that Baur bequeathed three fundamental principles to normative
biblical scholarship: (1) The New Testament should be studied
according to the standards of historiography, standards which
mandate skepticism when reading the Gospels and Acts; (2) The
documents of the New Testament should be interpreted in light of
the (reconstructed) history of the early Christian Church; (3) This
history is fueled by the conflict between theEastern, servile legalism

of Jewish Christianity and the Western gospel of Pauline freedom.[7] I have argued that two of these principles, (2) and (3) are essential to Baur's racialization of Christianity. By appropriating these principles, the discipline took over the category of race as well.

Before turning to racialization in more recent biblical scholarship, it might be helpful to dwell briefly on two of Baur's heirs who played particularly important roles in the racial discord of their day: Bruno Bauer and Ernest Renan. Attention to these two figures will bring to the fore some of the implications of Baur's racialized system.

Bruno Bauer and Ernest Renan: two case studies

> The birth of the new epoch which is now emerging will cost the Christian world great pains: are the Jews to suffer no pain, are they to have equal rights with those who fought and suffered for the new world? As if that could be! As if they could feel at home in a world which they did not make, did not help to make, which is contrary to their unchanged nature!
>
> Bruno Bauer, *The Jewish Question*

> One sees that in all things the Semitic race appears to us to be an incomplete race, by virtue of its simplicity. This race ... is to the Indo-European family what a pencil sketch is to painting; it lacks that variety, that amplitude, that abundance of life which is the condition of perfectibility ... The Semitic nations experienced their fullest flowering in their first age and have never been able to achieve true maturity.
>
> Ernest Renan, *Histoire générale et système comparé des langues sémitiques* (my translation)

Bauer and Renan both used the category race more freely than did Baur, Herder, or Hegel. Both have received some critical attention in the standard histories of the discipline. Their contributions have been identified, their positions have been evaluated, their shortcomings have been highlighted; yet the role that race plays in their thought has been virtually ignored. As a corrective to the standard histories of the discipline, it is important that this study briefly dwells on the ways in which race functions in their thought.

Bauer is often seen as a tragic figure in the history of the discipline, as a scholar driven from the field because of his intemperate theological views. He began his career as a theological conservative and a critic of Strauss's skepticism. He slowly turned leftward theo-

logically, embracing both Hegel and historical skepticism. In
1841–2 he wrote a respected three-volume study on the Synoptic
Gospels. By 1842, his academic career was suspended and he joined
up with the more radical young Hegelians, including Marx, whom
he influenced. As they turned from philosophical speculation to
revolution, he fell out of favor with them as well. In 1850 he wrote
another study of the New Testament, this time of Acts, which was
so radical that it was mostly ignored. At this point he drifted into
financial failure, anonymity, poverty, and bitterness, only to slowly
turn around his life. Such is Bruno Bauer's life and career as told by
theologians and biblical critics. What is missing from this is any
mention of his radically antiSemitic writings, particularly *The Jewish
Question*, which was one of the seminal texts in the development of
modern racial antiSemitism (see Rose 263–278). Rose explains the
significance of this text as follows:

> This propaganda process began with Bauer's notorious essay
> of 1843 on *The Jewish Question*, whose title effectively stand-
> ardized the very name of the debate on the status of Jews
> in Germany. As Bauer in his journalism translated his crit-
> ical revolutionism successively into more and more practical
> political terms, he developed the concept of a coherent
> "political antisemitism" that would implement the insights
> of critical revolutionary antisemitism in the real world.
> Political antisemitism . . . set the pattern of a modern popu-
> list revolutionary culture in Germany.
>
> (Rose 263)

We should note that *The Jewish Question* was published around the
same time as his still respected three-volume study of the Synoptics,
before his work turned idiosyncratic.

What is so striking about *The Jewish Question* is that many of its
philosophical arguments parallel those of Herder, Hegel, and Baur.
Unlike his later tirade *Judaism Abroad* (published in 1862 and 1863),
which was steeped in the language of blood and soil (see Rose
273–278), *The Jewish Question* is, in many important ways, consistent with his radical Hegelian philosophy. It may trade in philosophical speculation for philosophically grounded politics, and it
certainly is far nastier than anything we read in Herder, Hegel, or
Baur, yet it does not represent a fundamental shift in philosophical
perspective. In some ways it simply draws out one possible set of
political implications from Hegel's thought.

The Jewish Question is, primarily, a philosophical argument against granting civil rights to Jews. His basic argument is that Jews should not be granted freedom because they are incapable of being free, that freedom is opposed to their Oriental nature. It is in the Jewish nature to fight against history, art, science, progress (Bauer 5–12). This unhistorical Jewish nature is unable to recognize or embrace freedom, and instead must fight against it (13). Because Jews are cut off from history, they are also cut off from their fellow human beings and remain destined to embrace segregation and money-making (14–22). Since the days of Moses, Jews have been legalistic, backward, regressive, nit-picking, hopelessly contradictory, misanthropic, and arbitrary in their relationship to nature (Chapter 2). They are essentially despotic and servile, incapable of creating art or culture, or of thinking abstractly. They are "an unfree people" (Bauer 39).

As a result, he concludes that Jews are manifestly unfit for legal emancipation. Advocates of legal emancipation are looking at the question from the wrong perspective. They mistakenly assume that Jewish misery stems from an unjust social arrangement and argue that justice demands adjusting this social arrangement. The true cause of Jewish misery, however, is the fundamental spirit that animates the Jewish religion and people. It follows, therefore, that the solution to the Jewish Question is emancipation *from Judaism itself*. Until that occurs it would be foolish to offer them political emancipation (Chapter 5). Yet is this conclusion radically incompatible with Hegel's philosophical argument that Orientals are incapable of freedom while Europeans are incapable of being enslaved? Is it radically incompatible with Baur's claim that the principle of Christianity is freedom, which only occurs when Jewish elements are purged from the gospel? For that matter, is it all that far from Martin Luther's *On the Jews and Their Lies*? I think not. Bruno Bauer's *Jewish Question* simply draws the repulsive political conclusions implicit in the work of more mainstream philosophers, theologians, and scholars. Is it any wonder that it has met with silence in the conventional histories of the discipline?

Renan's status within the discipline is more secure than Bauer's. He is best known for two contributions: his *Life of Jesus* and his philology. His *Life of Jesus* was more popular than scholarly, and its sloppy sentimentality induced Albert Schweitzer to ridicule it mercilessly. His more scholarly work as a linguist, on the other hand, has earned him an honored place in the history of the discipline. While Baird does draw attention to the antiJewish stereotypes that inform Renan's historiography (Baird 382), he pays less attention to the more dramatic racial stereotypes that permeated his linguistics (see Baird 376).

Renan was a crucial figure in the development of the racialized discipline of Orientalism. Orientalism was developed as an academic discipline by Silvestre de Sacy, who was the founder of scientific Orientalism. According to Said, Sacy "put before the profession an entire systematic body of texts, a pedagogic practice, a scholarly tradition, and an important link between Orientalist scholarship and public policy" (Said 1979: 124). His major achievement was "to have produced a whole field" (Said 1979: 127) by doctoring, annotating, codifying, arranging, and commenting on Oriental texts. His anthologies were widely used for the remainder of the century, and they claimed to reveal what was typical and essential about Oriental language, culture, custom, and society (Said 1979: 129).

If Sacy was the originator of scientific Orientalism, Renan was the leading figure of the second generation. Renan's task was "to solidify the official discourse of Orientalism, systematize its insights, and to establish its intellectual and worldly institutions" (Said 1979: 130). Renan's major contribution to scientific Orientalism came by way of philology, which had recently taken to classifying human languages into large families. Renan explored the links between language, culture, and human development, producing a picture which, for all its positivism, is remarkably close to that of Hegel.

For Renan, the two most significant language families are the diametrically opposed Indo-European (i.e. Aryan) and Semitic (Said 1979: 143, see also Said 1979: 337 n. 26). The Indo-European race has, throughout the ages and from East to West, striven for thought that is independent, considered, courageous, severe, and philosophical. As a result, it uses a rational system to explain God, humanity, and the world, always bowing to the laws of logical development (Renan 1947: 145). The Semitic race is the antithesis of the Aryan. It bases its culture on intuition that is strong and sure, but ungrounded in reflection and argumentation. While this does help bring about the purest religious form known to antiquity, it also has long-term negative effects on the shape of Semitic culture (ibid.). Renan poses this fundamental, essential, unchangeable racial dichotomy and then uses it to explain every aspect of Semitic culture and society (see Renan 1947: 147–154). The monotheism of the Semitic race necessarily renders Semites intolerant and ensures that they will lack a scientific or philosophical culture, an analytic spirit, curiosity, and creative imagination. These defects are visible in every aspect of their culture: art, music, sculpture, and mythology. These defects also inform Semitic civil life, political life, military capabilities, and morality. Renan neatly summarizes the negative characteristics of the Semites, in the passage that I quoted to open this volume:

> Thus the Semitic race is to be recognized almost entirely by negative characteristics. It has neither mythology, nor epic, nor science, nor philosophy, nor fiction, nor plastic arts, nor civil life; in everything there is a complete absence of complexity, subtlety or feeling, except for unity.
>
> (Renan 1947: 155–156, trans. Bernal 346)

From this analysis, Renan concludes that "the Semitic race appears to us to be an incomplete race (*un race incomplète*) because of its simplicity" (Renan 1947: 156, my translation).

The incompleteness of the Semitic race, which informs every aspect of their culture, is reflected in their languages. "Unity and simplicity, which distinguish the Semitic race, can be found in the Semitic languages themselves. Abstraction is unknown to them, metaphysics impossible" (Renan 1947: 157, my translation). Language is the necessary vehicle which makes possible the intellectual operations of a people (ibid.), and the Semites have a defective language.

> The languages, in particular, offered a marked contrast. The languages of the Aryans and the Semites differed essentially, though there were points of connection between them. The Aryan language was immensely superior, especially in regard to the conjugation of verbs. This marvellous instrument . . . contained in the germ all the metaphysics which were afterwards to be developed through the Hindoo genius, the Greek genius, the German genius. The Semitic language, upon the contrary, started by making a capital fault in regard to the verb. The greatest blunder which this race has made (for it was irreparable), was to adopt, in treating the verb, a mechanism so petty that the expression of the tenses and moods has always been imperfect and cumbersome. Even at the present time the Arab has to struggle in vain against the linguistic blunder which his ancestors made ten or fifteen thousand years ago.
>
> (Renan 1888: 7–8)

The organic, dynamic Aryan languages, therefore, generate an ele-vated consciousness which makes possible culture, progress, art, and freedom. At the same time, the inorganic, ossified Semitic languages generate a narrow and rigid consciousness which is incapable of producing anything more than monotheism.

> Nearly all the roots of the Aryan languages thus contained an embryo divinity, whereas the Semitic roots are dry, inor-ganic, and quite incapable of giving birth to a mythology . . . It would be idle to attempt to derive a theology of the same order from the most essential words of Semitic languages . . . The physical imagery which, in the Semitic languages, is still almost on the surface, obscures abstract deduction and prevents anything like a delicate background in speech. The impossibility of the Semitic languages to express the mythological and epic conceptions of the Aryan peoples is not less striking . . . This is because, with the Semites, it is not merely the expression, but the train of thought itself, which is profoundly monotheistic.
>
> (Renan 1888: 40–41)

Mythology, art, commerce, and civilization all are made possible by the Aryan languages and, therefore, are found exclusively among the Aryan races. Monotheism and austere morality are made possible by the Semitic languages, and, therefore, originate among the Semitic races. While Hegelian philosophers and positivistic philologists disagreed on most points, they both hold remarkably similar views of race.

Conclusion

Throughout this chapter, I have traced the movement of racialized discourse from Herder to Hegel to Baur to mainstream biblical scholarship. The Tübingen school bequeathed to biblical scholarship a number of important critical principles and historical and aesthetic assumptions – principles and assumptions which became fatally entangled with racial ideology. While these racialized principles and assumptions were transformed in a number of important ways during the course of the twentieth century, they remain in some important ways anchored in Tübingen.

The late nineteenth century witnessed a decline in the prestige of philosophy and a rise in prestige of the social sciences, which gained an increasingly important place within the academic world. Within the field of theology, liberalism and the history of religions schools were the dominant intellectual trends. While Baur's racialized historical narrative remained unchallenged, his overt Hegelianism fell out of favor among theologians and biblical scholars. This decline in prestige greatly disturbed philosophers at the turn of the century, and a new movement arose which helped the discipline reclaim some of its former glory. This new movement, phenomenology, was developed by Edmund Husserl and nurtured the thought of Husserl's brightest student, Martin Heidegger. With the publication of Heidegger's first great work, *Being and Time*, a new era in German philosophy was born. Once again philosophy was asserting itself as *the* dominant intellectual discipline and as *the* most rigorous way of approaching the world.

Once again philosophy was seen, outside of its own walls, as a legitimate contender with the social sciences. And once again biblical scholarship would find itself enchanted by a philosopher who promised to reveal the fundamental nature of human existence. Certainly this time the rewards for biblical scholarship would be even more spectacular than they had been for Baur and his heirs. Martin Heidegger was going to turn out to be the greatest philosopher of the modern era, maybe even the greatest philosopher of them all. How could Bultmann and his heirs resist Heidegger's chaste proposition? What could possibly go wrong?

4

AESTHETIC FASCISM

Heidegger, National Socialism, and the Jews

Nazism was not born in the desert. We all know this, but it has to be constantly recalled. And even if, far from any desert, it had grown like a mushroom in the silence of a European forest, it would have done so in the shadow of big trees, in the shelter of their silence or their indifference but in the same soil.

Derrida, *Of Spirit*

Heidegger's decision for Hitler went far beyond simple agreement with the ideology and program of the Party. He was and remained a National Socialist.

Karl Löwith, "The Political Implications of Heidegger's Existentialism"

It is not Heidegger, who, in opting for Hitler, "misunderstood himself"; instead, those who cannot understand why he acted this way have failed to understand him . . . The possibility of a Heideggerean political philosophy was not born as a result of a regrettable "miscue", but from (his) very conception of existence.

Karl Löwith, "The Political Implications of Heidegger's Existentialism"

Martin Heidegger is a remarkably wide-ranging thinker whose influence has been felt both inside and outside of the discipline of philosophy. Literary criticism, postmodern theory, post-structuralism, deconstruction, biblical scholarship, theology – all can claim deep connections to Heidegger's complex body of work. His students (including Hannah Arendt, Hans Gadamer, Karl Löwith, Herbert Marcuse) and dialogue partners (Rudolf Bultmann, Karl Jaspers, Paul Tillich, Jean-Paul Sartre) remain influential in their respective fields.

89

Levinas, Lyotard, Derrida, and Foucault may seem a long way from Heidegger, but all four developed their positions in dialogue with his thought. He seems destined to remain one of the pivotal figures in the twentieth- and twenty-first-century intellectual landscape.

Heidegger was also a committed National Socialist and Hitler enthusiast. His commitment to Hitler and National Socialism has never been a secret. He went through two deNazification hearings and was severely reprimanded in the second (see Ott 325–345). Even his most impassioned defenders (with the possible exception of Jean Beaufret, recipient of the "Letter on Humanism", furtive Holocaust denier and champion of Robert Faurisson's thesis concerning "the Auschwitz Lie"; see Ott 8–9) have been confounded by his Nazism. One of the greatest, or at least most provocative and influential, thinkers of the age was, at least temporarily, a fervent supporter of one of the most destructive regimes of the age. There is something incomprehensible about all of this.[1] National Socialism evokes images of mindless violence, mass conformity, intellectual banality, sneering hatred, overt cruelty, and genocide. How can we even conceive of a way of reconciling this politics with his adventurous, probing, restless interrogation of the foundations of Western thought? How can we reconcile the horrors of Auschwitz with the profundity of his thought? What do Heidegger's political commitments mean for Heideggerian biblical scholarship? How can good Christians find something positive in Heidegger's writings? If we wish to come to terms with the role that race has played in modern biblical scholarship, then it is essential that we come to terms with the complex question of Heidegger's National Socialism.

To what extent is it fair to describe Heidegger as a National Socialist? Until recently, the inconceivability of associating Heidegger with fascism triumphed over the historical and textual record as weak or naive arguments were offered to fit predetermined conclusions (for an analysis of this position, see Kisiel 1992: 11–51; Sheehan 1988; Rockmore 1–122, 244–301; Wolin 1993a; 1993c). As the argument goes, a thinker of his caliber could not really have been a Nazi; therefore, his so-called fascism had to be accidental and unrelated to his philosophical work. Despite the best work of a small number of philosophers who did seek to relate his thought to his ill-fated political career (Adorno, Bourdieu, Löwith, Levinas, Derrida, Lacoue-Labarthe), most remaining philosophers were willing to draw a sharp line between his thought and his political actions. This sharp line was supported by Heidegger's deeply disingenuous version of the events of 1933 and 1934 (Heidegger

1993c; 1993d).[2] Heideggerian evasions were eagerly accepted by willing scholars as, together, they constructed an orthodox narrative of Heidegger's political "blunder". This orthodox story may have lacked intellectual vigor, but it served the very important purpose of temporarily brushing aside serious questions about the link between Heidegger's fascism and his thought. Exasperated Heidegger scholars could now put this embarrassment behind them and return to the more important matter of reading Heidegger with a good conscience.

This all came to a crashing halt, close to half a century after the events, with the research of Farias and Ott.[3] Farias's passionate, flawed book was met by shrill denunciations and charges of intellectual dishonesty in the transparent hope of maintaining the orthodox position.[4] Given the hysteria surrounding Farias's polemic, all eyes were on Ott's archival research. The results were even more devastating than Farias's sensational charges that Heidegger was a secret supporter of Ernst Röhm and the SA. By the end of *Martin Heidegger: A Political Life*, not a single aspect of the orthodox position remained unproblematic. With an abundance of detail, Ott showed that Heidegger was a committed Nazi who fought to Nazify the German universities as a first step towards Nazifying Germany itself. Ott also reveals Heidegger's shabby antiSemitism, his attempt at creating Nazi summer political camps, his enthusiasm for the SA and the SS and for martial rhetoric, his political denunciations of opponents to the authorities in Berlin, his unwavering support for the regime through 1945, and his lifelong refusal to acknowledge any error on his part. These revelations should not have come as a surprise to anyone who read the Rector's Address of 1933 and the reminiscences of former students and colleagues (particularly Arendt, Levinas, Löwith, Jaspers, Jonas, Müller). Nonetheless, Ott's research presents a crushing portrait of a foolish and banal Nazi. He resigned his position as rector and was replaced by men who lacked his academic credentials and abilities but who possessed superior connections within the Nazi party (see Ott 237–241).

Ott's research has led to an explosion of scholarship on Heidegger's political entanglement. While the traditional defenses of Heidegger's thought withered, some (e.g. Rockmore, Wolin) took to the offensive and indicted Heidegger and all things Heideggerian.[5] Deconstruction and postmodernism fell under this reductive critique, even though the relationship between Derrida and Heidegger is an extremely complex one. Those who had once been Heideggerians jumped into the fray (e.g. Caputo, Krell, Zimmerman), although the picture they began to develop was far different from the one that had held sway for half a century. It was proving to be as difficult to discard Heidegger as it was to acquit him. While Heidegger was a Nazi, he was not simply a Nazi and nothing more. Fascist motifs and arguments find their way into his thought, but there is more to his thought than fascism. The following question began to emerge in the scholarship: how, specifically, do we recognize and delimit the complicity between his thought and his politics? What is required is a way of reading that is capable of recognizing the specific points where Heidegger's thought intersects with, and parts ways with, fascism.

While some feared that the recognition of Heidegger's fascism would be the trump card that would put a stop to the discussion (Lacoue-Labarthe 136), it actually provided philosophers with the impetus for new inquiry into his thought. Unfortunately, no such reckoning has been forthcoming within biblical scholarship, where his thought has occupied such an important role. Given the historic importance of Heidegger in our discipline, the abundance of fine and readable scholarship on the topic, and the legitimate and difficult questions posed to biblical scholarship and to Christianity by the Holocaust, such a settling of accounts is long overdue. Such a settling of accounts would entail asking the following questions: How do we trace the process of ideological contamination from Heidegger to current exegetical, theological, and historical practice? What is the significance, and the cost, of our disciplinary embrace of Heidegger? How might Heidegger's thought import problematic ideological commitments into the field of biblical scholarship, *against the best intentions of current biblical scholars?*

Deconstructing Heidegger

Nothing which is vast enters into the life of mortals without a curse.

Sophocles, *Antigone*

There never was *a* Heidegger.

John van Buren, *The Young Heidegger*

After recovering from the shocking revelations of Heidegger's commitment to Nazism, scholarship began the laborious task of rethinking Heidegger's body of work. Following the explosion of Farias's work, a quiet revolution in Heidegger scholarship has taken place, a revolution with profound consequences for biblical scholarship. It is a revolution which seeks to trace the many complicated and nuanced ways in which Heidegger's thought is both complicit with, and a challenge to, the dominant versions of fascism. This scholarly revolution has finally forced Heideggerians to ask themselves the following question: Is Heidegger's philosophically complex, thoroughly idiosyncratic, version of National Socialism any more acceptable than the "vulgar" National Socialism of the Nazi party? This rethinking of Heidegger's politics merged together with two other critical forces: the publication of Heidegger's earliest lectures (Kisiel 1995; van Buren; Kisiel and van Buren eds.) and the gradual acceptance of Derridean deconstruction of philosophy itself, and of Heidegger in particular (Derrida 1978: 79–153; 1982b: 29–67, 129–136; 1989; 1991: 31–79, 279–309, 380–402).

Some of my readers may be surprised by my claim that Derridean deconstruction is a helpful tool in combating fascism. The conventional wisdom suggests that the opposite is the case. The revelations of de Man's fascism seemed only to confirm the view that deconstruction is structurally open to the lure of fascism or, at the very least, soft on fascism and on those intellectuals who fell under the spell of fascism (see Norris 1988: 178–182). The fascism of Heidegger (who was widely identified as an important predecessor of deconstruction) and of de Man (one of deconstruction's most accomplished practitioners) seems to confirm this conventional view, at least anecdotally.

Derrida's position on Heidegger has been particularly controversial. He has often been accused of throwing up an elaborate interpretive smokescreen designed to deny any culpability on Heidegger's part (see Rockmore 273–275; Wolin 1993c: 284–291; J. Young 135–139). Wolin implies that Derrida is guilty of whitewashing the crimes of Nazism, while Julian Young argues that "there is . . . something very wrong, even perverse about the overall argument" of Derrida's *Of Spirit* (135). This reading of Derrida is mistaken, but it grows out of the entirely understandable desire to condemn Nazism completely and unambiguously. Since traditional Heideggerian criticism did indeed turn a blind eye to Heidegger's Nazism, Wolin and Rockmore are on their guard for new and sophisticated attempts at whitewashing Heidegger. Since, according to Wolin and Rockmore, Derrida (and Lacoue-Labarthe) are insufficiently condemnatory, and since Derrida and Lacoue-Labarthe insist on continuing to find something of value in Heidegger's thought, Wolin and Rockmore rush to the unwarranted conclusion that they are motivated by a similar desire to whitewash Heidegger's political involvement. Wolin sees in Derrida's analysis a species of double-talk.[6] The legitimate desire to condemn Nazism in this instance leads to a reading of Heidegger that is oversimplified and insufficiently nuanced.

This mistaken assessment of Derrida is further complicated by a misunderstanding of the admittedly complex relationship between Heidegger and Derrida. Most importantly, Wolin and Rockmore confuse indebtedness with discipleship. This misunderstanding comes about, primarily, by a lack of attention to Derrida's larger project and by a lack of attention to his numerous studies of Heidegger's philosophy. Derrida is influenced by Heidegger and does indeed dialogue with him, but he is hardly a Heideggerian. Careful attention to the entirety of Derrida's engagement with Heidegger, an engagement that goes well beyond the text *Of Spirit*, reveals that Derrida undertakes a relentless and rigorous critique of every aspect of Heidegger's thought. Much of Derrida's thought is, indeed, made possible by Heidegger, but by Heidegger deconstructed. Long before the publication of Farias's *Heidegger and Nazism* and Derrida's *Of Spirit*, Derrida explains his relationship to Heidegger in the following way:

> I do maintain . . . that Heidegger's text is extremely important to me . . . That being said . . . what I write does not, shall we say, *resemble* a text of Heideggerean filiation . . . I have marked quite explicitly, in *all* the essays I have published . . . a *departure* from the Heideggerean problematic. This departure is related particularly to the concepts of *origin* and *fall*.
>
> (Derrida 1982a: 54, his emphasis)

The charge that Derrida is primarily concerned with exonerating Heidegger ignores the rigors of Derrida's deconstruction of Heidegger and ignores the variety of ways that Derrida takes on that which is central to Heidegger's thought. Rather than making excuses for Heidegger's political error, Derrida's deconstruction of Heidegger identifies where it is that Heidegger's writings open themselves up to Nazism and racialization.

Deconstruction has allowed criticism to recognize the contradictory and divided nature of the Heideggerian corpus. Derrida argues that Heidegger's extraordinary critique of classical ontology remains trapped within the world of metaphysics (see Derrida 1982b: 63).

Following Derrida, John van Buren argues that deconstruction shows that there never was a *single* Heidegger, because his thought "is caught up in an irreducible interplay of countertendencies and ambidexterities" (van Buren 394). Metaphysical strains wage war against, and are inscribed in, post-metaphysical strains; while ideological and authoritarian strains are inscribed within, and wage war against, more liberatory countertendencies. There is never a time in Heidegger's career when his thought is either entirely free from, or entirely consumed by, his fascist commitments. At the same time, his liberatory strains predominate in his earliest lectures of 1919 to 1921 (Caputo 1993: 39–44; Kisiel 1995: 15–68; Krell 1992: 147–157; van Buren 133–156, 250–361); *Being and Time* represents an ambiguous interval, replete with marked signs of authoritarianism and *völkisch* nationalism; while his fascist strains erupt and eventually capture his thought, with varying degrees of violence, from 1929 until the end of his career.

By reading Heidegger against Heidegger, we will be able to follow both aspects of his thought without denying the significance of either for Heidegger's corpus. We will also be able to identify some of those specific moments in Heidegger's argument when he turns towards Christian antiJudaism, *völkisch* nationalism, and racial antiSemitism. Deconstruction will help us recognize those moments when the text wages war against itself, when the contradictions thrust themselves into the open. These textual contradictions will, in turn, help us recognize and identify the ideological commitments that are embedded in the heart of Heidegger's fundamental ontology. For my argument to succeed I will need to pay careful attention to his philosophical argument and to pay attention to his specific ideological positions. Heidegger read with equal care shabby fascists and the great figures of Western philosophy, and it is important that we do the same. Our reading will prove to be inadequate if it fails to ground its critique in a careful reading of the often brilliant philosophical arguments or, on the other hand, if it confuses rigor with devotion.

My central claim will be this: embedded within Heidegger's purely formal ontology lurks a privileged mode of existence, a mode of existence that is, on some key points, aligned with antiJudaism, racial antiSemitism, and *völkisch* nationalism. The Christian antiJudaism is most clearly evident in the lecture courses he taught in the years leading up to *Being and Time*, although strong traces of this antiJudaism remain in *Being and Time*. The racialized nationalism and antiSemitism begin to emerge in *Being and Time*, become dominant themes in the years of his explicit commitment to Nazism, and remain stubbornly present in his post-Hitler, later philosophy. The analysis that follows will proceed through several stages. I will begin by showing how certain racialized themes of the fascist right find their way into some crucial categories of *Being and Time* ("falling", "the They", and temporality). This will be followed by an analysis of Heidegger's particular version of *völkisch* nationalism as found in *Being and Time* and in his postwar analysis of language, poetry, and Greek thought. The chapter concludes with a discussion of his postwar position on the genocide, a position which seems to fluctuate between indifference and implicit consent.

Authenticity in *Being and Time*

Dasein in Heidegger is never hungry.

Levinas, *Totality and Infinity*

Being and Time is Heidegger's ambitious rethinking of the relationship between the self and the world. It is essential that this rethinking avoid the fundamental errors made by modern philosophy. Modernity sought to erect its system of thought around the human subject, to make the subject foundational of the world, rather than a part of the world. Rejecting this foundational role for the subject, Heidegger is convinced that the subject needs to be decentered. Rather than being master of all that he or she surveys, Dasein (which, according to Heidegger, should not be confused with the subject of traditional metaphysics) is part of a network of signification. It is this network of signification, rather than Dasein him/herself, which creates meaning.

The subject is part of, and emerges from, a referential system that makes intelligibility possible. Philosophy should start its analysis with that referential system, rather than with the individual subject. To get at the subject, philosophy should start by analyzing the everyday world. By exploring the everyday world, we shall get at the referential system that makes intelligibility possible. By exploring how an individual, in his or her daily world, comports himself or herself, we shall begin the process which will culminate in an analysis of the referential system which makes that comportment possible. The goal of philosophy is to illuminate the structures that make daily activities possible, those structures which make possible communication, activity, and living. All of the specifics of *Being and Time* are supposed to be subsumed under this general goal.

Heidegger begins his analysis by watching the way individuals comport themselves. For Heidegger, everyday comportment is to be analyzed along the axis of authenticity/inauthenticity. Sometimes we comport ourselves authentically, while other times we comport ourselves inauthentically. This is a problematic move on Heidegger's part because, as Derrida explains, it pulls Heidegger back towards the metaphysical world that he is seeking to undo:

> The extraordinary trembling to which classical ontology is subjected in *Sein und Zeit* still remains within the grammar and lexicon of metaphysics. And all the conceptual pairs of opposites which serve the destruction of ontology are ordered around one fundamental axis: that which separates the authentic from the inauthentic and . . . primordial from fallen temporality . . . Now, is not the opposition of the *primordial* to the *derivative* still metaphysical? Is not the quest for an *archia* in general, no matter with what precautions one surrounds the concept, still the "essential" operation of metaphysics?
>
> (Derrida 1982b: 63)

The turn to the category of authenticity reveals a fundamental contradiction within the early Heideggerian project. *Being and Time* seeks to develop a fundamental ontology, the contentless conditions which make possible communication, intelligibility, and practical functioning. On the other hand, sections of *Being and Time* read like an existentialist manifesto with specific (i.e. "ontic" rather than "ontological") commitments to specific ways of life and behavior. Is Heidegger describing abstract, universal conditions which can be actualized in an infinite number of ways? Or, is he describing a specific way of life that all should follow? Is *Being and Time* a work of philosophy or is it a sermon? Is it a critique of the subject-centered orientation of modern thought, or is it an ever-more astute form of existentialist anthropology? While he posits a relationship between the ontological and the existential, he also denies that he is proscribing a specific way of life or developing a specific anthropology. He is emphatic in distinguishing his fundamental ontology from anthropology, psychology, and biology, arguing that anthropological thinking necessarily forgets the question of Being (*BT* chapter 10; Derrida 1982b: 111–136). "What stands in the way of the basic question of Dasein's Being (or leads it off the track) is an orientation thoroughly coloured by the anthropology of Christianity and the ancient world, whose inadequate ontological foundation has been overlooked" (BT 74). According to Heidegger, he is describing universal conditions, universal possibilities, and universal tendencies. He takes great pains to distance himself from existential specificity, relegating such sermonizing to the realm of religion (i.e. the ontic level) rather than of philosophy (i.e. the ontological level). Philosophers have long recognized that he does not seem to be able to keep the text at the purely ontological level (see Dreyfus 141–144, 225–237; Zimmerman 1986: 100–132). Being and Time often does read like an existentialist sermon on self-actualization precisely because of its concern with authenticity. Those philosophers who seek to elucidate the major arguments of Being and Time (Dreyfus, Mulhall, Zimmerman) develop a reading of the text that is more internally consistent than is Heidegger's own version. I am less interested in straightening out the contradictions than in identifying them and magnifying them. Behind this deconstructive move is an assumption that has borne fruit in the late writings of Paul de Man: gaping contradictions in the argument reveal hidden ideological commitments (see de Man 1982; 1984; 1986; Norris 1988: 28–64; 1990: 222–283). By identifying and tracing the argumentative contradictions we shall be able to identify and trace the ways that Heidegger's thought turns itself towards ideology and racialization.

Let us return to the question of authenticity. Rather than being aloof and autonomous, Heidegger's subject is situated in the world, which is the reason for his neologism "being-in-the-world". In authentic work, the subject is "being-in-the-world", while in inauthentic work, the subject is autonomous and cut off from the world. Heidegger illustrates the difference with the ideologically loaded example of the worker in the workshop (BT Chapters 15–18). The worker encounters equipment (not objects) by employing them, by being absorbed in activity. The worker works authentically when he picks up the hammer and uses it, and becomes inauthentic when he speculates and theorizes on the nature of the hammer. The former is authentic, lived experience, while the latter is inauthentic, objectifying experience. The former reveals an organic relationship between the worker and the hammer, while the latter reveals an inorganic rupturing of this relationship by the intrusion of stultifying theorizing. Both forms of comportment, the authentic and inauthentic, are forms of everyday comportment. This seemingly innocuous example provides a starting point for his analysis of the structure of meaning.

It would seem then that being-with others should function in the same way. Surprisingly, however, Heidegger does not draw this conclusion, because the category of authenticity pulls him in the opposite direction. Instead he concludes that "when Dasein is absorbed in the world of its concern . . . it is not itself" (*BT* 163). Absorption in the everyday actually means falling (*das Verfallen*) into "the They" (*das Man*, literally "the One"). This is because authenticity (*Eigentlichkeit*) is, for Heidegger, ownness or mineness (*eigen*).[7] "Dasein is an entity which in each case I myself am. Mineness belongs to any existent Dasein, and belongs to it as the condition which makes authenticity and inauthenticity possible" (*BT* 78). Authentic mineness is, for Heidegger, threatened by absorption with others in a way that it is not threatened by absorption with equipment. The everyday human world deprives Dasein of itself. *Being and Time* is laced with a bitter, hostile attack on conventional daily life. If meaning emerges from a network of intelligibility (as he has taken great pains to show), why does Heidegger equate absorption in this network with inauthenticity? With this move Heidegger begins drifting towards the very solipsism that *Being and Time* so emphatically rejects.

This sudden argumentative shift reveals a philosophical and ideological conflict hidden under the seemingly placid prose of *Being and Time*. This philosophical and ideological tension stems from Heidegger's reliance upon two sets of traditions (Dreyfus 141–143). The first (which he defines as "the hermeneutics of facticity" and "fundamental ontology") is rooted in Dilthey and Aristotle (Kisiel 1995: 221–361; van Buren 220–234). This tradition encourages Heidegger to ground philosophy in the dynamic flow of life because daily life, properly understood, is the basis for philosophical reflection. The second tradition is nurtured primarily by Paul as interpreted by Luther and Kierkegaard and biblical scholarship (Kisiel 1995: 69–219, 525–527; van Buren 113–202; Zimmerman 1986: 43–68).[8] Rather than continue following the clues provided by existence, Heidegger dons the camel hair garment and berates a dying culture. From this perspective daily life is drenched in inauthenticity, and philosophy must call us out of the fallen world.

The former tradition sees the public realm as necessary and positive (i.e. as an ontological structure, as that which makes intelligibility possible), while the latter sees the public as a site of decay, inauthenticity, and herd-like conformity (i.e. as ontically disastrous). In short, we are encountering conflict between Heidegger's *ontology* (his inquiry into the conditions which make existence possible) and his *existentialism* (his call to authenticity). It is this conflict which will provide race with the opportunity to enter into Heidegger's thought.

Authenticity, the public, and racial antiSemitism

> When the young farmboy drags his heavy sled up the slope and guides it, piled high with beech logs, down the dangerous descent to his house, when the herdsmen, lost in thought and slow of step, drives the cattle up the slope, when the farmer in his shed gets the countless shingles ready for his roof, my work is of the same sort. It is intimately rooted in and related to the life of the peasants.
>
> Heidegger, "Why Do I Stay in the Provinces?"

Like most forms of European antiSemitic racism, Heidegger's ideological commitments emerge in his quest for authenticity and organicity. As we saw above, organicity seeks to harmonize the linguistic, the natural, and the human. It seeks a harmonious, almost mystical, unity between language, nature, and the people. De Man concludes that "what we call ideology is precisely the confusion of linguistic with natural reality, of reference with phenomenalism" (de Man 1986: 11). Given the vicious antiSemitism of his youthful writings (see Carroll 248–261), the mature de Man is in a position to recognize where this ideology leads: to an aestheticized version of blood and soil racism (see Norris 1988: 177–198). Blood and soil racism seeks to distinguish between what is healthy and what is corrupting for each particular people (*Volk*), with the German version focusing upon the health of the German people. That which is healthy is rooted in the purity of the people's blood, while that which is corrupting stems from the intermingling of foreign, alien blood. The health of the German people has been threatened by the influx of foreigners and by racial miscegenation. The aestheticized version of this ideology ends up embracing the same sort of racialized politics, although it emphasizes purity of culture and language rather than of blood. The aestheticized version of blood and soil racism emphasizes that the health of the German people depends upon the cultivation of authentic German culture and upon the expulsion of those cultural forces which are impure, alien, and corrupting. Since the Jews are bilingual, resistant to assimilation, and without a homeland and a native soil, they became, throughout the first half of the century, *the* dominant symbol of parasitic inorganicity. The Jews came to symbolize the disruption of the dream of pure presence and organic harmony; they became that which must be purged.[9] Right-wing German racists, in the 1930s and 1940s, will rail against the intrusion into German life and German culture of all that is foreign, but will be obsessive in uprooting any traces of Jewish blood or Jewish spirit from German society (see especially Goldhagen 80–128; Friedländer 9–173; Herf 130–151; Katz; Weiss 206–255).

This quest for organicity, which connects Heidegger with common racists and the more elevated variety of modern philosophical racism, is the thread which we will be following through his early lectures and *Being and Time*. It is the thread through which the more disturbing ideological views of Heidegger's day find their way into his universal structures of human existence. This ideology contradicts other aspects of the text, including the text's claim that it steadfastly refuses to privilege any particular (i.e. ontic) perspective. Heidegger's quest for organicity is most visible in his position on the relationship between the subject and the world. In his view that absorption in the world of the public is inherently inauthentic. It is here that his thought and racialized discourse become entangled together.

In *Being and Time*, Heidegger weaves authenticity and inauthenticity through his analysis of the structure of meaning. To see how he does this, it is necessary to return, briefly, to his overall argument. As we saw earlier, he wants to account for comprehension, communication, and intelligibility. He wants to define these in terms of the structure of Dasein, the human subject, redefined as Dasein (Caputo 1993: 10–11; van Buren 363–367). *Being and Time*, therefore, wants to explain the structure which allows other entities and other humans to reveal themselves to us. He defines this as the "care-structure" of "Being-in-the-world". This care-structure has nothing to do with the ordinary meaning of care as compassion. Instead it means the structural openness of Dasein. The care-structure becomes the center which supports the argument of *Being and Time*.

The care-structure has three elements, each of which has a corresponding structure of human existence, an "existentiale", (see *BT* Chapters 29–34), a corresponding life event[10] (*BT* Chapters 39–53), and a corresponding temporal stance (*BT* Chapters 67–71). (1) In existing, I am usually ahead of myself, planning and preparing. My life is full of possibilities. This corresponds to the temporality of the *future*. Each individual is thrown into a life which is futurally moving, and which culminates in death. The corresponding existentiale (i.e. structure of human existence) is understanding, which emerges from openness to the future. (2) In facticity, I am thrown into a particular situation with limited possibilities. This corresponds to the temporality of the *past*. Each individual is born, and born into a particular fate. The corresponding existentiale is mood, which discloses the condition into which we are thrown. (3) In falling I conceal truth through absorption in worldly affairs. This corresponds to the temporality of the *present*, which is as closed as "existing" is open. The corresponding existentiale is *discourse* (*Rede*, which might be better translated as "talking" or "telling", see Dreyfus 215–224 and which should not be confused with Foucault's understanding of discourse), especially "idle talk".

As this sketch suggests, Heidegger's analysis of points (1) and (2) are neutral and descriptive, while his analysis of point (3) is closer to a denunciation. Despite his frequent denials, he is no longer neutrally describing ontological conditions of communication; he is now rebuking a particular way of life. He introduces the topic of "idle talk" by disclaiming that "our Interpretation is purely onto-logical in its aims, and is far removed from any moralizing critique of everyday Dasein" (*BT* 211); and by repeating the point that "the expression 'idle talk' is not to be used here in a 'disparaging' signi-fication" (*BT* 211). The ensuing description of idle talk, however, certainly seems to undercut these claims. He then defines idle talk as inability to communicate, uprootedness, banality, dominance, avoidance of struggle, and the lack of individuality. Gadamer found his teacher's claim of descriptive neutrality as "simply incredible" (see Zimmerman 1986: 62).

At the heart of the care-structure is an aesthetic judgment. Heidegger contrasts static/present-oriented aesthetic values with dynamic/future-oriented aesthetic values. The static is the embodi-ment of inauthenticity while the dynamic is the embodiment of authenticity. Phenomenology revealed that Being itself, properly understood, is dynamic flux, while nihilistic metaphysics reduced Being to a static object, eternal and unchanging. With each set of aesthetic values we have a corresponding temporality: inauthenticity is oriented to the past or present, while authenticity is open to the future. Each also brings a psychological stance as well: inauthen-ticity, by its absorption in the present, is closed to the possibilities (which are represented by the future) while authenticity is open to such possibilities. Heidegger does not even seem to recognize that these particular aesthetic values might be contested or challenged. He then takes them to be natural descriptions of life, as phenomenologically self-evident and beyond question. In doing so he argues that he is overcoming the destructive, and inauthentic, aesthetic assumptions of the West. Yet all the while he is importing deeply rooted and ideologically troublesome aesthetic values into his ontology of Being, without the apparent awareness that he is doing so.

According to Heidegger, inauthenticity is Dasein's everyday stance, which he defines as "the They". "The They" is a structure of human existence (i.e. it is "existential" instead of "existentiell"), and should not be confused with specific historically conditioned aspects of modernity, or so Heidegger claims. According to Heidegger, "the They" represents the permanent ontological tendency towards inauthenticity and fallenness. This category, which will be taken over by Heideggerian biblical scholarship (especially Bultmann, Bultmann's students, Funk, and Crossan), will become one of the unacknowledged gateways through which fascist political ideas find their way into Heidegger's thought.

Heidegger, Spengler, and racial antiSemitism

> The inner relationship of my own work to the Black Forest and its people comes from a centuries-long and irreplaceable rootedness in the Alemannian–Swabian soil.
>
> Heidegger, "Why Do I Stay in the Provinces?"

Heideggerians have long recognized his indebtedness to Kierkegaard, particularly for his development of the concept of the everyday.[11] They have been slower to recognize that Heidegger's everyday is also deeply indebted to Oswald Spengler's *The Decline of the West*, the influential text that launched German fascism. Spengler attempted to explain how modern Germany had fallen upon such hard times, how it had reached its current state of crisis. He sought to explain the inflation, the military defeat, the social divisions and the political instability of the immediate post-World War I years without relying on economic or conventionally political arguments. Instead he argued that Germany was facing a spiritual crisis caused by instrumental reason, racial impurity, jazz (i.e. black) music, Jewification (i.e. parasitic finance, rootlessness, urbanization), technology, inattention to the spirit, the avoidance of struggle, the quest for security, and a dictatorship of impersonal formlessness. (We should note the parallels between Spengler's degenerate Weimar Republic and Heidegger's "They".) These forces had conspired to bring the West into decline (see Herf 49–69). This position was widely accepted in a Germany that was both deeply antiSemitic (as was the rest of Europe) *and* in a state of seemingly permanent economic and political crisis (which differentiated Germany from the rest of Europe).[12] His disturbingly racist argument was influential because it seemed to explain the crisis of Germany in widely accepted terms. Since many of Germany's right-wing political theorists already equated Germany with the heart of Europe, a crisis for Germany was assumed to be a crisis of the West itself and, by implication, a crisis of philosophy which produced the West (see Heidegger 1959: 37–46; Sluga 53–74). Spengler had identified the crisis of Weimar as a crisis of philosophy, and had done so in overtly racialized terms. The right-wing critique of the Weimar Republic employed the terms and logic of racialized discourse and, therefore, was thoroughly racialized.

Spengler's version of Germany's post-World War I collapse contains strong echoes of the secularized version of the Ahasverus myth of the eternal, wandering Jew (see Rose 23–31). In the sixteenth-century version of the myth, Ahasverus referred to the Jew who mocked the crucified Jesus and who, in punishment, was forced to wander the world homeless. His eternal condemnation, his stubbornness, his cruelty, and his homelessness made him a powerful symbol of the stereotypically defined Jewish people. The myth was secularized in the early part of the nineteenth century. Rather than symbolize a jeering enemy of Jesus, Ahasverus now symbolized destructive self-love, egoism, rootlessness, and inorganicity. In both instances, Ahasverus was the embodiment of "Jewification". Rather than stubbornly rejecting the gospel and salvation, Jews were now seen as stubbornly rejecting authenticity and organicity, the secular versions of salvation. Revolutionary liberation from inorganicity meant, ultimately, liberation from Jewification.

While Heidegger did not mention Spengler by name in *Being and Time* (as he rarely mentioned any of his dialogue partners), he did discuss him often in other contexts (Ward 33–34, 53–63; Zimmerman 1990: 26–33). He paid particular attention to Spengler between 1919 and 1921 (van Buren 233, 321, 355), when he began constructing his phenomenological project; and again in 1929–30 (Heidegger 1995: 70), when redefining this project and explicitly turning to fascism. In both instances he criticized Spengler's unsophisticated philosophy and his incomplete radicality; but he praised Spengler's description of Western decline (Ward 33). Zimmerman concludes that the "early Heidegger began to conceive of his own work as an attempt to provide a philosophically sound account for the *symptoms* of decline popularized by Spengler" (Zimmerman 1990: 27, his italics). In other words, Heidegger assumed the same thing about Spengler that he did about Kierkegaard: they were both onti- cally insightful, but both failed to ground their insight ontologically (on Kierkegaard, see *BT* 278 n. vi).

Central to Spengler's argument is the claim that the West is in decline. Heidegger attempts to ground this claim ontologically without falling prey to the illusions that dominate Western philoso- phy. This means, first of all, redefining "decline". Early Heidegger agrees that post-World War I Germany faces a momentous spiri- tual crisis that can be solved only through radical reinterpretation of the entire history of the West and through a revolution properly grounded in that radical reinterpretation. He disagrees with Spengler's use of the term "decline" because it takes over a faulty view of temporality, a view indebted to the very decadent meta- physics that caused the decline in the first place (see *BT* Chapters 78–82).

Instead, Heidegger seeks to define the current state of affairs phenomenologically (i.e. in terms of the care-structure). Falling (*Verfallen*, which has the connotation of deterioration, decay, or collapse) is a permanent (i.e. ontological) possibility. Heideggerian falling is not a matter of historical decline, as Spengler would have it; nor a matter of falling into time, as Hegel would have it (see *BT* Chapter 82; Derrida 1989: 23–30). It is falling from authentic temporality (which is open to the future) to inauthentic temporality (which is so absorbed in the present that it is closed off to the future). Falling is the most common form of existing; it is our everyday way of existing. "(Falling is) that kind of Being which is closest to Dasein and in which Dasein maintains itself for the most part" (*BT* 220). Falling is an omnipresent possibility, like original sin, on which it is modeled. For Heidegger, Western culture can choose to exist primarily in the state of falling, as it did in the Weimar Republic and in other democracies; or it can choose to exist in something approaching authenticity, as it will when it opts for Hitler's revo- lution. Unlike Spengler, Heidegger does not think that we are doomed to witness the descent of the West and the ascendancy of lesser races. A proper revolution will purge the forces of fallen inauthenticity and save the West from this apocalyptic future.

If authenticity means having a sense of mineness or ownness, then inauthenticity means the antithesis of mineness. The everyday self thinks of itself as Cartesian ego rather than as existing Dasein (Zimmerman 1986: 43–52). This is the more profound meaning of egoism, and is in keeping with the definition offered by the German antiSemitic revolutionaries (Rose 23–43). This egoistical inauthenticity represents the triumph of the average, the leveling off of all possibilities of Being, the avoidance of struggle and decision, the loss of individuality (*BT* Chapter 27). This loss is so strong that Dasein does not even recognize that he/she is falling; Dasein confuses falling with ascendancy. This egotistical inauthenticity also means the triumph of public conventions, of "idle talk" over authentic communication. In idle talk, public opinion is approvingly passed along without comprehension or thought, and novelty is valued over depth (*BT* Chapters 35–37).

This shallowness emerges because of Dasein's uprootedness, because Dasein never dwells anywhere (see *BT* 217). Like inauthentic Dasein, inauthentic discourse "has lost its primary relationship-of-Being towards the entity talked about" as the primordial has been lost (*BT* 212). Inauthenticity represents the "*downward plunge* . . . into the groundlessness and nullity of inauthentic everydayness" (*BT* 223, his emphasis). In falling, Dasein loses its organic, natural relationship to language (which becomes idle talk), to other entities and other Dasein (which become present-at-hand objects) and to the world (which becomes an external space inhabited by objects). Inauthenticity is rootless inorganicity. How near is he to equating inauthenticity with Jewification?

Dasein inevitably drifts towards inauthenticity, groundlessness, and lack of primordiality. At its most stubborn, Dasein aggressively courts inauthenticity (*BT* Chapter 35). When this occurs, Dasein's initial lack of ground drifts towards ever-increasing groundlessness, ultimately resting in complete groundlessness and reveling in a state of constant uprooting. At this point there is complete inability to decide, complete lack of struggle, and the inability to communicate. New inquiry is suppressed, establishing a negative mood which overcomes the entire culture, as has happened in ("Jewified") Weimar (Heidegger 1993a; 1993b; 1993c; 1993d; Rockmore 49–53; Ward 46–81). As the Jews stubbornly refuse salvation, so Jewified inauthenticity stubbornly refuses organicity and authenticity. A spiritual revolution is required, a spiritual revolution rooted in radical insecurity and anxiety (*Angst*).

Let us now return to the examples of authenticity and inauthenticity that puzzled us earlier. For Heidegger, the man or woman absorbed in hammering is authentic. He or she is rooted, grounded, and maintains an organic relationship with the world. At the same time, the individual absorbed with other humans is inauthentic.

This latter absorbing activity is for the lost, the rootless, the inorganic, for those who flit from conventional topic to conventional topic and who carelessly circulate ideas. We paused earlier on this contradiction, noting that this sudden turn threatens to undo the ontological project. Maybe this turn is not as inexplicable as it first appeared.

Marxist critics have astutely argued that Heidegger's everyday represents a romanticized rebellion against late capitalist society, universalized into a fundamental ontology (see Adorno 53–110; Bourdieu 70–87). The authentic hammerer is laboring in a precapitalist workshop before the emergence of economic reification. In this idealized, illusory portrait, agrarian life comes to embody authenticity and primality (see Adorno 55). On the other hand, the inauthentic "They" is a dizzying capitalist city. The talk that is casually and rootlessly passed around parallels the rootless system of capitalist exchange. Two sets of maudlin *völkisch* stereotypes (the rootless urbanite versus the rooted peasant) are universalized into fundamental human traits. Conventional images are confused with universal traits of Dasein, and, in the process, *völkisch* conservatism is granted the status of universal truth. While Heidegger boasts about the rootedness of his own philosophy in the soil and peasant life of his native region, he communicates no awareness that this rootedness brings with it particular, and particularly noxious, political and ideological commitments (see Adorno 53–57; Beistegui 21–23, 37–39, 44–54; Derrida 1991: 279–309; Fritsche 1995: 136–142; Lang 40–59; Rockmore 45–49; Schama 93–120; Zimmerman 1986: 127).

This romantic revolution against urban modernity was conceived in racial, as well as economic, terms. The hammerer is not just precapitalist, he is also a German peasant rooted in the soil. The "They" (rootless, degenerate, intelligent but abstract, parasitic circulation) is not just urban, it is Jewified urbanity or Jewification itself. Rootlessness, degeneration, and circulation were designated as clear signs of Jewification by a century and a half of *völkisch* thinkers (Rockmore 35–39; Mosse 1–145; Sluga 75–124); by Spengler (Herf 55–61); by virtually all of Heidegger's compatriots in the Reactionary Modernist movement (see Bourdieu 46–50; Herf *passim*, especially 130–151); by nonGerman fascists (Carroll *passim*); by most European intellectuals (Bauman 31–82; Gilman 1993); and by the Nazi party itself (Weiss 222–341). Is it unreasonable to suggest that it means as much for Heidegger? In his earliest courses on religion, inauthenticity was made equivalent to the Jewish religion. Echoing

Hegel, he held that the great Greek beginning was made possible by overcoming the mythical Asiatic (Ward 13). By incorporating the terms and logic of racialized discourse he ensured that his own thought would become racialized.

Furthermore, there is evidence to suggest that he was personally racist, which suggests that, in his case, the gap between racialized discourse and racist intentions narrows, especially during the 1930s. The years leading up to and immediately following the Nazi seizure of power are replete with examples of personal antiSemitic statements and behavior. Many former friends and colleagues, including Löwith, Jaspers, and Husserl, report hearing antiSemitic (and antiblack) comments from both Heidegger and his wife (see Ott 185; Ettinger 33; Jaspers 140–143; Lang 65; Müller; Rockmore 33; van Buren 384–6). His infamous antiSemitic letter of 1929 dramatizes the way that these personal prejudices migrated into his thought.

> We face a choice between sustaining our *German* intellectual life through a renewed infusion of genuine native teachers and educators, or abandoning it once and for all to the growing Jewish influence (*Verjudung*, "Jewification") – in both the wider and narrower sense. We shall get back on the right track only if we are able to promote the careers of a new generation of teachers without harassment and unhelpful confrontation.
>
> (quoted in Ott 378; see also Lang 36)[13]

By 1929, the proposition of pervasive, pernicious Jewish influence was widely held (see Friedländer 107). This view was ascribed to both traditional, intellectual elites and the new, radical, revolutionary student groups that would play such an important role in Hitler's revolution (see Friedländer 49–60). On the face of it, therefore, it is not clear whether in this letter Heidegger is expressing the cultured Judeophobia of traditional elites or the revolutionary antiSemitism of the emerging Nazi party. This question can be answered by examining his career as a member of the Nazi party and as university rector. It is these activities that demonstrate that this antiSemitic letter reveals an emerging commitment to radical, revolutionary, racist antiSemitism. Even early on in Heidegger's career he advocated a radically new beginning for Germany. This radically new beginning could only come about by overturning the established intellectual order embodied in the elite, humanistic professoriate (see especially Safranski 86, 120, 183–188, 239, 259). Once Heidegger became rector he was able to put this policy in place by cracking down on the autonomy of the faculty (e.g. canceling the faculty senate, by rejecting the principles of academic freedom) and by elevating the authority of the student radicals. It is, therefore, unlikely that his antiSemitic letter reflects the genteel antiSemitism of the elites he rejected. It is far more likely that this letter reflects the revolutionary antiSemitism of the student radicals.

Furthermore, analysis of his statements and actions as rector demonstrate that he was supportive of the sort of revolutionary antiSemitism espoused by student radicals. By 1933 he explained the dangerous nature of the international alliance of Jews to Jaspers, who eventually lost his teaching position for being married to a Jewish woman (van Buren 385); he no longer accepted Jewish students, and he eventually removed the dedication to the Jewish Husserl from *Being and Time*, failing even to attend his funeral. As rector Heidegger enforced Nazi antiSemitic policies. According to Farias, as rector he oversaw

> the expulsion of all Jews on the teaching staff; a question-
> naire for each teacher showing racial origin; the new rights
> of students; the obligatory oath for all teachers concerning
> the purity of their race; the obligation to use the Nazi salute
> at the beginning and end of each class; the organization of
> the University Department of Racial Matters . . .; obliga-
> tory work service; economic help for student members of
> the SA and the SS, or other military groups, and refusal of
> aid to Jewish and Marxist students; the obligation to attend
> classes on racial theory, military science, and German
> culture.
>
> (Farias 119)

Throughout his political speeches as rector and his rector's address ("The Self-Assertion of the German University") he criticizes tradi-tional elites, calls for a radical revision of the university under National Socialist principles, embraces student radicals (including the SS and the SA), and endorses Hitler's revolution and Hitler as Führer (see Heidegger 1993a; 1993b). While it is true, as Heidegger's defenders insist, that in 1933 he had no way of intu-iting the coming genocide, it cannot be said that he was unaware of the antiSemitic nature of the regime. The antiSemitic boycott (April 1–4), antiSemitic legislation (April 7) and outbursts of antiSemitic violence had already occurred *before* he took over as rector in May.[14]

Thus Heidegger himself explicitly defines inauthenticity as Jewification, and does so a mere two years after *Being and Time* and a full four years before Hitler's rise to power. Even before his explicit turn to Hitler, his language (egotism, groundlessness, uprootedness, lack of primordiality) evokes most of the major themes of Spengler's reactionary modernism and secularized antiJudaism and anti-Semitism. This is not to suggest that Heidegger is doing nothing more than repeating popular racist tripe. He limits his overtly racist declarations to private and professional correspondences and to the political speeches he gave as rector. He is no simple biological racist, despite intimations to that effect in 1933, where he puts his philosophically sophisticated political theory to the service of blood and soil racism. The problem with biological racism, for Heidegger, is that it is *biological*, and therefore ontologically groundless; not that it is *racist*.[15]

To summarize, Heidegger's philosophy, even his early philosophy of *Being and Time*, is internally contradictory, divided, and unstable. Metaphysical and postmetaphysical ideas sit side-by-side while authoritarian beliefs wage war against liberatory convictions. The philosophical discord is most visible in the conflict between fundamental ontology (i.e. the conditions which make possible intelligibility) and existentialism. The ontology takes Heidegger away from subject-centered anthropology, which it rejects as a sign of a decadent philosophical system, while the existentialism returns him to a specific anthropology, complete with ethical prescriptions and political commitments.

Heidegger's existentialism, which clashes with his most important philosophical insights, provides ideology with one entrance into his philosophy. His overall goal was twofold: By clearing away the stultifying tradition-blocked access to the originary, he hoped to open a new path for access to the primordial (a concept which, since the days of Fichte, has deep roots in German nationalism). To get at the primordial, Heidegger employed the categories of authenticity and inauthenticity. Not only does this move reintroduce the centrality of the human subject, threatening to undo the complex ontological arguments; it brings along with it a series of ideological commitments interwoven in aesthetic categories. Inauthenticity is indebted to antiSemitic and antiJewish stereotypes, while "the They" (inauthenticity writ large) is structurally comparable to the Jewified city of right-wing nightmares.[16] The antithesis to the inauthenticity of "the They" contains echoes of both *völkisch* nationalism and secularized Christian antiJudaism.

These aestheticized ideological commitments find their way into Heidegger's most important category: the care-structure. This is Dasein's fundamental temporal structure of past, present, and future. Because of the temporal nature of the care-structure, Dasein's status as either authentic or inauthentic is revealed in its fundamental temporal stance. Authentic existence comes when Dasein, thrown into the past, is fundamentally open to the future. Inauthentic existence comes when Dasein is either weighted down by the past or absorbed in the present. In both cases, Dasein seeks security by closing itself off to demands of the future, leaving only idle talk, fallenness, decay, and Jewification.

Authenticity, the Greeks, and *völkisch* nationalism

Only by virtue of the most severe and creative confrontation with what was for them most foreign and difficult – the Asiatic – did this people (the Greeks) enter the brief period of their historical uniqueness and greatness.

Heidegger, "Wege zur Aussprache" (trans. Bernasconi)

I learned very early, perhaps even before 1933 and certainly after Hitler's huge success at the time of his election to the Reichstag, of Heidegger's sympathy toward National Socialism ... It cast a shadow over my firm confidence that an unbridgeable distance forever separated the delirious and criminal hatred voiced by Evil on the pages of *Mein Kampf* from the intellectual vigor and extreme analytical virtuosity displayed in *Sein und Zeit*.

Emmanuel Levinas, "As if Consenting to Horror"

I see the task of thought to consist in helping man in general, within the limits allotted to thought, to achieve an adequate relationship to the essence of technology. National Socialism, to be sure, moved in this direction. But those people were far too limited in their thinking to acquire an explicit relationship to what is really happening today and has been underway for three centuries.

Heidegger, "Only a God Can Save Us"

Blood and soil racism, in both its biological and aestheticized form, strives to create a healthy *Volk*. The fascist critique discussed in the last section (i.e. on the city, on Jews, on leftists) was an essential step in the process of reviving the German *Volk*. Freed from the unGermanic forces of corruption, the German *Volk* could finally emerge. The exclusions inherent in blood and soil racism are, for the radical right that nurtured Heidegger's politics, essential steps in the spiritual revitalization of the German *Volk*. The authenticity of the *Volk*, who are organically connected to the pure soil, comes about by excluding those spiritual influences (and those alien peoples) which corrupt the *Volk* from within.

Up until this point, my analysis has emphasized the role that racial antiSemitism plays in Heidegger's thought. It is now time that we turn to the concurrent question and identify the strain of aestheticized *völkisch* nationalism that runs through his writings. Heidegger's thought wants to identify and exclude the forces of corruption, but it is equally concerned with nurturing a healthy German people. Heidegger's aestheticized *völkisch* nationalism will be explicitly marked in the pages of *Being and Time* and in everything that will follow. If the signs of racial antiSemitism are subtle (but nonetheless potent), the signs of *völkisch* nationalism are anything but so. Heidegger employs the category of *das Volk* before, during, and after his years as an active spokesman for Hitler's regime. On top of that, as Johannes Fritsche demonstrates, Heidegger also employs the particular version of *völkisch* nationalism that is articulated by National Socialism. The logic of racialized discourse dictates that Heidegger must find an antithesis to the racialized category of "the They" (i.e. Jewification). Like others of the radical right, Heidegger seeks to confront the nefarious influences of Jewified urbanity so that he can better nurture a healthy German people. In making his case, he not only uses the racialized category *das Volk*, he also does so in such a way that he places himself in the orbit of National Socialism.

The Volk *in* Being and Time

> It is impossible to be stinting in our admiration for the intellectual vigor of *Sein und Zeit*, particularly in light of the immense output this extraordinary book of 1927 inspired. Its supreme steadfastness will mark it forever. Can we be assured, however, that there was never an echo of Evil in it?
>
> Levinas, "As If Consenting to Horror"

To understand the role assigned to the German *Volk* in *Being and Time*, we need to return briefly to Heidegger's overall argument. We have attempted to trace the conflict between authenticity and funda-mental ontology; between existentialism and ontology. One of the places where this conflict manifests itself is in Heidegger's con-flicting stance towards human absorption in the world. Fundamental ontology rejects the view that the individual is an aloof, autonomous, self-sufficient ego which creates meaning and intelligibility. Heideg-ger proposes the category of "Being-in-the-World" as a way of showing that the world precedes, and gives meaning to, the human subject. Existentialism, on the other hand, scoffs at absorption as a sign of lost authenticity. Being absorbed in the world means renouncing one's authenticity (i.e. "mineness") and becoming lost in the herd. Heidegger proposes the category of "the They" to convey the ways that public life strips the human subject of its individu-ality. This is because the public consists of falling, idle talk, lostness in the present, closedness to the future, rootlessness, and the para-sitical circulating unimportant information. Ontology insists that the human subject is defined in the world, while existentialism calls for the heroic renunciation of the shallow public. Heidegger's description of "the They", which dominates much of *Being and Time*, provides Heidegger with a fundamental philosophical problem. Ontology was supposed to avoid the dead-end of solipsism. Heideg-gerean authenticity, with its emphasis on mineness, however, seems to reintroduce the sense that the human subject is somehow onto-logically foundational and isolated. One seems to become authentic by withdrawing from others. So what becomes of "Being-in-the-world"? Is this not a return to the anthropocentrism that Heidegger is trying to escape?

Emphasis on "the They" and on authenticity backs Heidegger into a corner. If Heidegger does not return Dasein to the world, then *Being and Time* runs the risk of collapsing under the weight of its own contradictions. It is time for him to return Dasein to the world, and, in the process, to return some of the human specificity that has been lost in the analysis of anxiety. To do so he must return to the question of Dasein's possibilities and must provide a source for these possibilities. He must ground human possibility in some-thing other than the human subject, or he will fall subject to his own critique of modern (i.e. anthropocentric) philosophy. If he wishes to escape from the specter of anthropocentrism, then he must reintroduce a source of human possibilities that is both outside of Dasein and that precedes Dasein.

For much of *Being and Time*, Heidegger seems to envision these possibilities in terms of the category of "thrownness". Dasein is thrown into pure, groundless, anxious possibility, into a situation permeated with "nullity" (see *BT* 331). I am thrown into a particular situation, which provides me with my possibilities, and can become authentic by courageously making these possibilities my own. It would seem that, for Heidegger, human existence is permeated by random chance, by invariable contingency; and that authenticity depends upon the way a particular Dasein takes over that which presents itself. Instead of embracing chance, however, Heidegger draws back. He repeatedly comes to insist on the non-accidental nature of human existence (see especially *BT* 434–436). He insists that Dasein is thrown into a particular heritage (*Erbe*) and that it is this heritage that provides Dasein with its fate (*Schicksal*). As Caputo observes, with this move Heidegger turns away from "chance" and towards "vocation" and "call" (see Caputo 1993: 75–100); and as Caputo explains, "the economy of 'vocation' is deeply at odds with the economy of 'facticity'" (Caputo 1993: 79).

The economy of vocation, in the form of heritage and fate, continues to operate throughout *Being and Time*. "If fateful Dasein, as Being-in-the-world, exists essentially in Being with Others, its historizing is co-historizing and is determinative for it is as *destiny* (*Geschick*). This is how we designate the historizing (*Geschehen*)[17] of a community (*Gemeinschaft*), of the people (*des Volkes*)" (*BT* 436 (1929: 384)).[18] Heidegger seeks to situate Dasein socially as well as historically (in terms of heritage and fate). Far from being isolated and atomized, each Dasein is part of a community. Without explanation, Heidegger defines this community as a racialized nationality, a *Volk*. Most commentators find this move to the category of *Volk* as gratuitous (Beistegui 20–23; Caputo 1993: 81; Krell 1992: 177–179; Lacoue-Labarthe 108; Lang 49–56; van Buren 384–386). They argue that there is no compelling reason to equate community with a racially harmonized people rather than with some other form of collectivity.

While the move from community to the German *Volk* may, in some sense, be gratuitous and logically inconsistent, it is, in another sense, consistent with Heidegger's political and ideological views and with his unease in the face of Jewified urbanity. Rightist intellectuals constantly returned to these categories (fate, community, heritage, people) throughout the Weimar Republic (see Fritsche 1999: 68–148; Herf; Sluga 53–124; Wolin 1990: 23–35; Zimmerman 1990: 34–76). Since the 1920s, right-wing intellectuals had opposed the authentic world of community (*Gemeinschaft*) to the inauthentic world of collective society (*Gesellschaft*) (see Fritsche

1999: 68–69).[19] There is no need for Heidegger to explain these ideas in detail, since they had such wide currency in the social discourse of the age.[20] Heidegger self-consciously located himself as a member of the German radical right. It was widely held, on the German right, that inauthentic society, which was governed by the principles of liberalism, Jewification, and self-interest, was to be found in the cities. It was equally widely held, among the same intellectuals, that authentic community, which was controlled by fate and heritage, was to be found among the peasants. There was disagreement on the right as to what formed the basis of this authentic community. Was it the Christian community? Was it the love community? Was it the state? Was it the community forged at the front? Was it the *Volk* (see Fritsche 1999: 137–139)? It is telling that Heidegger employs the phrase *der Gemeinschaft, des Volkes*. In choosing the racialized community of the German people, Heidegger locates himself on the right by framing the argument as one of community (*Gemeinschaft*) over against society (*Gesellschaft*). By specifying that the community (*der Gemeinschaft*) is of the people (*des Volkes*), he opts for the racialized position of the National Socialists, who called for reviving the *Volkgemeinschaft*, rather than that of other radical rightists. He chooses to align himself ideologically with the radical right in general and with Hitler and the National Socialists in particular. He acknowledged as much, in 1936, when he met up with to his exiled Jewish former student, Karl Löwith.

> (I) explained to him that . . . I was of the opinion that his partisanship for National Socialism lay in the essence of his philosophy. Heidegger agreed with me without reservation, and added that his concept of "historicity" was the basis of his "engagement".
>
> (Löwith 1993b: 142)

Fritsche confirms this connection by undertaking his own meticulous analysis of Heidegger's text. He compares Heidegger's language and thought structure to that of a variety of Weimar intellectuals on the right and left. He concludes that "when one reads *Sein und Zeit* in its context, one sees that . . . it belonged to the revolutionary Right, and that it contained an argument for the most radical group on the Revolutionary Right, namely, the National Socialist" (Fritsche 1999: xv). Heidegger embraced the rightist notions of a racialized, *völkisch* German people, free from the corruption of the

Jewified city. Is it any wonder that he came to support Hitler's racialized revolution against urbanity, democracy, and Jewification?

Germans, Greeks, and Nazis: völkisch nationalism after Being and Time

> If we will the essence of science in the sense of *the questioning*
> . . . then *this* will to essence will create for our *Volk* a world of
> the innermost and most extreme danger, i.e., a truly *spiritual*
> world . . . And the *spiritual world* of a Volk is not its cultural
> superstructure . . .; rather, it is the power that comes from
> preserving at the most profound level the forces that are rooted
> in the soil and blood of a Volk, the power to arouse most
> inwardly and to shake most extensively the Volk's existence.
> A spiritual world alone will guarantee our Volk greatness.
>
> Heidegger, *The Self-Assertion of the*
> *German University*

Heidegger's attraction to the category of the *Volk* does not abate in the years following the publication of *Being and Time*. His later writings are even more emphatic in their aestheticized *völkisch* nationalism. This is particularly the case in his speeches of 1933 (both his rectoral address and his political speeches). His rectoral address makes clear that the fundamental bond that binds Germans together is the racial community (i.e. the *Volkgemeinschaft*) and that this racial community provides the German *Volk* with its authentic spiritual mission (see especially Heidegger 1993a: 35; 1993b: 43, 52–56). This racialized thinking is not limited to his pro-Hitler speeches. The category of the *Volk* continues to play an important role in his philosophical writings, even after his disappointment with the direction of the National Socialist revolution.[21] For Heidegger, the essence of a specific language is always intertwined with the essence of a particular *Volk* that is defined by that language. Heideggerian art also always finds itself intertwined with the triangle of essence, language, and *Volk*. The essence of a *Volk* is its voice, which is revealed through its great artists and poets. As in the case of Herder and Hegel, Heidegger's concept of the *Volk* is essential to his view of history, art, language, and poetry.

In *Being and Time*, Heidegger links his *völkisch* nationalism to his position on authentic historicality. Even though Heidegger disagrees with the general outline of Hegel's upwardly progressing narrative of world history (see *BT* 480–486), he does follow Hegel in seeing history (and the cultural artifacts that make possible the study of history) through racialized eyes. The link between the *Volk*, history, and race is particularly visible in Heidegger's analysis of the Greeks. Heidegger first pronounces his new position on history and on the Greeks in *The Self-Assertion of the German University*, his pro-Hitler Rector's Address (Caputo 1993: 82–90). Caputo offers the following, very telling, observation:

> It was only in the 1930s, in the period of Heidegger's active political engagement with National Socialism, that the twofold root of the tradition (Greek and Biblical-Jewish) was pruned to a single root, to a single, simple incipience (*Anfang*), a Great Greek Beginning, from which everything Jewish and Christian, everything Roman, Latin, and Romance, was to be excluded as fallen, derivative, distortive, and inauthentic . . . It cannot be forgotten that it was in the context of the National Socialist seizure of power that Heidegger narrowed down the beginnings of the West to a single "Origin" . . . purely Greek, without Jewish or Christian contamination . . . The first form of the myth of Being is a political myth tied to a hellish ideology, fully equipped with robust and quite bellicose Greek gods and their German heirs, in which Heidegger undertook to produce a thought of Being that was *Judenrein*, thereby reproducing on the level of thinking what the Nazis were doing in the streets.
>
> (Caputo 1993: 4)

As I argued in Chapter 2, eighteenth-century German reconstruction of classical antiquity was carried out within the context of debates about the identity of the German people and debates about the nature of the German state. With the rise of National Socialism, Germany is once again rethinking the issues of peoplehood, German identity, and the state. Once again a leading intellectual chooses to engage this debate by rethinking the essence of the Greeks and by reconfiguring the relationship between the Greeks and the Germans. Once again, the analysis of antiquity is part and parcel of the ongoing debates about peoplehood and race.

As Bernasconi argues (see 1995a; 1995b), Heidegger's radical turn to the Greeks necessarily implies an artificial and violent exclusion of much (i.e. Asian, African, Christian) from the world of philosophy/thought. This artificial and violent exclusion parallels the exclusions that become the cornerstone of Hitler's domestic and foreign policy. Heidegger makes it abundantly clear that not all peoples are created equal. The Germans are at the top and their spiritual, linguistic, and racial ancestors, the Greeks, are slightly below them. If there is some question about what Hegel means by "Germanic", there is no such question here. "For along with German the Greek language is (in regard to its possibilities of thought) at once the most powerful and most spiritual of all languages" (Heidegger 1959: 57). On the other hand, those peoples nourished by the Romance languages are significantly lower, and the original Romance language, Latin, played a particularly nefarious role in the history of Being. While I have been quoting from the days of his Nazi engagement, Heidegger says the same thing throughout the remainder of his career, right on down to his final interview. As Caputo observes, "for Heidegger's 'Greeks' are nothing merely historical (*geschichtlich*) at all, but something destining (*geschicklich*), something steering the very destiny (*Geschick*) of the West, which leaves merely historical research behind" (Caputo 1993: 1). It is at this moment that the ideological and mythical elements, which have taken hold of Heidegger's post-metaphysical "thought", become most visible (see Bernasconi 1995a; 1995b; Caputo 1993: 1–38; Foti 47–51, 65–67; Lacoue-Labarthe 55–58, 78–82).

This Greek/Roman/German triangle provides Heidegger with more than a means of constructing a clearly delimited racialized hierarchy. It also provides the structure of his grand, mythical narrative of Western history and its relationship to the crisis of modernity. While this narrative is in many ways idiosyncratic, we should notice its many points of contact with the similar mythical-historical narratives of Herder and Hegel. In all three metanarratives, the Greeks are the forerunners to the Germans and the Romans (and the Latin people, including the French) are a pale caricature of this Greek beginning. The barbaric Romans/Latins stultify and deaden the glory that was Greece, although there is a chance for revival in modern Europe (or, in Heidegger's case, in modern Germany). The fully blown mythical History of Being makes its first appearance in his pro-Hitler *The Self-Assertion of the German University*. In that speech he argues that modern Germany must submit to the power of the beginning of its spiritual-historical existence:

> This beginning is the beginning [*Aufbruch*] of Greek philosophy. That is when, from the culture of one Volk and by the power of that Volk's language, Western man rises up for the first time against *the totality of what is* and questions

it and comprehends it as the being that it is. All science
... remains bound to that beginning of philosophy and
draws from it the strength of its essence, assuming that it
still remains at all equal to this beginning.

(Heidegger 1993a: 31)

Heidegger did not want to recreate the lost values of the Greek
world nor did he advocate crass imitation of the Greek way of life.
Instead he wished to repeat that Greek beginning in a new, authentically German way (see Bernasconi 1995a; 1995b; Lacoue-Labarthe
55–58, 78–82). Only such an authentic repetition of the great Greek
beginning could bring about a reversal of that which haunted the
modern world: technological nihilism, intellectual and disciplinary
fragmentation, and human groundlessness. Only the Germans are
capable of this authentic repetition, and only after they "destroy"
the dead weight of the Latinized West that continues to block off
access to primordiality even among the sole, modern race capable of
profundity. As late as 1966, in an interview designed to put to rest
rumors of his fascism or racism, he asserts the following. "I have in
mind especially the inner relationship of the German language with
the language of the Greeks and with their thought. This has been
confirmed for me today again by the French. When they begin to
think, they speak German, being sure that they could not make it
with their own language" (Heidegger 1993d: 113).

The West has been in a state of perpetual decline since this great
Greek beginning. The decline was visible during the Greek era
(1959: 145), even in the writings of Plato and Aristotle, who had
fallen away from the primordiality of the pre-Socratics.[22] This is
because it is at the moment of origin, and only that moment, that
the purity of the essence is revealed. "Origin here means that from
which and by which something is what it is and as it is. What something is, as it is, we call its essence. The origin of something is the
source of its essence" (Heidegger 1977a: 149). Since essence and
origin are intertwined in Heidegger, the further one drifts from the
point of origin the more obscure becomes the essence. But there is
more to this than temporal drift from the vibrant moment of life-
giving origin. There is, indeed, a decisive turning away from the
inceptive and from the moment of origin. This decisive turning away
is the source of all later decline. All of the ills that Heidegger sees
in modernity (nihilism, technology, groundlessness, etc.) are
inevitable results of this turning away, and this decisive turning
away took a *racial* form. It occurred when the authentic, vibrant,

dynamic Greek terms, already in a state of decline, became translated into Latin.

The process begins with the appropriation of Greek words by Roman-Latin thought. *Hypokeimenon* becomes *subiectum*; *hypostasis* becomes *substantia; symbebēkos* becomes *accidens*. However, this translation of Greek names into Latin is in no way the innocent process it is considered today. Beneath the seemingly literal and thus faithful translation there is concealed, rather, a *trans*lation of Greek experience into a different way of thinking. *Roman thought takes over the Greek words without a corresponding, equally original experience of what they say, without the Greek word.* The rootlessness of Western thought begins with this translation.

Heidegger (1977a: 153–4, his emphasis)

This Latinization of the originary Greek experience sets in motion the decline of the West. "What happened in this translation from the Greek into the Latin is not accidental and harmless; it marks the first stage in the process by which we cut ourselves off and alienated ourselves from the original essence of Greek philosophy" (1959: 13). The Latinized decline is the root of all contemporary problems: humanism (1977a: 201), philosophy (1977a: 232), nihilism (1977b: 62–63), technology (1977b: 1–5, 30–35), and the resultant political decline that the Nazis had failed to properly diagnose or solve (1959: 36–37, 62–63). We have been declining since we began, and have now hit rock bottom, as revealed by the reduction of humanity to "standing reserve" *(Bestand)*.

With this move Heidegger radicalizes the fascist argument of the decline and regeneration of the West by locating the moment of decline all the way back in antiquity. As Caputo argues, this temporal meeting of Heideggerian fascism and historico-mythologizing is hardly coincidental (Caputo 1993: 27–28). As Heidegger falls under the sway of the myth of Being, his dialogue partners change. Gone are the nonGermans (Paul, Kierkegaard) and those Greco-Germans not properly attuned to the call of their Greco-Germanic destiny (Luther, Bultmann, Plato, Aristotle, Kant, Nietzsche, the Jewish Husserl, the miscegenist Jaspers, the cosmopolitan Goethe). In their place we find those Greco-Germans whom he assumes to be attuned to the mythical, mystical, poetic voice of *aletheia* (the pre-Socratics, Sophocles, Hölderin, Rilke). Not only are the Jews missing as dialogue partners, they are missing from his world history. Both Herder and Hegel may have allowed antiSemitism and racism to affect their description of the Jews and the Orientals, but at least they included them in their history of the world. The East existed and was worth mentioning. This is not the case for Heidegger. His history of Being is a history of the West, and his West is a Greco-German one. All other figures, from the East or the West, can be dismissed as contaminates. This racialized decontamination and purgation is one of the essential strategies of aestheticized racialization; and it is hardly limited to his Nazi years. He may introduce this mystifying metanarrative in 1933, but he holds on to it long after the regime itself has collapsed. He holds on to it before the war, during the war, after the liberation of Auschwitz, and well after Germany's defeat. It is, indeed, one of the few stable aspects of the final forty years of his thought. Heidegger's later thought remains as racialized as it was during his years as a supporter of Hitler. Race plays an essential role in the economy of the thought of the later Heidegger.

As if Consenting to Horror

Doesn't this silence, in time of peace, on the gas chambers and death camps lie beyond the realm of feeble excuses and reveal a soul completely cut off from any sensitivity, in which can be perceived a kind of consent to the horror?

Levinas, "As if Consenting to Horror"

Many of us have long awaited a statement from you, a statement that would clearly and finally free you from such identification, a statement that honestly expresses your current attitude about the events that have occurred. But you have never uttered such a statement . . . Is this really the way you would like to be remembered in the history of ideas?

Herbert Marcuse to Heidegger

In the years after the war, a number of Heidegger's colleagues and former students pleaded with him to renounce the Nazi regime and to condemn the genocide. The most moving of these pleas came from Rudolf Bultmann (see Ott 168), Paul Celan (see Foti 78–98) and Herbert Marcuse (see Marcuse and Heidegger). They wanted him to explain his actions, distance himself from the barbarism of the regime, and save his thought from the taint of Auschwitz. Unmoved, Heidegger consistently and adamantly refused to offer apologies, retractions, or condemnations. For a long time, Heidegger's apologists sought to find dignity and profundity in his silence. What, after all, can one say in the face of such monstrous evil? When words are inadequate to the task at hand, is not silence appropriate? This position was rooted in the discredited view that Heidegger himself had become a courageous and vocal critic of the regime. Once the degree and extent of his political commitment and activities were revealed, it became difficult to believe that Heidegger's silence was a form of poetic mourning for Hitler's many victims. Instead his silence began to look like poetic mourning for the opportunities that were lost and callous indifference to the fate of the victims.

To make matters worse, Heidegger was not really silent at all. He did offer a number of self-serving and evasive defenses of his own behavior. Both in his statement to the denazification committee and in his response to Marcuse he seemed to be unwilling to concede that there was anything particularly or exceptionally evil about the genocide or anything misguided about his public endorsement of Hitler (see Heidegger 1993c; Marcuse and Heidegger 163; see also Ott 309–351; Safranski 332–352). If he had trouble acknowledging the reality (or severity) of the genocide, then he would have infinitely more trouble thinking through the philosophical issues involved. What he had to say on these matters is offensive enough to make one long for scandalous silence.

Recent research has revealed that he did speak of the regime and, on a few occasions, of the genocide. His inflammatory philosophical comments have kindled a scholarly debate so fierce that it has threatened to overshadow his work completely. It is the following quotes, taken from the unpublished version of the seminal essay "The Enframing" ("*Das Gestell*"), which have set the debate aflame.[23]

> Agriculture is now a motorized food industry – in essence, the same as the manufacturing of corpses in gas chambers and the extermination camps, the same as the blockading and starving of nations, the same as the manufacture of atom bombs.

> Hundreds of thousands die en mass. Do they die? They perish. They are cut down. They become items of material available for the manufacture of corpses. Do they die? Hardly noticed, they are liquidated in extermination camps. And even apart from that, in China millions now perish of hunger.

One recoils in horror long before beginning the arduous task of deciphering this particular enigma. Are there really essential similarities

between the manufacturing of food and of corpses? Is it not repre-
hensible to imply, in terms taken from *Being and Time*, that those
slaughtered in the camps died the inauthentic death of those lost in
"the They"? Is this a sophisticated form of defending the regime?
Even if one gets past the initial shock and attends to Heidegger's
argument, there is no decrease in the scandal. This intentionally
shocking quote is designed to illuminate the fundamental truth of
the era: the metaphysical essence (i.e. "in essence the same . . .") of
technology. In Heidegger's schema, Auschwitz is one of many symptoms of how technology has transformed the natural and human
world into standing reserve (i.e. *Bestand*) ripe for manipulation and
exploitation. For Heidegger the question of the essence of technology is truly vital. All other considerations distract us from the
true source and essence of the danger.

One cannot help but notice the absolutely crucial questions that
Heidegger avoids. He does not ask about the identity of murderers
or the victims; nor does he ask why the extermination happened;
nor what it has to say to philosophy or what philosophy has to say
to or about it. Many very serious and sympathetic scholars have
argued that Heidegger's thinking breaks down here even on the
terms that he himself employs. They argue that the logic of the
extermination does not fit with the logic of technology as outlined
in *"Das Gestell"* (see Beistegui 146–157; Lacoue-Labarthe 34–37).
Heidegger's argument, even on its own terms, fails to take the extermination seriously. Why might that be?

Perhaps the victims were too alien and unGermanic to merit any
sympathy or to occasion any philosophical reflection (see Beistugi
157; Lang 57). If the victims were German soldiers or patriots,
whom he freely and eloquently eulogized, one wonders whether he
might not have been so cavalier in his remarks. Since the greatest
number of victims were Jews, the great corrupters of German life,
he remained unmoved, determinedly focused on the great issues
behind the slaughter. Perhaps he was also seeking to rub out the
memory of Auschwitz, to wink to his audience as he let them, and
himself, off the hook. This is the rigorously argued position of
Johannes Fritsche, who concludes as follows:

> Many Germans were all too willing to forget about Ausch-
> witz and to "whitewash" themselves as well as Heidegger.
> Also as with regard to his strategy – the oblique references
> which expel themselves once they have done their job – he
> was very successful . . . How would it have looked to other

countries if *Der Denker* openly advised Germans that one should forget about Auschwitz? Besides, it was much more efficient to silence Auschwitz silently.

(Fritsche 1995: 155)

Heidegger's position here resides somewhere between gross insensitivity to genocide and covert Holocaust denial. The problem runs deeper than that, striking at the very heart of Heidegger's philosophy. As Caputo argues, the later Heidegger renounces mere human (i.e. factical) life in a misguided quest for spiritual purity (see Caputo 1993: 118–130). Heidegger, especially in his later thought, seeks a purified essence so decontaminated that it remains untainted by human existence. The two statements quoted above demonstrate the worst consequences of this essentialist mythologizing. Heidegger is so removed from human (i.e. factical) life, that he is rendered indifferent to human suffering (Caputo 1993: 131–132). He mourns the scarring of Hölderlin's skies, but not the mass slaughter carried out in Hölderlin's name. Essentialized thinking "is accompanied by an ominous, unearthly indifference to concrete historical life" (Caputo 1993: 131). Heidegger's fundamental error stems from his need to place the spiritual over, above, and apart from the merely political and material (see Beistegui 10, 158–160; Lacoue-Labarthe 13). This fundamental error means that he has no way to come to terms with the specificity of political or cultural life. It renders him susceptible to mystification and racialization. It forms the core of his thought, leading him to posit a purified peasant economy corrupted by Jewification and technology and to posit a single, great Greek beginning capable of being repeated only by the spiritual Germans. It first leads him into Hitler's arms and then renders him incapable of coming to terms with the genocide.

Heidegger's thought, with its racialized myths and monstrous indifference to human life, is hopelessly blind and deeply deficient. Despite Heidegger's astonishing brilliance, at the center of his thought resides a fundamental flaw and an equally fundamental blindness. The flaw comes in assuming that human existence can be thought in the abstract, without paying attention to the material world. The blindness encourages him to continue philosophizing after the genocide as if nothing had changed. He writes and thinks as if the Holocaust presented philosophy and humanity with no new questions and no new challenges. Heidegger wanted to identify the essence of technology and used the extermination as a particularly arresting example of this fundamental problem. That assumes that Auschwitz poses no problems of its own, that once the problem of technology has been addressed one can be done with thinking about the genocide. Yet is there not more to Auschwitz than the problem of technology? Auschwitz eclipses the question of technology and replaces it with questions of its own; questions about racism and imperialism, questions about ideology, evil, and indifference, and questions about the forcible exclusions (carried out in the name of racial and aesthetic purity) that function throughout the modern project that Heidegger both embraced and challenged.

Heidegger's public, philosophical statements about the genocide turn out to be extremely revealing, although not in the way that he himself intended. He wanted them to help him reveal, in a particularly provocative way, the essence of technology. In the end, however, they help to raise lasting questions about the entire project of essentialized thinking – questions which threaten to undo Heidegger's entire project.

Conclusion

> One must always ask oneself whether Heidegger doesn't speak
> a language which has become impossible.
> Otto Pöggler, "Heidegger's Political
> Self-Understanding"

Heidegger is one of the twentieth century's most perplexing thinkers because his thought is *simultaneously* profound and ideologically contaminated. There are no moments when his thought is entirely free of racialized mystification; yet there are also few moments when his serious writing is unremittingly consumed by these same disturbing tendencies. Both are always at work in his text, occasionally at the same time. If this makes strict discipleship no longer conceivable, it also makes discarding him altogether equally inadequate. His best insights are too valuable to repudiate, while his worst tendencies are too disturbing to endorse and too pervasive to ignore. Perhaps, in this ironic way, he truly is emblematic of our age; not as our incontestably greatest thinker, but as a man whose brilliant thought can never escape the tinge of imperialism and racism.

Despite the strongly critical tone of this chapter, I do wish to insist that there is much that is worthwhile, even exhilarating, in Heidegger's work: his decentering of the subject, his call for the "destruction" of the West, even his passionate insistence that philosophy be a way of life rather than a dry academic discipline. All of this is eminently worthwhile, and it is difficult to imagine the careers of Levinas, Foucault, and Derrida without his ground-breaking quest.

On the other hand, there is as much to be condemned in Heidegger as to be admired. Even his most insightful writings are not unproblematic. For most of his career he does not succeed in his decentering project, and he finally succeeds in decentering the subject only with the help of a racialized aesthetic and an equally racialized, and thoroughly mystified, history of being. His actual destructive analysis is always tied to his quest for pure, uncontaminated origins and essences. This desire for purity is deeply connected to his quest for organicity, which opened philosophy's door to every manner of rank antiSemitism and racism. It is a short step from aesthetic purity to racial purity. Finally, his passion quickly turned to arrogance and poor judgment, leading him to confuse Hitler with a Messiah and leading him to hope that the National Socialists were bringing about a truly revolutionary response to the philosophical crisis of the West. With this inconceivable act he not only placed his entire career under a permanent cloud, he helped prop up a truly monstrous regime. He may not be guilty of supporting genocide, since he had the good fortune to fail as rector well before the implementation of the final solution; but he certainly is guilty of endorsing and justifying philosophically a totalitarian regime that later committed genocide. To top it all off he refused to admit that this was a fundamentally flawed, perhaps evil, act on his part and he consistently refused to condemn the genocide that was carried out by a regime that he actively supported. If Heidegger's brilliance opened a space for Foucault, Levinas, and Derrida, his enormous transgressions and philosophical errors made them necessary and inevitable.

The most interesting recent work being done with Heidegger is as concerned with contesting his thought as it is with implementing it. Influenced by Derrida's influential essay "Violence and Metaphysics" (Derrida 1978: 78–153), in which he puts Levinas in dialogue with Heidegger and Husserl, several recent studies (especially Caputo, Krell, van Buren) have attempted to rescue that which remains fruitful in Heidegger's thought. I have repeatedly appropriated Derrida's insight to argue that Heidegger's thought is internally divided and self-contradictory, filled with liberatory strains as well as metaphysical and authoritarian strains. I have used this insight to trace the ways that Heidegger's thought turns itself towards racialization. Caputo, Krell, and van Buren have made similar arguments, but have also taken up the task of liberating Heidegger's *topic* without exonerating the Heideggerian version of this topic. Caputo sums up his goals nicely. "If the myth of Being is tied up with National Socialist mythology, then demythologizing (i.e. deconstructing) Heidegger is likewise an operation of denazification and of putting Heidegger's thought in the service of other, more honorable ends, ends that he himself would likely have abhorred, given his own disastrous judgment in political matters" (Caputo 1993: 5). These studies hope to take up the liberatory strains of his thought and use them as weapons to subdue those aspects of Heidegger that are less admirable.

These philosophers are again raising the questions that preoccupied Heidegger, but are doing so without giving in to the desire for pure origins and pure essences. For these thinkers, the obsession for purity gives way to a recognition of the inherent impurity and hybridity in all cultural artifacts. The single great Greek beginning gives way to the multiple beginnings and multiple ways of thinking about the self and the world (see Derrida 1978: 152–153, and the "Jew–Greek" economy). These scholars are dissatisfied with the notion that modernity has fallen from the dizzying heights of philosophy's primordial birth and they seek to think about the past without recourse to the categories of origin and fall. They seek a way of thinking that has as much compassion for the suffering of the victim as for the absence of Being. At the same time, and this is worth noting, their analysis emerges from, and is deeply indebted to, the Heideggerian texts that they simultaneously appropriate and critique.

It is also worth noting, however, the distance between the Heidegger of biblical scholarship and Heidegger deconstructed (at the hands of Derrida, Levinas, Caputo, Krell, and van Buren). I hope to show that some, but not all, of Heidegger's nefarious racial views found their way into the very heart of the discipline. Furthermore, the biblical scholars who embraced him did not do so because he was a simultaneously problematic yet brilliant thinker. They embraced him because he was purported to be the greatest thinker of the age, the man who had seen through to the core of human nature and passed his wisdom on to his followers. Bultmann's Heidegger is the existentialist philosopher rather than the Buddhist, the postcolonial, or the deconstructed Heidegger. To what extent is Bultmann's existentialist genius also the antiSemitic, Nazi

Heidegger? To what extent did his disastrous political and humanitarian judgments follow from his existentialist thought? Is there any way to take the existentialist Heidegger and to leave the racist Heidegger behind? What else did biblical scholars tacitly and unconsciously accept when they allowed Bultmann to turn them into Heideggerians? These are the questions that will occupy us over the course of the next two chapters.

5

IN THE SHADOW OF HEIDEGGER

Bultmann, race, and the quest for Christian origins

At the university there is nothing happening, no stimulus at all. The only real human being here is the theologian Bultmann, whom I see every week.

Heidegger, 1924

I am personally convinced that theology is *no* science . . . And so my work in Marburg was always consciously doublesided – helping and yet quite disconcerting – and I freed more than one from theology.

Heidegger, 1928[1]

Rudolf Bultmann is responsible for giving shape to much of twentieth-century biblical scholarship. It is he who established the terms that would be employed, the issues that would be debated, and the historical and exegetical framework that would be adopted. Bultmannian form criticism redefined the scholarly approach to the Synoptic Gospels and, in the process, redefined the scholarly understanding of Jesus and his place in early Christian history. Not content with this momentous achievement, he shocked the theological world with his World War II essay on demythologizing. For the next twenty years, Protestant theologians of all stripes were forced to reckon with Bultmann's provocative challenge to Christian faith. Around the same time, Bultmann's students (Conzelmann, Haenchen, Bornkamm, Käsemann, Fuchs, to name a few of the most prominent) began their own successful scholarly careers. Indebted to their teacher but independent of mind, they helped reshape the discipline of New Testament scholarship. Their methodological, theological, and exegetical innovations dictated the scholarly agenda through the 1960s and beyond.

Even as biblical scholarship in the 1970s began to move geographically (towards America) and methodologically (towards structuralism, narrative criticism, postmodernism, feminism) the Bultmannian perspective remained profoundly influential. Despite significant shifts in historical and exegetical perspective, one can still detect in current scholarship revised versions of the ideological, theological, and aesthetic perspectives of the Bultmannian school, even among scholars who do not consciously invoke his name. His presence in current scholarship is so strong that he has become something of a mythical father, implacably lodged in the disciplinary subconscious. It remains to be seen whether for current scholarship he is closer to Laius or Abraham, whether he is positioned at the crossroads or is binding his offspring to the sacrificial altar.

Bultmann was convinced that the New Testament was best understood from the perspective of Heidegger's philosophy. He was largely responsible for introducing Heideggerian terminology and categories into the practice of the discipline. His limitless faith in the early Heidegger proved infectious, as Heideggerian terminology slowly began to permeate the nooks and crannies of scholarly discourse. He not only dictated *that* Heideggerian terminology would be employed by serious New Testament scholars, he dictated *how* Heidegger would be employed. I argued, in the previous chapter, that *Being and Time* contains competing and contradictory strains, where the ontological analysis of the conditions of intelligibility (rooted in Dilthey) was in tension with the existentialist themes (rooted in Kierkegaard) of authenticity and "the They". While the former challenged the anthropocentrism of modern thought, the latter allowed anthropocentrism to return to the foreground. In the wake of *Being and Time*, Heidegger became increasingly dissatisfied with the anthropocentric strain of his earlier argument and began to avoid the language and categories of existentialism. Bultmann's Heidegger possessed none of this philosophical sophistication or maddening ambiguity. Bultmann shows little interest in Heidegger's philosophical analysis or in his later rejection of existentialism. Bultmann's Heidegger was an existentialist who had discovered the formal structures of human existence. Long after Heidegger had renounced his formalized analysis of the structure of Dasein, Bultmann remained convinced of its validity. Long after Heidegger had renounced *Being and Time* and Christianity, Bultmann continued to preach the Heideggerian gospel.[2]

Bultmann created a useful Heidegger, one who sounded simultaneously profound and comfortable, and passed him along to biblical scholarship. Some of Bultmann's students sought to reconfigure Heidegger by means of his later philosophy, although they were unable to imagine a Heidegger fundamentally different from Bultmann's. The Heidegger of biblical scholarship is at heart an existentialist, a philosopher of authenticity and freedom. This is true of Bultmann's Heidegger, of the New Hermeneutic's Heidegger, and of the Heidegger of parable scholarship.

There is much in Bultmann's career that is worthy of critical appraisal. This study shall be forced to limit itself to the relatively narrow issue of Bultmann's relationship to Heidegger, which is most visible in his theology and his program of demythologizing. Many recent scholars have taken up the issues of antiJudaism and racism in the New Testament and in biblical scholarship. Many of these same scholars remain deeply indebted to Martin Heidegger, who was a Nazi. The as-yet unasked question could be framed as follows: To what extent are biblical Heideggerians influenced by the disastrous ideological and political values embedded in Heidegger's thought? This is the question which will occupy us for the remainder of this book. We shall begin by looking at Bultmann's initial attraction to Heidegger.

Heidegger, Bultmann, and liberal theology

One may call such interpretation "anthropological" on the condition that what one understands by "anthropology" is existentialist analysis of human being and does not confuse such an analysis with the kind of anthropology offered by objectifying scientific thinking.

Bultmann, "On the Problem of Demythologizing"

What if the aforementioned approach, starting with the givenness of the "I" to Dasein itself, should lead the existential analytic, as it were, into a pitfall?

Heidegger, *Being and Time*

Bultmann seems to believe that a language which is no longer "objectifying" is innocent. But in what sense is it still a language? And what does it signify?

Paul Ricoeur, "Preface to Bultmann"

In 1923, Heidegger joined Bultmann on the faculty of the University of Marburg. While Heidegger was distinctly unimpressed with most of the faculty and with the university's intellectual climate, he did find an exception in Rudolf Bultmann. They soon began attending each other's seminars[3] and developed a friendship that endured after Heidegger's departure in 1928. Despite Heidegger's growing suspicion of religion and theology, he collaborated with Bultmann throughout the entirety of his stay at Marburg. While the two men drifted apart intellectually and politically after Heidegger left for Freiburg, their friendship continued unabated. They took radically different positions during the Nazi years, with Heidegger joining the Party and Bultmann joining the Confessing Church. While they had no contact during the war, Heidegger phoned Bultmann immediately after the war ended and the two soon spent an afternoon together. During this meeting, Bultmann tried unsuccessfully to get Heidegger to retract his Nazi affiliation. Bultmann recounts the story as follows:

> The past was forgotten. If he had once been drawn to National Socialism for good reasons, they had soon turned to disillusionment. Nothing more stood between us . . . "Now you'll have to write a retraction, like Augustine", I said ". . . not least for the sake of the truth of your thought". Heidegger's face became a stony mask. He left without another word.
>
> (quoted in Ott 168)

Despite this disconcerting refusal on Heidegger's part, Bultmann remained unwavering in his devotion to the validity of Heidegger's early phenomenology. Neither Heidegger's rejection of *Being and Time* and of theology, nor his steadfast National Socialism was enough to get Bultmann to reconsider his own commitment to Heideggerian existentialism. Bultmann may have recognized that early Heidegger had given way to later Heidegger, but this recognition had little effect on Bultmann's own position (see Achtemeier 68–69; Robinson 1963: 63–68). Bultmann's Heidegger is every bit as solid as the philosophical Heidegger is fractured. Bultmann encountered Heidegger on the terrain of religion and theology and developed a position on Heidegger's thought drawn from their collaboration, a position which remained unmodified in over thirty years of scholarly writings. He remained convinced, for all that time, that early Heidegger had uncovered the purely formal structure of human existence. He spent much of his career grounding his theology and exegesis in this purely formal structure. He was not going to let anything, including the renunciation of the position by its author or the unrepentant fascism of that same author, stand in the way of applying Heideggerian existentialism to the New Testament. This devotion needs to be explored, as does the particular version of Heidegger it produced.

Bultmann maintained that philosophy establishes the formal structure of human existence and theology articulates the particular structure of Christian existence. "Philosophy shows that my being a man uniquely belongs to me, but it does not speak of my unique existence; this, however, is exactly what theology does" (EF 93). It is the task of philosophy to determine the general structure of existence and the task of theology to determine how to actualize that structure to elicit faith. It is the task of philosophy to define the conditions that make possible authentic and inauthentic existence, and the task of theology to summon the individual to the particular mode of authentic existence that is faith. Philosophy does not replace faith, but it does give faith the conceptual tools necessary for proper self-definition.

Bultmann was also convinced that he had found in Heidegger the proper philosophical ground for his own views on the New Testament:

> When critics have occasionally objected that I interpret the New Testament with the categories of Heidegger's philosophy of existence, I fear they have missed the real problem. What ought to alarm them is that philosophy all by itself already sees what the New Testament says.
>
> (NTM 23)

This assertion is as revealing as it is inaccurate. While one strain of Heidegger's thought did genuinely ground Bultmann's position, I will show that the more dominant (ontological) argument directly challenges Bultmann's anthropocentric reading of Heidegger. Furthermore, Heidegger hardly arrived at this position independently of the New Testament. His position was directly influenced both by Kierkegaard and by a number of nineteenth- and early twentieth-century biblical scholars (see Kisiel 1995: 87, 102–105, 525–527). Bultmann was attracted to the religious/theological aspect of Heidegger's thought, yet was unmoved by the rest of Being and Time. He shows no interest in Heidegger's engagement with Aristotle or Dilthey (i.e. with the hermeneutics of facticity) or in Heidegger's destruction of Western ontology. This exclusive devotion to Heidegger's theologically inspired ideas goes a long way towards explaining Bultmann's disinterest in the later Heidegger, which directly challenges those tenets of *Being and Time* that Bultmann finds most appealing. Bultmann knew that Heidegger was a philosopher, of course, and he appropriated his work, in part, because he was a philosopher of considerable distinction and stature. The philosophical rigor and profundity of *Being and Time*, however, were not what attracted Bultmann, nor did they find their way into Bultmann's existentialism.

Bultmann responded to more than Heidegger's philosophy. He also responded to Heidegger's unflinching radicality, a radicality which was not limited to Heidegger. Radicality emerged from a number of distinct sources and seemed to define the *Zeitgeist* of the Weimar Republic (see Sluga 53–75, 125–153). Bultmann was hardly alone in responding enthusiastically. As Löwith explains, the early Weimar years were a time of crisis that seemed to call for radical revisions of the established intellectual order:

> The extraordinary fascination that Spengler, Barth and Heidegger – despite their various divergences – exerted upon a generation of young Germans following the First World War derives from a common source. Their shared position can be seen in the clear awareness of being situated in a crisis – a turning point between epochs; and thus being obliged to confront questions whose nature was too radical to find an answer in the enfeebled, nineteenth-century belief in progress, culture, and education. The questions that agitated this young generation, devoid of illusions, yet sincere, were fundamentally questions of faith.
>
> (Löwith 1993a: 172)

Karl Barth and Martin Heidegger may both share a sense of revolutionary zeal, a sense of the crisis of the day, and a sense of revulsion at the total inadequacy of nineteenth-century liberalism. Despite these aesthetic similarities, they make for rather strange bedfellows. They both are attractive partners for Bultmann, but for different reasons and in different ways. Barth becomes an ally in his quest to restore the primacy of God's grace. Heidegger becomes an ally in his quest to overthrow the old order.[4] The two goals sit uneasily together in Bultmann's theology.

Bultmann and Heidegger found themselves in the same socio-political environment and in the same institutional setting. They were both convinced that they were responding to a crisis, and were equally contemptuous of established certainties and inherited critical practices. They shared a similar *narrative* of origin, fall, crisis, and revival; a narrative which would prove to provide Bultmann's thought with its essential structure. On the other hand, they were from different disciplines and were seeking to overthrow different intellectual traditions. Having aligned himself with Husserl and Jaspers, Heidegger sought to return to the origins of Western philosophy, to wage war against modern, liberal individualism, and, in the process, to revive a dying culture. Bultmann, however, had his eyes elsewhere. Having aligned himself with Barth and Gogarten, he sought to return to the origins of the Christian faith, to wage war against the tepid and feeble forces of liberal theology, and, in the process, to revive a moribund faith. Heidegger helped Bultmann wage his own war by providing him with categories and terminology, with revolutionary zeal, and with an increasing degree of intellectual prestige; but the two men were fighting a different war, against different opponents, who were seen as causing different kinds of damage. They may have shared a general narrative structure, but they were telling altogether different stories.

If Heidegger traced the woes of the modern world to the philosophy of Descartes and his heirs, Bultmann traced the crisis of modern faith to the flaws of recent, liberal theology,[5] which forgets that God is wholly other and assumes that God is a given entity which can be analyzed like other entities in the world (*F&U* 45–47). In so doing it commits the most egregious of all possible sins: idolatry. Modern theology thereby eliminates the stumbling block of faith and encourages humans to justify themselves before God. Bultmann sees liberal theology as religiously flawed, idolatrous, and sinful.

For Bultmann, any statement about God is objectifying and profoundly sinful (*F&U* 53–58). Bultmann wishes to restore the primacy of theological language in critical scholarship (note his emphasis on sin, grace, justification, the law, the kerygma, etc.), yet by defining objectification so stringently, he seems to leave little room for this theological language (see Ricoeur 395–397). For Bultmann one must talk about God, yet virtually every statement about God is intrinsically sinful. How, then, can one honestly talk about God without objectifying, defining, or analyzing God and without falling into sin? Bultmann's answer to this question determines virtually the entirety of his theological project and is equally determinative for his theological heirs. "It is therefore clear that if a man will speak of God, he must evidently *speak of himself*" (*F&U*

55). Thus, the statement that "God is merciful to sinners" is not a statement about God's merciful nature but about my experience of God's mercy. Likewise, the grace of God means nothing more, or less, than that "God is gracious to me" (*F&U* 145–148). Or, to put it more bluntly: "Only such statements about God are legitimate as express the existential relation between God and man. Statements which speak of God's actions as cosmic events are illegitimate" (*JCM* 69).

Bultmann avoids objectification by launching a theological program that is utterly anthropocentric and individualistic, perhaps even solipsistic. This move ensures that Bultmann's theological program contradicts the central arguments of *Being and Time*. As I argued in the last chapter, Heidegger's entire project could be summarized as an attempt to decenter the subject. While *Being and Time*'s use of existentialist language ensured that he was unable to successfully decenter the subject, the goal remained essential to his overall argument. It was his own inability to avoid anthropocentrism that led to his eventual repudiation of *Being and Time*. He was convinced that anthropocentrism was the decisive philosophical error that made possible all that was wrong with modernity, including objectification. The crisis of the West, for Heidegger, was brought on by anthropocentrism. The solution, for Heidegger, was to develop a philosophical program which reconceives the subject from the ground up (hence being-in-the-world and all that follows from it). On the other hand, Bultmann's thought, which seeks to be Heideggerian, is necessarily, compulsively anthropocentric. Bultmann was convinced that objectification was the decisive spiritual error that made possible all that was wrong with modern faith. The crisis of modern Christianity, for Bultmann, was brought on by the human need to objectify itself and God. The solution is anthropocentrism. For Bultmann, any language about God which is not exclusively about the individual is illegitimate, objectifying, and sinful. All theological language is, therefore, necessarily anthropocentric.

The two thinkers are on a collision course with each other, with Heidegger straining to remove the human subject from the center of the world and Bultmann straining just as hard to anthropologize all theological language. It is no wonder that Bultmann shows little interest in the philosophical arguments of *Being and Time* and even less in the later Heidegger. Bultmann's anthropocentrism, which is essential to his entire project, guides his reading of Heidegger, who becomes equally important to his project. He repeatedly and sincerely maintains his allegiance to Heidegger, who, despite his own claims to the contrary, apparently has defined the essence of human existence. It is to Bultmann's precarious reading of Heidegger that we shall now turn.

Bultmann reading Heidegger

> Demythologizing as existentialist interpretation seeks to make
> clear the character of scripture as personal address.
> Bultmann, "On the Problem of Demythologizing"

If Heidegger sought to decenter the subject, Bultmann, inspired by a demythologized Paul, sought to *de-objectify* the individual and God. If Heidegger turned to being-in-the-world to reach his goal, Bultmann turned to *relationality*. The individual in *relation to God* becomes the centerpiece of Bultmann's nonobjectified theology.

> For Paul, *God* is not a metaphysical being and thus is not an object of speculation, but rather is the God whose action does not take place primarily in cosmic occurrences, but in relation to man in history. On the other hand, he does not understand *man* as an isolated being within the world, but rather always sees him in his relation to God. Therefore, it follows that what God and man mean for Paul can only be understood together as a unity and that this "theology" can be presented as anthropology.
>
> (*EF* 127–128)

Like Heidegger's being-in-the-world on which it is modeled, Bultmannian relationality is designed to liberate the individual from atomism and isolation. "If I have my authentic being, my existence, in being personal – and this means also in personal relations – it can be said that my existence is not objectifiable" (*NTM* 140–141). Bultmann's individual is not an isolated, objectified subject, because he/she is always situated in relation to God; just as his God is not a metaphysical object of speculation, because God is always in relation to humans. "I cannot talk in an objectifying way about God, who only encounters me in the word of God that affects me in my existence. I can talk of God only out of my existence" (*NTM* 143–144).

The individual exists in history, which is the realm where my unique possibilities of existence are revealed. Since these possibilities are uniquely my own, I must seize them myself and make them my own. The crucial moment of authenticity comes through my own *decision*. I must decide to claim my own unique possibilities as my own. "It belongs to the historicity of man that he gains his essence in his decisions" (*HE* 44). History, therefore, is the site of decision, the place where I decide to exist authentically (by seizing my own possibilities) or inauthentically (by failing to do so). The New Testament, as a historical document, is also a site of decision. "The issue is whether the New Testament offers us an understanding of ourselves that constitutes for us a genuine question of decision" (*NTM* 15).

I seize my own authentic possibilities in history, which means in time. Like Heidegger, Bultmann constructs temporality around the category of the care-structure. Temporality, as defined by the care-structure, and authenticity become as closely intertwined for Bultmann as they are for Heidegger. Indeed one may say that this is the point where Bultmann follows Heidegger most closely.

> Martin Heidegger's existentialist analysis of human exist-
> ence seems to be only a profane philosophical presentation
> of the New Testament view of who we are: beings existing
> historically (*geschichtlich*) in care (*Sorge*) for ourselves on the
> basis of anxiety (*Angst*), ever in the moment of decision
> between the past and the future, whether we will lose
> ourselves in the world of what is available (*Vorhandenen*) and
> of the "one" (*des "Man"*), or whether we will attain our
> authenticity (*Eigentlichkeit*) by surrendering all securities
> and being unreservedly free for this future. Is that not how
> we are also understood in the New Testament?
> (*NTM* 23 (1951a: 33))

Bultmann and his heirs have dedicated themselves to finding the Heideggerian care-structure in the New Testament. This raises a number of interesting methodological, exegetical, historical, and ideological issues. Given the task of this book, I wish to emphasize the latter. As I argued in the previous chapter, the Heideggerian care-structure (i.e. Heideggerian temporality) is infused with troublesome ideology. This certainly has implications for our reading of Bultmann.

Bultmann and the origins of Christianity

> *Where and how does it begin . . .?* A question of origin. But a
> meditation upon the trace should undoubtedly teach us that
> there is no origin, that is to say simple origin; that the ques-
> tions of origin carry with them a metaphysics of presence . . .
> The question of origins is at first confused with the question
> of essence.
>
> Derrida, *Of Grammatology*

Bultmann's theology has been guided by two disparate sets of
commitments: his critique of liberal theology and his embrace of
Heidegger. His critique of liberal theology dictates that theological
language must be primarily anthropological and must affirm the
radical stumbling block of the gospel. His embrace of Heidegger
dictates a rejection of all forms of objectification, a commitment to
existentialism and authenticity, and an anthropology that is temporally structured. These commitments (to a temporally defined
anthropology, existentialism, authenticity, and de-objectification)
form the pre-understanding which Bultmann brings to the reading
of the New Testament. They form "the life relation to the subject
matter" (*NTM* 74). This life relation to the subject matter taken
up by the New Testament (i.e. salvation through the act of God)
makes possible a reading of the text which Bultmann regards as
proper. It guides his theological reading of the New Testament.
All of the major themes we have been analyzing (Heidegger's
ideologically infused ontology, Bultmann's anthropocentrism,
Heideggerian/Bultmannian authenticity and temporality, the care-
structure, the radicality of the stumbling block) come together in
Bultmann's theological reconstruction of the origins of Christianity.
It is here, in the Heideggerianized reconstruction of Christian
origins, that the issues of antiJudaism and of racialized identity come
to the fore.

For Bultmann's exegetical program to succeed he needs a means
of bridging the gap between his theology and the text. Surprisingly,
his essays on demythology do not provide methodological principles
for existentialist interpretation. Demythology does not provide a
rigorous means for bridging the gap between theory and practice.
The gap is bridged, instead, with the category of *eschatology*. This is
the category that will bear the weight of Heideggerian temporality.
For Bultmann, eschatology is temporal self-understanding, which
is necessarily defined around care-structure. "The general human
understanding of the insecurity of the present in the face of the

future has found expression in eschatological thought" (*JCM* 24–25). Eschatology becomes the bridge between the care-structure, his theological program, and the New Testament. It is eschatology that helps Bultmann import Heideggerian existentialism to the New Testament and it is eschatology that provides Bultmann's thought with its (Heideggerianized and, therefore, racialized) structure. For Bultmann, the care-structure, temporality, and eschatology all mean the same thing. This conflation will help Bultmann construct his Heideggerian narrative of Christian origins.

An existential morality tale

> The idea of freedom has in actual fact given our western civil-
> ization its peculiar character – or at least it is one of the chief
> forces to which this civilization owes its stamp.
>
> Bultmann, *The Significance of the Idea of*
> *Freedom for Western Civilization*

As we saw earlier, the care-structure has three parts: a past into which we are thrown, a present in which we live, and a future which is bursting upon us. These three temporal moments provide us with three possible temporal stances, each with varying degrees of authenticity or inauthenticity: one can live weighed down by the past, which is closed to the future and, therefore, inauthentic; one can live authentically, where the present is always open to the future; or one can live lost in the present, and, therefore, can drift back to the inauthenticity that had been formerly overcome.

These three stages of authenticity fit nicely into an existentialist morality tale. First, I live inauthentically, perhaps blindly so, un-aware of the existence of other possibilities. Suddenly I encounter that primordial moment, shocking me out of my blindness, shat-tering my devotion to "the They" and conventionality, and opening up the way to authenticity. Unfortunately I am unable to maintain this high level of openness and, weighed down by the cares of the world, I slowly drift back into an inauthenticity of a different sort. A pattern develops: first blindness, then vibrancy and liberation, which is eventually tempered by lethargy and indifference. This lethargic state holds sway until my next encounter with the prim-ordial, when it happens all over again. My experience of God needs to be claimed anew each day, and without constant vigilance it falls prey to the temptations of objectification, merit, and pride. Life consists in three existential moments: habitual inauthenticity, existential encounter producing exhilarating moments of authenticity, and slothful fall back into convention. Even those who have awakened from the intoxicating slumber of inauthentic conventionality can only move between authenticity and its opposite. Even they cannot perpetually maintain their heightened state of existential awareness.

This narrative may, at first blush, seem to be ideologically innocent. When it is applied to Christian origins, however, it shifts from the idiosyncratic to the disturbing and becomes the bridge between racialized thinking and Bultmannian existentialism. It is particularly disturbing if we accept that the terms "inauthenticity", "conventionality", and "fall" all contain unsettling echoes of "Jewification" and that the term "authenticity" contains equally troublesome echoes of escape from Jewification. The problem here is one of discourse rather than intention. Bultmann's benign intentions are no match for a discourse capable of steering his analysis in the direction of racialization. I am not arguing that everyone who employs these terms (i.e. "inauthenticity", "conventionality", "fall") is consciously affirming antiSemitism and I have no wish to taint Bultmann with the accusation of Heideggerian fascism. I am arguing, however, that these terms do indeed ensure that Bultmann's historical reconstructions are racialized, *irrespective of Bultmann's intentions*. When this narrative is applied to the origins of Christianity, it will be all too easy to equate inauthenticity with Judaism and to equate authenticity with a purified form of Western Christianity, with Christianity before it became corrupted by the (Jewified or Roman) forces of convention and tradition.

Bultmann's narrative of early Christian theology was as indebted to F.C. Baur and the Tübingen school (see Chapter 3) as it was to Heidegger. Most especially he inherited an architectonic structure of early Christianity from Tübingen (see *Essays* 209–215, 226, 305–306). While the specifically Hegelian aspects of Tübingen had long been stripped away (i.e. the simultaneously upward and Westward movement of *Geist* and of human consciousness), the fundamental structure (i.e. the oppositions between the servile East and the free West) continued to persevere. Bultmann's achievement was to revitalize this magnificent structure by infusing it with Heideggerian existentialism.

While form criticism radically reconfigured the scholarly view of primitive Jesus traditions, Bultmann's theological reconstruction of early Christianity remained within the orbit of Tübingen. His early Christianity breaks down into the same three phases: legalistic,

Eastern Judaism and Jewish Christianity; radically free, Western Hellenism; compromised, tepidly universalist, early Catholicism. Rather than being defined by the inevitable upward movement of spirit, however, Bultmann's three phases are defined by the existentialist morality tale. This means that Bultmann will organize each period by self-understanding (graded by the standard of authenticity) rather than by levels of consciousness (graded by the standard of *Geist*). Despite these differences, the Bultmannian version of Christian origins will be remarkably similar to the Tübingen version of the Christian origins. As we saw above, the existential morality tale also has three stages: *inauthenticity, encounter, fall*. Just as Hegel dictated the development of Baur's Christianity (from servile consciousness to subjective freedom to compromise), so existentialism dictates the terms of Bultmann's Christianity. In Bultmann's schema authenticity can only erupt from a sea of mediocrity and conventionality, and authenticity must inevitably fall back into lethargic conventionality.

The existential morality tale and the narrative of early Christianity correspond to each other nicely: inauthenticity/late Judaism, existential encounter/Paul, fall/early Catholicism. We should not be surprised by this correspondence, which is neither accidental nor coincidental. Both the existentialist morality tale and the narrative of early Christian theology have been constructed around the category of temporality. Existentialism has been constructed around the care-structure and early Christian history has been constructed in terms of eschatology defined as temporal self-understanding. If Heidegger has properly understood the essence of human nature (as Bultmann claims) and has accidently defined the essence of the New Testament (as Bultmann also claims), then the eschatology (i.e. temporal self-understanding) of the New Testament time period quite literary *must* divide itself into the threefold category of inauthenticity, encounter and fall. It cannot be otherwise. This threefold narrative of the origin and fall of primitive Christianity provides Bultmann's thought with its structure and identifies that which is to be defined as originary (and, therefore, nurtured) and that which is to be defined as alien (and, therefore, excluded). It is, therefore, this threefold, temporal structure which ensures that Bultmann's thought remains Heideggerianized and racialized. It is to this threefold division that we shall now turn.

Bultmann's Palestinian Judaism: inauthenticity

> As interpretation of the will, the demand, of God, Jesus'
> message is a great *protest against Jewish legalism* – i.e. against a
> form of piety which regards the will of God as expressed in
> the written Law and in the Tradition which interprets it, a
> piety which endeavors to win God's favor by the toil of
> minutely fulfilling the Law's stipulation.
>
> Bultmann, *New Testament Theology*

> If God himself had introduced salvation by sending the
> Messiah and permitting him to be crucified, then he had
> destroyed the Jewish way of salvation and had thereby passed
> judgment against everything human, which had reached its
> highest point in Judaism.
>
> Bultmann, "Paul"

It should not surprise us to recognize in Bultmann's thought most
of the tenets of traditional Christian antiJudaism (see especially *PC*
59–86; *EF* 111–157; *Theo* I). As Heschel argues, the historical critical realization that Jesus was fundamentally Jewish had the ironic
effect of increasing the role of antiJewish stereotypes within the
discipline of modern biblical scholarship, especially in Germany
(see Heschel 1998: 9–13, 63–68, 226–228). The exaggerated denigration of first-century Judaism ("late Judaism") made it easier to
separate Jesus from the corrupt Jewish environment which Jesus
came to challenge. It also made it easier, in an age of doubt about
the nature of German identity, for Protestant theologians to separate authentic Germans (i.e. Christians) from inauthentic Germans
(i.e. Jews and, to a lesser extent, Catholics). Jewish critics repeatedly pointed out to no avail that this uninformed view of Judaism
confused racial and religious polemic with serious scholarship (see
Heschel 1998: 222). The social need to cement German identity at
the expense of the Jews overrode the scholarly need to reconstruct
antiquity with fairness and objectivity.

E.P. Sanders has convincingly identified the views of post-exilic
Judaism that permeated Bultmann's theological sources and that
find their way into his overall argument (E.P. Sanders 1977: 3–4,
39–47; 1985: 24–29, 130; see also Heschel 1998: 232). According
to this widely held view, late Judaism suffered from an inner contradiction in its sense of election, a contradiction which loosened
Israel's ties to God and which prevented God from becoming a
vital factor in the life of Israel. God, in the days of late Judaism,

had become inaccessible, remote, distant, and absent. This inner contradiction grew out of the belief that salvation could be earned and was the necessary result of justification by works. Salvation became equated with merit, with the constant piling up of good works in the hope of offsetting the negative results of sin. This flawed view of the mechanics of salvation left Jews in a constant state of spiritual anxiety and unease. They could never do enough to earn salvation or to attain forgiveness for their sins. They could never rest assured, confident that they had achieved salvation. Devout Jews had no certainty, no security, no inner peace. Unable to achieve security or certainty, yet simultaneously convinced of their own chosen status, Jews become increasingly delusional, hypocritical, judgmental, proud and shrill. They compensated for their inability to achieve salvation with increasing *legalism*. They compensated for the loss of the prophetic voice with an idolatrous devotion to the written text. They compensated for their lack of security through haughty self-importance, through rabid nationalism, through scribal scribbling, and through apocalyptic fantasies of world destruction.

Bultmann's major contribution to this common view of late Judaism was to give a Heideggerian structure to it. Bultmann's postexilic Judaism is structured around an inner contradiction, a contradiction which provides the clue to our whole understanding of Israel (*PC* 60–71). This contradiction is fundamentally *temporal*. By binding herself to her past, Israel had loosened her ties to the present and her responsibility for the present. "God was no longer really the God of history, and therefore always the God who was about to come. He was no longer a vital factor in the present: his revelations lay in the past" (*PC* 60). As a result, history was brought to a standstill and the Israelites' moribund culture began to degenerate. With no history, no vital culture, no experience of God in the present, no hope for the future, late Judaism fell into idle, apocalyptic speculation about the cosmic events at the end of the world (*PC* 80–86; *HE* 23–30; *F&U* 194). All that remained was legalism and the ensuing stereotypes: alienation, ritualism, stunted spirituality, formal obedience rooted in fear. The Law, which had been perverted from its original intention as revelation of divine will, became instead the basis for Jewish self-security and boasting (*F&U* 214–219, 222–239, 254; *PC* 71–72; *Essays* 136; *Theo* I. 11–18, 262–269), the most serious of all sins. "The *real sin of man* is that he himself takes his will and his life into his own hands, makes himself secure and so has his self-confidence, his 'boast'" (*F&U* 228).

In both theological and existentialist terms, the Jew is the embodiment of sin and inauthenticity.

> The height of illusion is that man thinks he can separate himself from the "world" and bring himself to a being beyond it.
>
> (*EF* 129)

> Sin is the care, boasting and confidence of the man who forgets his creatureliness and tries to secure his own existence. It reaches its acme in the Jew.
>
> (*EF* 133)

The circle is closed: Heidegger created the category of authenticity with the help of secularized antiJewish stereotypes, culled from biblical scholars, philosophy and traditional theology. Bultmann then, in taking up Heideggerian existentialism, appropriates these secularized antiJewish categories and applies them to Judaism itself. Jews are inauthentic and inauthenticity is Jewification.

Bultmann's Hellenistic Paul: originary authenticity

The most unusual aspect of Bultmann's work comes in the relatively limited role he assigns to Jesus (see *Theo* I. 3–32; *PC* 71–79; *F&U* 220–246). Bultmann's Jesus is, of course, a positive figure. He overcame the flaws of late Judaism, incorporated its virtues into his teaching, and fulfilled its possibilities in a way that Judaism itself never could. It is through Jesus that Christians are able to recognize that the ethical commands of the Old Testament remain valid, even though they are incapable of providing justification. At the same time, Bultmann's Jesus remains fundamentally within the Jewish worldview and his teachings are inessential to Christian faith. While the teachings of Jesus can be recovered through scientific criticism, one should not place too much stock in them. To do so is, for Bultmann, to seek security for faith and is the intellectual equivalent of Lutheran justification by works.

For Bultmann, it is Hellenistic Christianity in general, and Paul in particular, who provides the antidote to legalism, self-security, and inauthenticity. Even more than Jesus and the Jerusalem church, the Hellenist Paul articulates the existential nature of sin and salvation, of law and grace, of inauthenticity and authenticity, of freedom and enslavement.[6] It seems that such ideas can only be articulated on Western, Hellenistic shores.

> This idea of freedom has its *origin* where western civilization itself has its origin, in the *Greek world*. It is here that it is comprehended and developed along definite lines. It then acquired a peculiar stamp in Christianity, and both forms – the humanistic and the Christian idea of freedom – have unfolded their effect in the history of the West.
>
> (*Essays* 306)

According to Bultmann, Paul clarified the theological motifs he inherited from Hellenistic Christianity and raised them to the level of genuine theology, thus making him the founder of Christian theology (*Theo* I. 187). Paul may have employed mythological categories from the larger culture, but not without submitting them to the rigors of demythologizing (*JCM* 32–34). Most especially, it is Paul who goes beyond cosmology and recognizes that theology is primarily anthropology. For Paul, even God as Creator is an existential statement, "a proposition that concerns man's existence" (*Theo* I. 228). Paul assumes an existentialist anthropology, but is specifically interested in the antithesis between authenticity and inauthenticity, between faith and its opposite. "Paul's theology can best be treated as his doctrine of man: first, of man prior to the revelation of faith, and second, of man under faith" (*Theo* I. 191). This general anthropological–existential framework (i.e. humanity prior to faith versus humanity under faith) becomes essential to Bultmann's entire project. It is the organizing principle around which he interprets Paul (*EF* 128–146; *Theo* I. 190–352), around which he carries out his demythologizing program (*NTM* 15–20, 105–110), and around which he builds his own theology.[7] It is here, in his demythologized reading of Paul, that we find all of Bultmann's major concerns: existentialism, demythology, justification by faith alone, eschatology as self-understanding, history as anthropology, authentic self-understanding as freedom. For Bultmann, and for some of his heirs, a demythologized Paul will become the central moment in early Christian history and in modern New Testament scholarship. He will define the essence of early Christianity and, in the process, will become the standard against which other New Testament writings, and other New Testament scholars, will be judged.

For Bultmann's Paul, pre-faith humanity abides in a fundamentally illusory state of existence, a state of existence which flows from a fallacious self-understanding. Denying our creatureliness, we think that we can secure our own existence. "Hence the ultimate sin reveals itself to be the false assumption of receiving life not as the gift of the Creator but procuring it by one's own power, of living from one's self rather than from God" (*Theo* I. 232; see also *EF* 115). As a result of this false assumption, humanity develops anxiety for the things of the world and loses itself in mundane, daily existence. The individual becomes part of Heidegger's "the They". This fallacious self-understanding, this refusal to accept that life is a gift, is what Heidegger calls inauthenticity and what Paul calls sin. It manifests itself in a variety of ways: in pagan wisdom (*Theo* I. 240–241, 327; *EF* 137), in mythological objectification (*NTM* 9–17), and most especially and most tragically in Jewish legalism (*Theo* I. 259–269; *EF* 135–137). This is because the Jewish people are indeed chosen and the Jewish Law is indeed from God. The problem comes with the assumption that one can achieve righteousness from the Law (*Theo* I. 240). The truth is that no one can produce righteousness by means of the Law – that the very effort is doomed to fail. *"Man's effort to achieve his salvation by keeping the Law* only leads him into sin, indeed this effort itself in the end *is already sin*. It is the insight which Paul has achieved into the nature of sin that determines his teaching on the Law" (*Theo* I. 264, his italics).[8] Legalism leads to inauthentic, *servile* self-understanding. "The period before faith, that is, was under the sway of fear. This sentence also shows that it was a period of '*slavery*' (*eine Zeit der Knechtschaft*)" (*Theo* I. 243 (1948: 239)). The period before faith, as represented by the Jewish Old Testament, has no true sense of freedom (*Essays* 306). This servility stems from the inauthenticity, from the failure to, or the inability to, decide.

Pagan wisdom, mythological objectification, and Jewish legalism all share the same characteristics. In all three, the individual seeks to secure his/her own existence falsely. All three share the characteristic of "boasting" (see *Theo* I. 242). What is required is a new form of self-understanding, one which recognizes the shattering of all human standards of greatness, which recognizes the groundlessness of all human self-security, which accepts that life is a gift. This new form of self-understanding will overcome the human desire for self-delusion, self-glorification, objectification, boasting, and self-security.

This new form of self-understanding is what Paul calls faith. Authenticity occurs when I "understand myself existentially here and now as God's creature" (*NTM* 112). Bultmann's actual depiction of the state of Christian authenticity gets rather fuzzy. This fuzziness may be inevitable given his fear of indulging in objectification. He reverts to existentially tinged terminology like "event", "eschatological deed", "gift-character", "presentness", "eschatological Now", "eschatological occurrence", and "being created anew" (*Theo* I. 288–289, 319, 330). It is the product of a *decision* and it brings with it *freedom*, freedom in the form of a new self-understanding.

Freedom comes in the form of a new, authentic self-understanding. This new self-understanding is, in important ways, aestheticized and existentialized. As such, it emerges from and is linked up with the racialized, aestheticized ideology that we have been tracing throughout this book. According to this ideology, authentic self-understanding and/or higher consciousness come about by a twofold move of expulsion and of nurturing. A healthy individual, and, by extension, a healthy people, are made possible by the expulsion of the corrupting and the alien and by the simultaneous nurturing of the originary and the primordial. Only by expelling the corrupting forces of Eastern, despotic Jewification can an authentic culture emerge. For a radical nationalist like Heidegger, it is only the Germans who are capable of thinking primordially and creating an authentic culture. For the more tolerant Hegel, all Europeans who are free from the spirit of Roman Catholicism are capable of creating an authentic culture. In both cases, authentic freedom comes about by means of excluding the non-European spirit and by excluding those aspects of the European spirit (i.e. Latin-Catholic) deemed to be inferior. This racialized ideology is deeply infused in the discourse being employed by Bultmannand finds its way, perhaps unconsciously, into his own views of authentic self-understanding.

For Bultmann, Christian authenticity is diametrically opposed to and profoundly antithetical to Jewish legalism. A series of anti-Jewish and Orientalist oppositions (i.e. Jew/Christian, ritual/prayer, law/grace, East/West, slave/free) have found their way into the writings of Hegel, Baur, and Heidegger. They also find their way, unchallenged and unchanged, into Bultmann's own thinking. Bultmannian inauthenticity might not be reducible to Jewification, but Jewification and inauthenticity correspond with each other in fundamental ways. In the same way, there may be more to faith than fleeing from Jewish boasting, but such fleeing is indeed an essential part of Bultmannian-Pauline faith. "*'Faith' is the absolute contrary of boasting*. . . . (Boasting) is the fundamental attitude of the Jew, the essence of sin, and the radical giving up of boasting is faith's attitude" (*Theo* I. 281, his italics; see also *Theo* I. 242). Judaism and the Jew play very important roles in the economy of Bultmann's thought and theology. They represent the highpoint of human delusion, sin, self-assertion, and pride. They make it possible for Bultmann to define authenticity and Christian faith. They embody that which must be left behind, which must be expelled and excluded, if faith and authenticity are to be found.

Once the spirit of inauthenticity has been expelled, authentic self-understanding is possible. For Bultmann, this authentic self-understanding is fundamentally *eschatological*. As we saw above, Bultmann interprets apocalypticism and eschatology existentially, anthropologically, and temporally. Eschatology reveals a fundamental temporal stance. The inauthentic temporality of late Judaism situates divine revelation in the past and defers hope to some specific point in the future. In both cases, Judaism turns the ineffable, fleeting experience of the divine into something visible, tangible, objective, and, therefore, inauthentic. In both cases, the present is devoid of meaning, devoid of the experience of God (who acted in the past), and devoid of the experience of salvation (which will occur at some date in the future). In authentic Christian faith, however, the past, present, and future are profoundly intertwined. Hope for the future is experienced in the present, as are events that occurred in the past. In authenticity, there is no deferral of the experience of revelation or of grace, as both are experienced in the present. The authentic Christian experiences grace and freedom as "nothing else than being open for the genuine future, letting one's self be determined by the future. So Spirit may be called the power of futurity" (*Theo* I. 335). It is the cross which is the salvific event, which renders "God's judgment upon all self-righteousness and 'boasting'" (*F&U* 214; *EF* 115).

Bultmann takes over from the aestheticized ideology the logic of expulsion of the alien in the name of nurturing the originary. He does distance himself from Heidegger's aestheticized *völkisch* nationalism and does not fall prey to the sort of strident nationalism that was so prominent during the Nazi era. He never limits authenticity to members of the primordial German *Volk* and, unlike Heidegger, he is uninterested in establishing a Greco-Germanic dialogue (see *NTM* 80–81; *Essays* 226–227, 291–292; *EF* 158–162). All who are open to the Pauline–Lutheran gospel are capable of freedom. At the same time, the cross does represent God's judgment on Eastern Jewification, which means that authenticity and freedom are implicitly (and sometimes explicitly) limited to the West (see *Essays* 305–306). For Bultmann, it is the expulsion of the servile and despotic spirit of the East which makes possible the emergence of Western authenticity and freedom.

Bultmann's institutional Church: falling into early Catholicism

> We can only make a just estimate of it if we approach it from the aspect of the antithesis between *theologia crucis* and *theologia gloriae* and, in so doing, raise the central problem of all Christian proclamation.
>
> Käsemann, "New Testament Questions of Today"

The existential morality tale being spun by Bultmann includes a fall from grace every bit as surely as it includes an exhilarating eschatological encounter. While static Jews are consistently inauthentic, the dynamic Christian is in a constant state of flux, perpetually moving in and out of authenticity. The individual is tempted on a daily basis by the forces of convention, tradition, and stultification. These same temptations threaten the eschatological Church itself, the body of Christ. Christianity (Hellenistic, Western, forward-looking, dynamic, eschatological, authentic, free) found its way by breaking free from the moribund world of Judaism (Eastern, backward-looking, alienated, static, decayed, apocalyptic, inauthentic, servile); yet Christianity is also consistently tempted to tame the radicality of Paul's originary insight and to return to the sort of security provided by Judaism. Even after successfully breaking away from that world, Christian Judaizers constantly tempted primitive Christianity with the siren call of objectification, ossification, self-justification, legalism, ritualism, and worldly power.

When the eschaton did not materialize, apocalyptic hopes began to dim and the sense of eschatological urgency began to slacken. The pure freedom and radicality of Paul were inevitably tamed by later generations of Christians (see especially *Theo* II. 95–118, and "History of Salvation and History", in *EF*). A decisive shift occurred at this point as the eschatological community was transformed into the institution of the Church. Rather than being the instrument of eschatological summons, the Church saw itself as the embodiment of divine law and as a transcendental institution of salvation. This process of eschatological slackening and emerging institutionalization brought with it a profound shift in the Church's self-understanding. With the emergence of the Church as an institution, we have a temporal and existential fall from the heights of the Pauline gospel. Paul's sense of eschatological urgency is tamed, as salvation history (*Heilsgeschichte*) replaces the summons of faith. Paul's universalism is tempered, as Christians become smug in the security of their salvation. Paul's devotion to radical freedom is undermined, as the institutional Church replaces kerygmatic preaching. The pure spirit of the Greeks gives way to the impoverished spirit of the Romans.

This spiritual lapse is most noticeable in the shifting temporal stance. The future/present tension, so essential to Paul's primal eschatology, is tempered and objectified. The hope for fulfillment is pushed further into the future and the moment of revelation is pushed into the past. The fundamental character of decision is lost as salvation becomes guaranteed (*Theo* II. 110–114). We should note the role that existentialist terminology and conceptions play here. The loss of decision, the shifting temporal stance, the slackening of primal urgency, the emergence of security and guarantee; these are all signs of inauthenticity and of Jewification. The gospel, which had liberated itself from Judaism, is being reJudaized. In the process Christians surrender true radicality, openness, authenticity, freedom, and identity. As Käsemann explains, "we are in danger of giving up our own identity if we do not remain faithful to this tradition, which has so often been viewed with great suspicion" (Käsemann 1969b: ix). Surrendering the true gospel means a loss of identity and will lead the West into a state of crisis.

The historical process of surrender and compromise culminates in the development of early Catholicism, which, since the days of Tübingen, was seen as a step backwards from all that was pure about early primordial Christianity. As in the days of Tübingen, early Catholicism appears in the New Testament (rather than in the post-biblical era) and is most vividly visible in Luke–Acts. Bultmann is not terribly clear about how he comes to recognize Luke's early Catholicism. He does mention that in Luke, Christianity becomes an event in world history and one religion among many, that Jesus becomes a figure from the past, the kerygma gets historicized, and eschatology is transformed into salvation history (*Theo* II. 116–119; *EF* 238–239). It would be up to his students to take up his programmatic statements and apply them, in a systematic manner, to the text of Luke–Acts.[9] In the process, they set the agenda for Lukan scholarship for the second half of the century and made Luke, at least temporarily, one of scholarship's "storm centers".[10]

According to Bultmann's students, Luke responded to the delay of the parousia (Conzelmann 1961: 14, 97; Haenchen 94–98; Käsemann 1969b: 21; Vielhauer 45–49) by replacing primitive eschatology with salvation history (Bornkamm 199–201; Conzelmann 1961: 23, 105, 113, 135; Käsemann 1964: 28–29; 1969a: 116–117; 1969b: 21; Vielhauer 46–47). According to Conzelmann, whose text was acclaimed as definitive, Luke's Gospel is an exercise in de-eschatology, in removing the sense of ultimacy and existential urgency from the primitive and more authentic gospel. Conzelmann's indebtedness to Heidegger's temporal care-structure is evident in every aspect of Conzelmann's influential book, including its title (*Die Mitte der Zeit*).[11] According to Conzelmann's influential schema, Luke divides history into three epochs: the epoch of Israel, the epoch of Jesus, and the epoch of the Church (Conzelmann 1961: 16–17). This schema locates Jesus in the middle of time and pushes the eschaton to the distant future, separating Jesus from the Church and separating the believer from the eschaton. Jesus is now irrevocably in the *past* (Conzelmann 1961: 14, 28, Part IV; Käsemann 1969a: 116–117), offering timeless teachings rather than historic summons (Conzelmann 1961: 14, 104). At the same time, the eschatological end is reduced to a *future* hope (Conzelmann 1961: 37, 105). Like late Judaism, which Paul had left behind, Luke's generation was living on hope and memory rather than on the experience of God in the present. "The Good News is not that God's Kingdom has come near, but that the life of Jesus provides the foundation for the hope of the future Kingdom. Thus the nearness of the Kingdom has become a secondary factor" (Conzelmann 1961: 37). Jesus' life and the salvation it offers are transformed into mere facts of history, as Luke writes the first history of the life of Jesus. In Bultmann's theological terminology, the authentic *Geschichte* (historicity) of the primitive Church has degenerated into mere *Historie* (see also Käsemann 1964: 18–24, 29). Mighty deeds replace mighty words (Conzelmann 1961: 36–41, 192–193; Haenchen 362–363; Käsemann 1964: 29), as security stands in the place of the purity of the summons.

Perhaps Luke's greatest transgression, even more egregious in the eyes of the Bultmannians than his mistreatment of the life of Jesus, is his misunderstanding of the true nature of the death and resurrection of Jesus. This misunderstanding on Luke's part determines his interpretation of Jesus and, more tellingly, his interpretation of Paul. To state matters succinctly, Luke misunderstands the true nature of Paul's theology of the cross (see Conzelmann 1961:

196–201; Haenchen 92; Käsemann 1964: 29, 91–92; 1969a: 124; 1969b: 22; Vielhauer 40–42). "Luke could cling to this only because he did not feel deeply enough the offence of Jesus' cross" (Käsemann 1969a: 124). Because Luke does not understand the true nature of the cross, he swaps a theology of the cross for a theology of glory. As Bultmann explained, Paul's theology of the cross is the condemnation of all human achievement. Paul's enemy is Jewish legalism and Jewish boasting. Since Luke does not understand the nature of the cross, he does not understand the real nature of Paul's critique of legalism (Conzelmann 1961: 160; Vielhauer 42; Bornkamm 198). As a result Luke has a disturbingly positive attitude towards Judaism and towards the Law (Haenchen 115–116). He does not recognize that the cross marks the condemnation of the Law (Vielhauer 37–43), and he borrowed heavily from Jewish Christianity (Käsemann 1969b: 248). As a result, he reinscribes the gospel back into the spirit of Judaism.

In Luke's world there is no theology of the cross, no summons to faith, no immediate experience of the nearness of God, no freedom from legalism, no authentic independence. God's presence, when not temporally deferred, is mediated through the Church. Luke's Gospel is temporally and theologically defective, existentially inauthentic, spiritually barren, and essentially unfree. Luke's Gospel, as conceived by the Bultmannians, is structurally similar to Heidegger's "They" and bears remarkable similarities to Bultmann's Judaism. Luke's taming of the primordial gospel represents the reJudaizing and reOrientalizing of the authentic, Western gospel.

Despite the bleak situation, all is not lost. Buried beneath the ossified shell of the (Roman) institutional Church lies the (Hellenistic) Pauline gospel, waiting to be rediscovered. One must be willing to peel away the layers of debris that stand in the way of a radical encounter with the kerygma: the stultifying traditions and practices, the perpetual quest for self-security, the willingness to sacrifice the intellect. Only if I am willing to strip away all that is inessential can I encounter the primordial, radical summons of faith that makes up the Pauline gospel. As Bultmann's student Käsemann explains, "whenever he (Paul) is rediscovered – which happens almost exclusively in times of crisis – there issues from him explosive power which destroys as much as it opens up something new" (1969b: 249). When Paul's gospel is properly understood, creative anarchy is unleashed. It disturbs the piety of Christians, it shatters the false security of those in authority, it grounds the Church in the creative Word, it restores worship in the place of the cult, it wipes out superstition and it reinvigorates true faith. The gospel loosens the chains of uniformity and boasting, as freedom reigns (Käsemann 1969b: 249–250). Unfortunately, as Heidegger long recognized, this situation cannot continue forever. The tepid forces of orthodoxy and pietism are unable to live authentically and are equally unable to allow others to achieve authenticity. They will necessarily reassert themselves and will, in the process, domesticate Paul's image and turn away from the power of his writings.

As in the days of Tübingen, Jewish legalism and Hellenistic freedom are seen as existing in a state of permanent warfare. Great is the temptation to reach a compromise in the form of tepid universalism and self-satisfied piety. It is the task of radical criticism to fight, on behalf of Pauline primordiality, against those forces in the ancient and modern world that would compromise the principle of Christian freedom, that would taint the Hellenistic gospel by compromising with the spirit of Eastern Judaism. Radical criticism necessarily rejects this dangerous compromise in the name of the West, of freedom, of higher consciousness, and of authenticity. In the nineteenth century, the Tübingen school stood up for radical freedom, but was eventually domesticated by the accommodating spirit of theological liberalism. In the early part of the twentieth century, the Bultmann school, assisted by insights that he learned from Martin Heidegger, once again took up the case for freedom. Once again, modern Europeans could put themselves in touch with their pure, Christian, Hellenistic essence, an essence which could be found by purging from the New Testament the Latinic tendency to compromise and by waging war against the legalistic, inauthentic, corrupt, servile, Jewified spirit of the East.

Bultmann, Heidegger, and the Holocaust

> From the catastrophe which has broken in upon our western civilization, what is it that we must salvage at all costs for the future?
>
> Bultmann, "The Significance of the Idea of
> Freedom for Western Civilization"

> When I try to decipher a text I do not constantly ask myself if I will finish by answering *yes* or *no*.
>
> Derrida, *Positions*

Behind Bultmann's theology one can detect the longing for a pure Western essence untainted by the corrupting spirits of the East or of Rome. Bultmann neither invented this longing nor is his attraction to it unique. I have argued that this longing permeates much modern thought, both in philosophy and in New Testament scholarship. To put the matter more precisely, I have argued that this longing is infused in the discourse that underlies some aspects of both philosophy and modern New Testament scholarship. There is, therefore, nothing unusual about finding this particular longing (for purity untainted by the alien) in the work of a biblical scholar who is deeply influenced by the history of his own discipline and by the philosophy of Martin Heidegger. The situation is made more complex, however, by the unfortunate fact that Bultmann's career exists in the shadow of Nazism. Much of Bultmann's writings, including his seminal essay on demythology, appear during the Nazi era. Furthermore, his own theological work is deeply and self-consciously influenced by a philosopher who was also a Nazi. Given the historical context out of which he was writing, it seems important to ask about the interaction between Bultmann's theology and National Socialism. Throughout the course of this book I have tried to distinguish between racist intentions and racialized discourse. Once again I find this distinction helpful in posing the particular question of Bultmann's relationship to Nazism.

It is important to begin the discussion by recognizing that Bultmann, unlike Heidegger, never flirted with Nazism and was, instead, a member of the Confessing Church. After the war it was commonly asserted that the Confessing Church actively resisted Nazi racism and oppression. I am persuaded by the revisionist view that the Confessing Church was far more ambiguous in its attitudes towards Jews and towards the regime (see especially Baranowski; Barnes; Barnett). Even if one accepts these scholarly revisions, as I do, this does not change the fact that, when faced with a choice, Bultmann did not choose Nazism. Unlike many intellectuals, Bultmann was not a supporter of the National Socialist "renewal" of the German *Volk*. Furthermore, Bultmann, who rarely talked about politics, did make a series of statements critical of National Socialism.[12] Bultmann's postwar statement, made after the regime's many atrocities had come to light, was far more critical than the statement of 1933. At the same time, his statement of 2 May 1933, made the day after Heidegger officially joined the Party (see Friedländer 55), stands in striking contrast to the numerous public statements made by intellectuals and religious leaders in support of the regime (see Sluga 6–7, 154–157; Friedländer 9–14, 34–39, 49–55). He spoke out against the mistreatment of Jews (*EF* 165), against nationalism's excesses (*EF* 159–162), and against the dismissal of non-Aryan Christian ministers (Bultmann 1966). He was never tempted to join the German Christian movement, which radically deJudaized the Bible, the hymns, and the Churches (see Bergen 1999: 50–59; Heschel 1999: 73–80). Instead he was, from the beginning, deeply concerned that such a new folkish religion (*völkische Religiosität*) would replace or dilute Christianity (*EF* 165 (Bultmann 1933: 166)). After the war he complained that the regime had oppressed both Jews and Christians (*EF* 165, 285) and had been hostile to scientific research (*EF* 285, 288). He also argued that blood and soil racism reduces humanity to the level of the beast (*Essays* 291–292) and that totalitarianism is radically opposed to the principles of human freedom (*Essays* 296–297). National Socialism took the most radical position possible on a variety of issues. There is no evidence that Bultmann himself was personally attracted to their fanatical racism, their rabid antiSemitism or their unequivocal nationalism.

If the question is "Was Bultmann a Nazi?", then the answer is an emphatic "No". This does not mean, however, that he is diametrically opposed to everything they represent. There is a distinct ambiguity that comes through in his discussions of these issues, even in his criticisms of Nazism. So, for example, he argues that nationalism is a perfectly legitimate issue, but that the absolute nationalism of Nazism threatens to turn the people into an idol. Christians owe allegiance to the state and the *Volk*, but it should be ambiguous and critical (*EF* 158–160).[13] This framework leads him to ask the following question, "Is our present struggle on behalf of the ideal of nationality (*Volkstums*) a struggle for an abstraction or for something concrete?" (*EF* 163 (Bultmann 1933: 165)). This question seems to confirm Baranowski's conclusion that while the Confessing Church wanted to defend itself against the encroachment of the Aryanized German Christian movement, it "was equally concerned to avoid the appearance of a sectarian breakaway" (Baranowski 103).

Let us also look more closely at his defence of the Jews. He takes as his starting point the Nazi slogan, "We want to abolish lies."

> As a Christian, I must deplore the injustice that is being done precisely to the German Jews by means of such defamation. I am well aware of the complicated character of the Jewish problem (*das Judenproblem*) in Germany. But "We want to abolish lies" – and so I must say in all honesty

that . . . this beautiful sentiment was not sustained by the
spirit of love. Keep the struggle (*den Kampf*) for the German
nation (*das deutsche Volkstum*) pure, and take care that noble
intentions to serve truth and country are not marred by
demonic distortions.

(*EF* 165 (1933: 166))

There are several important but contradictory aspects of this quote
that are worth highlighting. It is important to recognize that, in
May of 1933, few Germans publicly defended Jews and even fewer
described the actions against Jews as unjust. At the same time, while
he is speaking out against unjust antiSemitic actions he acknowledges the legitimacy of the Jewish problem and he accepts the need
for national renewal and for the struggle for the German *Volk*. In
other words, he seems to separate the violent antiSemitism, which
he blames on defamations, from the policies of the government, from
Hitler himself, and from the Nazi revolution. The implication is
that something important is going on but it is in danger of being
transformed into something ugly. Although there is no evidence that
he supported legalized antiSemitism, he limits his criticisms to
antiSemitic actions without speaking out against the antiSemitic
laws that had already been promulgated. My point is not to criticize Bultmann's actions from the safety of my own study. His
statement on behalf of Jews was both courageous and, given the
spirit of the times, highly unusual. Instead I wish to emphasize that
when Bultmann thinks about the issues of racism and antiSemitism,
he necessarily employs the same intellectual resources that he
employs in his theology and his exegesis. These intellectual
resources, which emerge from a discourse which is racialized, limit
his ability to repudiate, in a comprehensive manner, the central
tenets of Nazi racism and antiSemitism. His intentions are praiseworthy, but his intellectual resources severely limit the kind of
critique he is able to launch.

This contradiction between intention and discourse arises most
especially from Bultmann's continued reliance upon the thought of
Martin Heidegger, who was himself an active member of the
Nazi party. I have argued that Heidegger's philosophy contains strong
links with his own political commitments. Heidegger's "authenticity"
echoes the themes of theological antiJudaism, his "They" echoes the
racialized phobia of the Jewified city, both *Being and Time* and his later
thought explicitly employ categories drawn from *völkisch* nationalism,
and an aestheticized and racialized ideology permeates his views of

language, poetry, and the Greeks. Heidegger's philosophy seems like an unlikely place to ground a critique of Nazism. It is not surprising, therefore, that Bultmann's critique of Nazism, which is deeply in-debted to Heidegger's thought, is itself ambiguous and contradictory. When Bultmann rereads Heidegger, he ignores Heidegger's *völkisch* nationalism and his aestheticized ideology. As a result, Bultmann is able to be unsparing in his critique of blood and soil racism and is able to express concern about excessive nationalism. At the same time, Bultmann's theology is deeply indebted to the Heideggerian category of authenticity and of "the They", both of which contain strong traces of theological antiJudaism and racialized antiSemitism. When Bultmann criticizes Nazism with the help of these categories, his critique, perhaps inevitably, becomes contradictory and divided.

For Bultmann, Nazism is fundamentally an inauthentic mode of existence. Most especially, totalitarianism represents a flight away from the angst of authentic existence and towards security. "The seductive element in the totalitarian state lies in the fact that it appears to guarantee to the individual the greatest possible security. The price paid for this is the freedom and personal responsibility of the individual and so the true community of the people" (*Essays* 296–7; see also *Essays* 314 n. 2). The false, inauthentic freedom attained through Nazism comes at the expense of the true self. This desire for security arises when people forget their creatureliness and forget that God, the Creator, is not immanent in the ordinances of the world (*EF* 160). Forgetting this, humans seek security by denying the necessity of a critical relationship to the world. Forgetting himself as creature, the human understands himself as lord over his/her own life. The result is sinful striving, boasting, and legalistic confusion of the paradoxical nature of existence. What the Nazis forget, according to Bultmann, is that "all of the ordinances in which we find ourselves are *ambiguous*. They are *God's* ordinances, but only insofar as they call us to service in our concrete tasks. In their mere givenness, they are ordinances of *sin*" (*EF* 160, his italics). This description of Nazi inauthenticity should sound familiar to anyone who has read Bultmann. It repeats the essential themes of his analysis of inauthentic, servile, unfree, sinful existence. Striving, boasting, sinful, self-secure, unfree; this is how Bultmann defines inauthenticity throughout his theology, and it is not surprising that it is the same understanding of inauthenticity that he applies to the Nazis. It is also worth recalling, however, that, according to Bultmann, such inauthenticity is a fundamental aspect of the essence of

Judaism. Indeed, for Bultmann, *Judaism represents the pinnacle of this inauthentic mode of existence.* Bultmann seems to imply some sort of similarity between Jewish and Nazi forms of inauthenticity. In case this conclusion on my part seems unjust to Bultmann, we can return to his own argument. He criticizes Nazism for sinfully equating human ordinances with the will of God and offers biblical examples (i.e. the prophets, Jesus) to bolster his argument. In both examples he underlines the centrality of the divine attack on *Jewish* inauthenticity. He argues that the prophetic critique arose in opposition to "an age that imagined it satisfied its duty to God by pompously carrying on the cult and that permitted unrestrained self-will to rule the common life" (*EF* 161). He also argues that Jesus' more extensive critique of Jewish ceremonialism and legalism "protests against ordinances of justice that have become ordinances of sin" (*EF* 161). In a disorienting move that could please neither German Jews nor the Jew-hating Nazis, Bultmann implies that the Nazis have become inauthentic in precisely the same way that late Judaism became inauthentic.

How is it possible that Bultmann could imply that there was some sort of existential–structural connection between Judaism and Nazism? How could he do so in a statement designed to criticize the injustice against the Jews? His intellectual resources, developed in a deeply antiJewish and racialized context, give him little other choice. More than a thousand years of theological antiJudaism, hundreds of years of German cultural antiSemitism and Eurocentrism, and the inner logic of Heidegger's thought all lead to the conclusion that the Eastern, Jewish spirit is the antithesis to true, Western freedom. When Bultmann tries to confront a regime that he finds to be despotic and unfree, the entire weight of this tradition leads him, perhaps unconsciously, to equate this unfree regime with the eternal symbol of the unfree: the Jews.[14] Given his fully developed and consistently articulated theological position, could he have argued otherwise? Bultmann is to be praised for daring in 1933 to defend Judaism and to criticize Nazism. At the same time, the Heideggerian temporal structure and categories employed by Bultmann, when combined with the traditional antiJewish theological categories that are also employed, pull his thought in an unfortunate and curious direction. Bultmann's courageous yet contradicatory criticism of Nazism reveals how difficult it is to use traditional theological and Heideggerian categories, categories which provide Bultmann's thought with its fundamental structure, to shed light on Nazi racism, antiSemitism, and nationalism.

Conclusion

At the end of the last chapter, I argued that Heidegger's thought was hopelessly blind and deeply deficient – blind to human suffering and susceptible to mystification and racialization. Bultmann's Heidegger is certainly not as deeply flawed as the Heidegger who wrote elegant philosophical tracts in support of Hitler. This does not mean, however, that Bultmannian existentialism is entirely free from the problems associated with Heidegger's politics. Bultmann has bequeathed to modern scholarship a problematic view of early Christianity as well as a problematic way of thinking of the role of the biblical scholar.

Bultmann and early Christianity

Bultmann infuses into NT scholarship a series of existential and aesthetic values that are themselves deeply racialized (originary/ derivative, primordial/compromised, dynamic/static, security/ insecurity, authenticity/inauthenticity, theology of history/theology of word, concrete/abstract, free/enslaved). These values play an essential role in Bultmann's historiography and theology and also deeply inform his extremely influential readings of the various texts of the New Testament (John, Paul, Luke–Acts, the traditional material that makes up the Synoptics).

These aesthetic values play a role in the larger, aestheticized and racialized narrative of world history that informs Bultmann's thought. In this narrative the East represents corrupt despotism, the Jew represents the antithesis of freedom, the Hellenistic West represents originary freedom, and the Catholic (which contains echoes of Hegel's Romanic and Latinic) represents tepid compromise with the spirit of Eastern Jewification. This narrative of world history, which goes back to the early nineteenth century, is closer to Hegel's view of history than it is to Heidegger's. It is not, therefore, rabidly nationalistic in the way that Heidegger's thought is. Bultmann's Hellenistic freedom is not limited to the German people, nor are authenticity and primordiality embodied in Hitler's state. At the same time, Bultmann's narrative of world history does assume that freedom is found in the European West, or, more precisely, in those parts of Europe not tainted by the Latinic spirit of Rome and of Catholicism. Furthermore, in this narrative, freedom is attained by overcoming the despotic spirit of the East and by overcoming the corrupt and inauthentic spirit of Judaism. Bultmann's version of this narrative is not tangled up with the zealous nationalism, the fanatical racism, or the pathological antiSemitism of Nazism. It is, however, explicitly Eurocentric and substantially racialized.

Bultmann's narrative of world history may not come directly from Heidegger, but he does take over Heidegger's views of temporality. It is through the category of authentic temporality that Bultmann translates Heidegger into the New Testament. Bultmann constructs his narrative of the origins of Christianity around what I have called "the existential morality tale", a morality tale deeply indebted to Heidegger's temporal care-structure and, therefore, to the racialized values outlined above. According to this morality tale, authenticity is available only in those moments of primordial encounter with the originary, moments which call us out of our daily, inauthentic mode of existing. According to Bultmann and his students, early Christian history followed the general movement of authentic/inauthentic existence. Habitual inauthenticity becomes equated with Eastern, Judaism; primordial encounter becomes equated with the Western, Hellenistic gospel of Paul; and the post-encounter slide back to inauthenticity becomes equated with the tepid compromise of early Catholicism. In philosophical terms, Bultmann, with the help of Heidegger's existentialist terminology, was able to rejuvenate the Hegelian–Tübingen view of world history and of early Christianity. Bultmann offers, in other words, an existentialized version of Tübingen's Hegelianized, and racialized, history of early Christianity.

This general structure profoundly influences the Bultmannian reading of the major texts of the first century. Jewish texts from the time become the pinnacle of Eastern despotism and inauthenticity, Jesus and especially Paul become the embodiment of Western freedom, and Luke–Acts becomes the embodiment of tepid Catholic compromise. These views of Jewish texts, of Paul, and of Luke–Acts became the dominant ones for much of the rest of the century. While competing readings of Judaism, Paul, and Luke have always existed, they have had to struggle with and against the dominant, Bultmannian position. It is only relatively recently that these competing views have moved from the margins to the center of the disciplinary discourse.

Because of Bultmann's prominence in the field, these racialized ideas, categories, and habits have been widely disseminated throughout the discipline. Whenever a scholar takes up these sets of values, this narrative of world history, this reading of a particular text, or the existentialized narrative of early Christianity, he/she incorporates into his/her scholarship this larger, racialized ideological system.

This happens whether or not the scholar consciously works out of Bultmann's framework and whether or not the scholar intends to write explicitly racialized analysis.

Bultmann and the task of modern biblical scholarship

> It is the idea of the *spiritual freedom* which leads as a consequence to freedom in political, communal and social life, and which is basically freedom of the individual. It is the idea that freedom is irrevocably bound up with being an individual and being one's self – indeed, that "being free" and "being one's self" are identical.
>
> Bultmann, "The Significance of the Idea of Freedom for Western Civilization"

Even though Bultmann did not like to speak about politics, his scholarship does contain a deep political commitment. We should recall that the essay on demythology was written in 1941, in the middle of the Nazi era. It was written well after the Nuremberg Laws and well after *Kristallnacht*. It was written after the well-publicized murder of the handicapped and right around the time that the regime began to implement the final solution of the Jewish problem.[15] It is my contention that demythologizing the New Testament, therefore, is a spiritual–political act which is designed to make possible authentic freedom in a troubled age.[16]

For Bultmann, New Testament criticism is designed to allow the originary power of true freedom (i.e. the Pauline gospel) to erupt into the modern world. This true freedom is buried under years of misreading (particularly through Catholicism) and through the early Catholic texts of the New Testament that fled the power of the gospel. It is the task of the radical critic to see behind the centuries of misreading and to scrape away the despotic or compromised husk that has obscured the originary core that lies at the heart of the gospel. In so doing, the radical critic is trying to make it possible for modern Christians to become truly free. Is there not, then, a political position implicit in the existentialist reading of these ancient texts? Does not this political position inevitably emerge when such readings occur during or in the wake of the Nazi era?

It is freedom that holds together Bultmann's political analysis and his interpretation of antiquity. It is Bultmann's particular views of freedom that render his thought problematic and open to racialization. For the Heideggerian Bultmannians, freedom is the defining essence of the Hellenistic, Christian West. The opposite of freedom is also, therefore, in opposition to this pure, free Christian essence. The alien is the source of and the embodiment of unfreedom. Since the beginning of the eighteenth century, the alien, particularly the alien Jew, has been identified as the source of and embodiment of servility and despotism; and there is little in Heidegger that encourages the Bultmannians to see things any differently. The antithesis of freedom is the alien and the pinnacle of unfreedom is the alien Jew. This conception of freedom produces an analysis of Nazism and its fallout that can be quite jarring. Existentialist, essentialized thinking encourages Bultmann to employ antiJewish stereotypes in his criticism of Nazism. The Bultmannian analysis of Nazism and its aftermath begins by seeking the deeper spiritual and existential meaning of Nazism. According to the Bultmannian position, those forces which are opposed to Christian freedom are existentially similar to Judaism, which represents the pinnacle of opposition to Christian freedom. In other words, Nazism (which is radically despotic) is existentially similar to Judaism. This conclusion is perfectly consistent with the existential morality tale which Bultmann so carefully constructs. Indeed, given the role that the existential morality tale plays in the economy of Bultmann's thought, what other conclusions could he draw? For if the existential morality is correct, then the enemies of Paul's gospel of radical freedom (whether totalitarian enemies of freedom or compromised enemies of radicality) must necessarily be existentially similar to Paul's essential enemy: the Eastern Jew.

Bultmann's goal, to read the gospel in such a way as to bring about freedom in a troubled modern world, is a noble one. There are, however, some very serious problems with the way that he tries to achieve that goal. I have already mentioned the way that racialization and antiJudaism are incorporated into his thought, and have argued that these aspects of his thought ensure that his critique of Nazism, while in some ways noble, remains powerless and contradictory. There is one more related problem that is worth identifying. Bultmann's Heideggerianized existentialism prevents him from confronting the problem of antiJudaism, antiSemitism, and racism. The question of race is, for the Bultmannians, necessarily an irrelevant one. The intellectual framework that the Bultmannians have developed with such care is structurally incapable of addressing those problems which are fundamental to our current age.

I can only conclude that existentialism and theological radicalism for its own sake are unable to speak to the fundamental concerns of the post-colonial, postmodern, post-European age. I am convinced that current biblical scholarship should speak to the fundamental concerns of postmodern humanity and that this means directly confronting the troublesome legacy of European oppression and racism. If this is the case, then current biblical scholarship needs to stop looking to Bultmann's racialized construction of Heidegger for inspiration and to ground its thought in something other than Bultmannian existentialism.

Before taking up this question, however, we need to return to our history of twentieth-century scholarship. Bultmannian existentialism continued to exert immediate influence in the 1960s and 1970s, by translating itself into a new environment (America) and by assuming a new form (parable scholarship). It is to the continuing influence of a transformed demythologizing program that we shall now turn.

6

PORTRAIT OF THE ARTIST AS A YOUNG MESSIAH

Jesus comes to America

Welcome, O life! I go to encounter for the millionth time the reality of experience and to forge in the smithy of my soul the uncreated conscience of my race.

James Joyce, *A Portrait of the Artist as a Young Man*

The construction of American biblical scholarship

This Europe, in its ruinous blindness forever on the point of cutting its own throat, lies today in a great pincers, squeezed between Russia on one side and America on the other. From a metaphysical point of view, Russia and America are the same; the same dreary technological frenzy, the same unrestricted organization of the average man.

Heidegger, "Introduction to Metaphysics" (1935)

The international character of scholarship, which ought to be ground for joy and thankfulness, is gradually growing into a pest and is causing nightmares. The time when German exegesis dominated the field is gone for ever.

Käsemann, "New Testament Questions of Today"

The Second World War dramatically shifted the political, economic, and cultural landscape for much of the world. Europe and Great Britain were greatly weakened economically, making possible the spread of decolonization movements throughout Asia and Africa – decolonization movements that played a role in the development of the American civil rights movement.[1] The United States and Russia emerged as world powers that towered over the traditional European powers of France, England, and Germany. The emergence of these

165

two superpowers confirmed Heidegger's worst nightmares and fed the poetic resignation of his later philosophy. The United States was one of the few participants to emerge from the great war strengthened economically and militarily. Primed for world leadership, locked in ideological conflict with the Soviet Union, eager to reward its white combatants with a college education and middle-class housing, and desperate for academic contributions to the growing defense industry, the United States pumped enormous resources into its universities and colleges (see Said 1994: 47, 340 n. 48). American universities were further nurtured by intellectuals emigrating from Hitler's Europe (e.g. Hannah Arendt, Albert Einstein, Paul Tillich) and, a little later, by distinguished scholars who were invited to split their time between European and American institutions (e.g. Derrida, Foucault, Paul Ricoeur). By the 1960s, American universities had begun to stake a claim on the world stage. Gone were the days when elite American universities lacked the stature of their European counterparts. American universities, no less than the American State Department, had taken up the burden of empire.

Not coincidently, American biblical scholarship was finally ready to assert itself on the world stage. Before the 1960s, serious scholarship was thought to take place primarily on the Continent and in Great Britain. By the end of the 1970s, biblical scholarship had established itself in America. Contemporary American biblical scholarship took shape during this time period, and it did so by confronting German scholarship. American biblical scholarship of the 1960s was profoundly and self-consciously shaped by the work of both Bultmann and his students. The ground for dialogue between American and German scholarship was prepared in the 1950s. Bultmann lectured at a number of American colleges and universities in the early 1950s; a number of American scholars followed closely the most recent developments inside Germany (James Robinson, Robert Funk, Amos Wilder); and Norman Perrin and, a little later, J.D. Crossan emigrated to the United States. The dialogue with German scholarship was, most explicitly, a dialogue with Bultmann and his students; and it had the effect of making the Bultmannian position the starting point for much American scholarship. As Robinson argues, "Bultmann's works and ideas have become Germany's dominant theological export throughout the world" (Robinson 1959: 11–12). Under the influence of Robinson, Funk, Perrin, and Crossan, American scholarship further normalized the assumptions of Bultmannian existentialism.

Appropriating a rehabilitated Nazi

> The experience of war and of the concentration camps is
> equally a distinctive mark of this generation. They utterly
> destroyed in it the attitude of bourgeois individualism and of
> detached historicism.
>
> Käsemann, "The New Testament Questions of Today"

The dialogue between American and German scholarship was greatly spurred on by a number of crucial texts: Robinson's *A New Quest of the Historical Jesus* (1959), Perrin's *The Kingdom of God in the Teaching of Jesus* (1963) and *Rediscovering the Teaching of Jesus* (1967), Keck and Martyn's *Studies in Luke–Acts* (1966), and Funk's *Language, Hermeneutic and Word of God* (1966). An even more important contribution was made by the series *New Frontiers in Theology*, which was designed to bring German scholarship to the center of current research. In the foreword, James Robinson and John Cobb explain the importance of German criticism in the creation of modern theology. While American theology has assimilated much German theology, it has also often lagged behind the most recent theological movements. "As long as this relationship was characterized by a considerable time lag in the translation and introduction in America of theological trends from the Continent, the American role was of necessity often that of receiving the results of a largely terminated discussion, so that the ensuing American discussion could hardly affect the ongoing German discussion" (Robinson and Cobb 1963: vii). *New Frontiers* was designed to change that. It was specifically intended to provide a means for American scholars to participate actively in German theological debates and to prove that American scholars had the nerve and ability to intervene in Continental scholarly debates as they occurred.

New Frontiers was designed to intervene in cutting-edge theological debates. For the first two volumes of the series, that meant debating the hottest trend in German theology of the late 1950s and early 1960s: the New Hermeneutic.[2] The New Hermeneutic was an attempt, by some of Bultmann's students, to surpass their teacher by grounding theology and exegesis in the philosophy of the later Heidegger. By intervening in this debate and by appropriating the questions posed by the New Hermeneutic, the series helped bring existentialism and Heidegger to American ears.

Translating Heidegger's obscure and philosophically dense musings into American diction is no easy task. In the first place, American intellectuals tend to be far less concerned than their

European counterparts with abstract philosophy. German biblical scholars had a difficult enough time reading Heidegger philosophically. American biblical scholars will tend to be content following Bultmann's lead. Bultmann's assertion that Heidegger is an existentialist philosopher will become part of the conventional scholarly wisdom.[3] The later Heidegger will be read through Bultmannian eyes, as his mature philosophy is read from the perspective of an existentialism that he himself had left behind.

Furthermore, there exist enormous cultural and political differences between the Weimar Republic and 1960s' America. When Heidegger wrote *Being and Time*, the Weimar Republic was crumbling and stormtroopers ran roughshod through the streets. Radicalism in Heidegger's time was youthful and fascist. The first two volumes of *New Frontiers* were published in the same years that Martin Luther King led the Birmingham campaign and the March on Washington, that urban racial rioting erupted, that Betty Friedan published *The Feminine Mystique*, and that John Kennedy was assassinated. When Bultmann turned to Heidegger for help in defining the needs of modern man, he could safely assume that modern man was male, European, Christian, and Protestant. By the time that Heidegger was transplanted to the United States, that still common assumption was in the process of being challenged. Certainly all of this affects the way that his difficult texts are perceived.

Furthermore, there exists a huge gap between dominant racial views of Weimar and the dominant racial views of 1960s' America. Heidegger inscribes particularly German racial anxiety into his thought: *völkisch* nationalism, racial antiSemitism, and the fascism of Spengler and Jünger. If Heidegger wrote as part of Germany's radical right, he will be appropriated by American biblical scholars who swing towards the left. Furthermore, America has its own distinctive racial history and ensuing racial anxieties. Heidegger's racially coded categories will remain invisible and, therefore, all the more potent. Because the New Hermeneuts are trolling in the waters of the later Heidegger, who self-consciously worked within the orbit of National Socialism, the question of their philosophical fidelity to (later) Heidegger is even more pressing, and more perilous, than it was for Bultmann. In hindsight the New Hermeneuts faced a dilemma about which they seemed to be unaware. If they misread the later Heidegger (as Bultmann did for the early Heidegger), then the legitimacy of their position is open to question, as Bultmann's position suffered from his overly anthropocentric reading of *Being and Time*. On the other hand, if they did correctly understand and apply the later Heidegger, then they ran the risk of reading the New Testament through the eyes of a National Socialist. This seems to be one of those rare instances when their anthropocentric misreading turned out to be a blessing in disguise. It is far better to be philosophically unsound than to be vouching for Hitler, even inadvertently.

To his credit, Robinson did not attempt to evade the question of Heidegger's fascism. Instead he sought refuge in the then mainstream position that there may have been a negligible relationship between Heidegger's early thought and his fascism, but that connection disappeared in his later thought. In this view, his later philosophy has a clean ideological bill of health and his much ballyhooed turn signifies a complete and rigorous repudiation of National Socialism. This is certainly the implicit position of those biblical scholars who embrace the later Heidegger. According to Robinson, "Heidegger's notorious address as Rector of the University of Freiburg in 1933 on 'The Self-Assertion of the German University' was still prior to the turn. But the lecture on 'The Origin of the Work of Art' in 1935 and the lecture at Rome in 1936 on 'Hölderlin and the Essence of Poetry' reflected the turn taking place" (Robinson 1963: 8–9). This is one of the few times when a biblical scholar directly acknowledges that Heidegger had been in the Nazi party and had spoken out on Hitler's behalf.[4] Despite this acknowledgment, we see remarkably little analysis of Heidegger's political decision and its implication for reading his thought. At the very moment when biblical scholarship is to be infused, for the second time, with a massive dose of Heideggerian philosophy, this absence of critical reflection on Heidegger's political folly is certainly significant.

It is interesting to note, however, that Robinson does cite one philosopher (Karl Löwith) who was highly critical of Heidegger's politics. Löwith was a Jewish student of Heidegger's who was forced into exile in 1934 and who did develop an extensive critique of the later Heidegger. He defended Heidegger's earliest philosophy, but concluded that some of *Being and Time* and much of the later philosophy was politically and philosophically dangerous. In short, his view of the turn (a turn towards fascism) is diametrically opposed to Robinson's view (a turn away from fascism). Robinson rejects Löwith's interpretation by arguing that Löwith, who had been teaching *Being and Time* outside of Germany when the turn occurred, was upset to discover that the official Heideggerian position had changed in his absence. Robinson seeks a psychological explanation for Löwith's philosophical critique. I would concur that psychology may have played a role here, but would offer a different explanation for Löwith's disenchantment with his former teacher. If Löwith's absence from Germany is significant for his reading of Heidegger, the reason for his absence is even more significant. The Jewish Löwith was forced into exile by the rise of Hitler. Like Heidegger's other Jewish students (Arendt, Marcuse), Löwith was deeply disturbed by Heidegger's enthusiasm for Hitler and for Nazism. Furthermore, Löwith was in Italy in 1936, when Heidegger was lecturing on Hölderlin. We should recall that Heidegger's turn to Hölderlin is one of the essential features of his later ("post-turn") philosophy and that Heidegger's analysis of Hölderlin's poetry is one of the texts that is essential to the New Hermeneutic (see Robinson 1963: 7–10; Funk 39–40). According to Löwith's first-hand account, after the Hölderlin lecture, a swastika-clad Heidegger met with his Jewish student in exile. During the course of that conversation, Heidegger confirmed that his fascism grew out of his philosophy, particularly out of his view of historicity (see Löwith 1993b). It was Heidegger's Nazism, not his philosophical change, that led to Löwith's rethinking of Heideggerian thought.

Bultmann's student Ernst Fuchs, who was instrumental in the appropriation of the later Heidegger, even manages to enlist Heidegger in the antiNazi camp, at least by implication. He composed the essay "The New Testament and the Hermeneutical Problem" (Fuchs 1964a: 111–145) specifically for the *New Frontier II*. It is designed to introduce the New Hermeneutic to an American audience. He begins this important introductory task with some autobiographical reflections, suggesting that these reflections are essential to understanding the New Hermeneutic. His central autobiographical claim is that the seminal figures of Barth, Bultmann, Heidegger, and Schlatter introduced a new academic era (112). Then, much like Käsemann, he describes how that new era inspired the theologians to resist Hitler. "In Germany there arose a new and brutal régime which terrified the world and the German nation as well. Even the church was put in a completely new situation, since it was severely persecuted. The enemies of the church brought about what the professors would perhaps never have achieved . . . Many persons . . . became inwardly more alive than they had ever been before" (113; see also Achtemeier 85).[5] While the theologians and philosophers made the best case possible for the necessity of their radical position, it was the experience of wartime persecution that proved that they were right. This experience breathed new life into the churches and into the study of the New Testament. Fuchs describes the situation this way:

> We also learned to read it (the New Testament) differently from before. To be sure, the problems remained to a large extent the old problems. But we were now (after the Nazi era) able to see the work of our teachers with sharpened eyes, simply because the time compelled us to do so. And since we had such good professors, new insights emerged, which appear to us as the fruit of the work of our great teachers.
>
> (Fuchs 1964a: 113)

While he does concede that not all stood the test (ibid.), he does not pursue the implications of Heidegger's own wartime behavior.

The analytical problem which we are facing comes in trying to maintain two seemingly contradictory positions. On the one hand, we need to recognize that many theologians did resist Hitler and defended Christian doctrine from ideological infection. Many of these same theologians were inspired to do so by existentialist radicality, and did so at considerable personal risk. On the other hand, the philosopher on whom they had relied and whom they now praise, was inspired by the very principle of radicality to embrace Hitler. Furthermore, some of those who resisted Hitler, inspired by their wartime experience, later sought to reconfigure their own position with the help of the later Heidegger. Ironically enough, the philosopher who had vocally supported Hitler is transformed, in the years after the war, into an enemy of fascism and a voice for freedom. It is time that biblical scholars come to terms with this contradiction.

Given the pace of Heidegger's rehabilitation and the state of philosophy in the early 1960s, this inability to come to terms with Heideggerian fascism is understandable. If those most qualified to analyze Heideggerian fascism were unable or unwilling to do so, those of us who rely on their expertise can hardly be expected to perform this Herculean task. Times change, however, and current philosophy has been particularly preoccupied with the question of Heidegger's politics. A new Heidegger has emerged in the scholarship of the last two decades, a Heidegger who is personally disreputable and intellectually problematic. It is time for biblical scholarship to squarely face the following question: What is the cost of embracing Heidegger's philosophy, particularly his later philosophy?

Funk, Wilder, and the poetry of authenticity

> Generations live in it (language) as a habitat in which they are
> born and die . . . The language of a people is its fate. Thus the
> poets or seers who purify the language of the tribe are truly
> world-makers.
>
> Amos Wilder, *Early Christian Rhetoric*

While our analysis of later Heidegger in American biblical scholarship could begin in any number of places, it seems wisest to begin with Robert Funk's *Language, Hermeneutic, and the Word of God*, which is one of the seminal texts in establishing current parable scholarship. This book helps us see, with utmost clarity, how the Bultmannian–Heideggerian legacy is both appropriated and redefined by an ambitious and extremely influential American scholar. It is clear that Funk takes very seriously the German theological and exegetical debates and that he develops his own position by means of a dialogue with Bultmann, Heidegger, and the New Hermeneutic (see Funk Part I). At the same time, it is equally clear that his seminal analysis of, and definition of, parable seek to go beyond the New Hermeneutic (see Funk Part II). Funk's theoretically informed reading of the parables is instrumental in both disseminating the Bultmannian–Heideggerian position throughout some aspects of American scholarship and in translating that position into a new idiom.

Like Bultmann, Funk opens his book by declaring a state of crisis. Bultmann's crisis was rooted in the particular social situation in which he found himself – the crumbling Weimar Republic and the failure of liberal theology to acknowledge the postwar social and intellectual situation. Funk's is less culturally specific. There is no mention, even implicitly, of the genuine crisis that was rocking American society in the mid-1960s. Nothing is said in this book about the Vietnam War, racial unrest, civil disobedience, the radicalization of the black power movement under the influence of Malcolm X, the emerging feminist movement. Even the civil rights movement, which was being led by a dialectical theologian fond of quoting biblical scholarship, merits little attention. As the New Hermeneutic lands on American soil, the civil rights movement, in the name of the gospel, is forcing a racist society to reexamine its fundamental principles and is engaging Christians, both white and black, in a fierce debate about the essence of the Christian faith. While the racial debates of fascist Germany did find their way into mainstream biblical scholarship (via Heidegger), these homegrown racial debates did not. Questions about white racism and civil rights were marginalized while Heidegger's racialized themes of "primordiality" and "authenticity" seized the day. By speaking to the existential crisis facing modern "man", American existentialist biblical scholarship would find itself unarmed in the face of the particular social conflict facing American society.

According to Funk, the fundamental problem is ultimately theological. "Theology and the way we experience reality have indeed come apart at the seams . . . Theology has abrogated its responsibility for touching and being touched by the real" (Funk xii). Apparently this crisis, like Bultmann's, is best diagnosed by a heavy dose of Heidegger-speak. Funk's foreword is laced with Heideggerian terminology: "temporality", "historicality", "responsibility for the past and future", "seized as his ownmost", "destiny", "primordial", "authentic", and "submit to destiny" (Funk xi–xiv). It is not just the terminology that is Heideggerian, the entire diagnosis of the crisis is influenced by the later Heidegger. "The first task is to expose the roots of our linguistic tradition and the second, which is wholly concomitant, is to liberate language from the hegemony of prescriptive thought" (Funk xiii). With this, Funk repeats the strategy of expulsion of the alien and nurturing of the authentic. In other words, his parable scholarship repeats the same gesture of the racialized, aesthetic ideology; the very ideology which is so central to the racialization of the discipline of modern New Testament scholarship. He infuses this racialized strategy into the very heart of modern parable scholarship.

The problem is, once again, the problem of objectification. Yet, following the New Hermeneutic rather than Bultmann, Funk's target is objectified and degraded language rather than objectifying worldviews. According to Funk, language tends towards becoming "conventional", "commonplace", "banal", and "ossified" (Funk 1–6). This is true of all language, but is most dangerous for religious language. The degradation of religious language is responsible for a great deal of misery and misfortune, including the absence of God and the inability to hear God's parabolic word. "The testimony to the death of God bears witness to a correlative tragedy, namely, the failure of language" (Funk 8). Contemporary churches have strangled biblical discourse, which has gone dead and which "forecloses rather than discloses understanding" (Funk 6). God is dead and Christ remains entombed. The problem originates in language itself, which is mundane and conventional. Religious discourse is so degraded and static that it "betrays its own emptiness" (Funk 8–9); it has fallen into "mere verbalization, vain prattle without ultimate reference" (Funk 8). This prattle stems from a deeper existential malaise. "Common parlance appears to presuppose a common view of reality" (Funk 3), which, in turn, "fosters sedimentation in language" (Funk 4). This degraded, ossified, static language produces a tradition that is "worn out and used up, that is broken down" (Funk 55) and that, in turn, necessitates a false existence. Inauthenticity stems from degraded language, which produces ineffectual religious traditions drenched in conventionality. It is this inauthenticity which leads to a thorough misunderstanding of the parables of Jesus.

Indeed, conventional language serves the same function in the economy of Funk's thought that objectification does in Bultmann's. Increasingly in American scholarship of the past thirty years, conventionality would serve as the enemy of authenticity, as that which New Testament scholars (and the Jesus constructed therein) must steadfastly oppose. Self-consciously radical American scholarship would not so much *demythologize* the Word of God as it would *de-conventionalize* it. Objectification was once considered the root of all evil and was embodied in the Eastern Jew. Now the conventional is the root of all evil. In whom shall it be embodied?

With this provocative shift from objectifying worldviews to conventional language, Funk produces a reading of Heidegger which goes beyond Bultmann's strictly Lutheran-theological interpretation yet which remains fundamentally existentialist, thereby ensuring continued resonance among biblical scholars. Funk's position on the degradation of language emerges from an alluring mixture of early and later Heidegger. His confidence about the centrality of language clearly emanates from the later Heidegger, as mediated by the New Hermeneutic (see Achtemeier 85–100; Ebeling 85, 94, 99–110; Fuchs 1964b: 207–212; Funk 20–26; Robinson 1964: 46–48). On the other hand, his actual analysis of language, particularly of its degradation, is fundamentally rooted in *Being and Time* – most especially in the category of "the They" (*das Man*), which we analyzed in considerable detail earlier in the study. This intriguing mixture of early and later Heidegger, of Bultmannian and nonBultmannian Heidegger, represents a significant theoretical and theological achievement. Its combination of daring improvisation and indebtedness to what was fast becoming a traditional position struck a chord with later readers. Unfortunately, the Heideggerian category "the They", which he has chosen to employ, is extremely problematic both ideologically and philosophically. A brief recapitulation of this volatile category is in order.

"The They" lies on one of the major fault lines of Heidegger's philosophy. As I argued earlier, *Being and Time* is caught between an Aristotelian/Dilthean analysis of the everyday conditions that make communication possible (i.e. being-in-the-world), and Lutheran–Kierkegaardian existentialism that rejects the everyday as drenched in herd-like conformity (i.e. authenticity). In the former, the everyday is that which makes life possible and in the latter the everyday is that which makes life tedious and unbearable. In the former, the public is an essential aspect of life while in the latter the public is degenerate and trite. "The They", which grows out of Heidegger's arguments about authenticity and authentic absorption, belongs firmly in the latter camp. The ownness (*eigen*) of authenticity (*Eigentlichkeit*) is threatened by the convention and conformity that categorizes "the They". By reaching for "the They" Funk ensures that his seminal position will be fundamentally existentialist. Parable criticism will be every bit as indebted to Heidegger and his ideological commitments as was demythology. Authenticity comes from calling us out of a fallen world, a world marked by idle talk (i.e. Funk's "prattle"), the inability to communicate, uprootedness, banality, dominance, avoidance of struggle, the lack of individuality, and the lack of freedom. Any crisis which Funk faces stems from the fundamental nature of "the They".

If language is constructed around the authentic/inauthentic axis, there must be some form of language that is actually authentic, that escapes the drudgery of "the They" and which founds genuine existence. For Funk, it will be the parables of Jesus that serve as Christian versions of this authentic language. For Heidegger, both in *Being and Time* and in his later thought, authentic language is rooted both in the *German* soil and in the *German* language. The true German poet, Hölderlin, founds and gives voice to the German *Volk*, which emanates from the primordial essence of the German language as revealed in the Greco-Germanic tradition. It is my contention that this emphasis on the authenticity of the German language, people, and culture is downplayed among Heideggerian biblical scholars, who do not seem to recognize that Heideggerian language is culturally and nationally specific. Despite this, there remains in Heideggerian biblical scholarship traces of Heidegger's racialization – traces which help structure the thought of Bultmann and his heirs (including Funk). "The They" represents Oriental Jewification corrupting the modern West from within, while aestheticized authenticity represents its aesthetic, racial, and spiritual opposite: Western, Hellenistic freedom.

If inauthentic language is static, conventional, mediated, and ossified, then authentic language is its opposite: dynamic, unconventional, unmediated, and vibrant. It is essential that authentic language break away from conventional language, that the old house of language be dismantled and replaced with something else. "The language that sets the limits for understanding is not common parlance, but an idiosyncratic language or even a language as yet unborn" (Funk 2). Following Heidegger, Funk equates authentic language with the language of the artist and the poet. We should recall that, for Heidegger, the authentic German poet (Hölderlin) gives voice to the primordial essence of the German *Volk*; and that, for Heidegger, the Germans are one of two peoples (along with the Greeks) capable of primordial thought or of speaking a primordial language. The originary word of the authentic poet creates the German *Volk*. Funk follows Heidegger here, without underlining the *völkisch* nationalism implicit in Heidegger's aesthetic. Funk declares that "the poet is one who names by allowing being to speak. Authentic language is the voice of being naming itself through the mouth of the poet" (Funk 40). It is the authentic poet who breaks free from the tyranny of the conventional and who hears the primordial call of being. Authentic language is aestheticized language, as authenticity is transformed into creative poetry.

I have been arguing that the central strategy of racialized aestheticism involves the expulsion of the alien (Eastern, Jewish, African, Latin) along with the nurturing of the primordial (Western, Hellenistic, European, Germanic) essence. Funk follows Heidegger's racialized aesthetic without acknowledging, or perhaps even recognizing, that he is doing so. This leads him to aestheticize, rather than confront, the antiJudaism he inherits from the Bultmannians. For Funk, the authentic core of the Christian faith is buried under two millennia of inauthentic language, rather than under two millennia of inauthentic religious experience (as it is for Bultmann and his school). The millennia of ossified, static, failed linguistic debris (rather than existential malaise) must be scraped away before this authentic Christian core can be recovered. The Lutheran faith–works dichotomy which Bultmann and Käsemann (and Fuchs, for that matter) found to be essential in Paul, however, remains essential for Funk as well. Now it is simply poeticized. Grace itself is aestheticized as justification by faith alone gives way to justification by poetry alone. The Word of God, properly understood, is "like a great work of art" (Funk 11) and Jesus becomes the poet of radical grace. If we wish to revive a decayed and degraded tradition

and resolve the existential crisis of the modern era, then we must
return to the intuitive Word which "creates, brings into being . . .
brings man from death to life . . . By it men are lost, and by it men
are saved" (Funk 13). Resisting the grace which is revealed in
authentic language is a form of justification by works. For Funk, the
Pharisees symbolize the (Jewish) desire to master and objectify
the text. "To use the pejorative analogy of the New Testament, the
Pharisee is the one who insists that he is the interpreter of the text,
whereas the sinner allows himself to be interpreted by the text"
(Funk 59). This desire for mastery and objectification, which is
apparently part of Jewish nature, ultimately stems from resistance
to grace. *"The Pharisees are those who insist on interpreting the word of
grace rather than letting themselves be interpreted by it"* (Funk 17, his
emphasis). No matter how elaborate, complex, and profound the
theory appropriated by Heideggerian New Testament scholars, it
seems quite difficult to escape the idea that there is a Jewish nature
which rejects grace and revels in self-righteous inauthenticity. At
the very moment that Krister Stendahl had forced Pauline scholarship to reexamine the law/grace dichotomy, Funk was reinscribing
that dichotomy into the heart of Gospel criticism. This does not
bode well for the American response to the challenge of demythologizing the Word of God: parable criticism.

Jesus the poet: the parables and the language of authenticity

> Heavenly God! cried Stephen's soul, in an outburst of profane
> joy.
>
> James Joyce, *A Portrait of the Artist*

> If in the parable we encounter the logos incarnate, the theo-
> logical justification for extended reflection on the parable is
> that theology is driven perennially back to its source and
> ground . . . in order to refurbish its thought out of the litter
> of the primordial event.
>
> Funk, *Language, Hermeneutic and Word of God*

Funk's general theorizing provides the interpretive framework for
his more concrete exegetical analysis. Like Bultmann, his existentialism becomes the lens through which he interprets the New
Testament. Funk, along with the New Hermeneuts, Amos Wilder,
Robinson, and Perrin, shifts the locus of salvific words from the
primitive, Pauline kerygma to the teachings of Jesus.[6] For Funk, as

for many who will follow him, it is the parables which are most worthy of attention. By the time that Funk was writing, the parables had already been accepted as the royal road to the historical Jesus.[7] As kerygmatic theology became attached to the words of Jesus, more and more would have to be expected of the parables. Not only are they asked to reveal the actual words of the historical Jesus, they are also to engender salvation. For self-styled radical critics in Germany, the Pauline kerygma held the key to Christian salvation and held out hope for the crisis-ridden modern world. The fate of the modern world depended upon modern humanity's ability to hear Paul's radical challenge to our self-understanding. For self-styled radical critics in the United States, this crucial task would fall to the parables. It is parables which will provide the indispensable challenge to modern self-understanding. It is worth asking how scholarship came to think that these simple stories were capable of bearing that kind of weight. The answer to that question tells us more about the dynamic of modern scholarship than about the parables themselves.

Funk has already argued that it is the authentic poet who breaks free from the tyranny of the conventional and who hears the primordial call of being. The challenge is to construct the teachings of Jesus in light of this already established presupposition about poetry, language, and the herd-like nature of mass society. The simplest way to begin is through sheer assertion, with a statement of faith. Amos Wilder paved the way by describing Jesus' language, in strikingly Romantic terminology, as *naive, unstudied, direct, dynamic, actual, immediate, inimitable, oral, live, face-to-face, free, unformulaic, fresh, fluid*, and *novel* (Wilder 13–17). This language opens up "a new dimension of man's awareness, a new breakthrough in language and symbolization" (Wilder 10). It is "not a matter of words on a tablet but a word in the heart, not a copybook for recitation but winged words for life" (Wilder 15).

It will be up to Funk, and later to Crossan, to translate Wilder's programmatic claims into persuasive exegetical conclusions. Funk will read parables through the lens of established scholarly categories, beginning with Dodd's deeply Romantic definition of the parable (see Funk 133ff.). According to Dodd:

> the parable is a metaphor or simile drawn from nature or common life, arresting the hearer by its vividness or strangeness, and leaving the mind in sufficient doubt about its precise application to tease it into active thought. (Dodd 16)

Funk begins by asking how a parable can be simultaneously drawn from common life and strange. "Why should a commonplace, even if fetchingly depicted or narrated, be vivid or strange? . . . And why should such a vivid vignette be argumentative, precipitating the hearer's judgment? Why should it call for, even compel, decision?" (Funk 152–153). The common/strange dichotomy immediately gains considerable importance in Funk's argument. It will turn out to be a critical ingredient in the translation of existentialist, kerygmatic theology into an idiom more amenable to American ears.

Parables and everyday existence

The parables are drawn from nature or common life. This seems to call out for a literal interpretation, where the parables concern themselves with nature (e.g. the growth of seeds, weeds, the harvest) and with daily events (e.g. lost coins, relations between parents and children, wedding feasts). Funk offers a nifty redefinition of common life which fundamentally reconfigures the analytical terrain while remaining faithful to the idiom of Bultmann. Funk's parabolic world is the world of everyday life and, following Wilder, is fundamentally *secular* (see Funk 153; Wilder 1971: 73–77). By employing intrinsically secular language and imagery, Jesus shows that every person's destiny is at stake in his or her ordinary everyday existence (Funk 155) – an existence which is best defined existentially. "The everydayness of the parables is translucent to the ground of man's existence", because "man's destiny is at stake *in his everyday creaturely existence*" (Funk 155, 156, his emphasis). It suggests that the central teaching of Jesus is primarily secular rather than conventionally religious or pious.

While the movement from "common life" to secularity may seem like quite a leap of logic, it is perfectly consistent within the logic of existentialism, which Funk has already claimed as his own. Funk can live with a parabolic world that is fundamentally secular, that is concerned with the everyday rather than the miraculous or the pious. These theological assumptions were long ago normalized by Bultmann, to whom Funk is clearly indebted. On the other hand, as a Bultmannian existentialist he must be uncomfortable with the seeming elevation of the everyday world. As we have repeatedly seen, the everyday may be the only place where the individual can meet God, but it is also the locus of custom, the conventional, ossification, degeneration, decay, and uprootedness. The everyday world is both the only place wherein God can be found and the place from which we must escape if we wish to reach authenticity. Funk has constructed a contradiction every bit as intractable as anything found in Bultmann. The recourse to "paradox" cannot be far away. The parabolic world of everyday existence must also be defined around the axis of authenticity/"the They". The authentic world of the parables (and it must be authentic) is in opposition to the inauthentic world of "the They". "The parabolic imagery lays bare the structure of human existence that is masked by convention, custom, consensus. It exposes the 'world' in which man is enmeshed and to which and for which he must give account" (Funk 155). The parable is in the everyday but not of the everyday.

The everyday secularity of the parable is, for Funk, extremely significant theologically. "The secularity of the parables may give expression to the only way of legitimately speaking of the incursion of the divine into history: metaphorical or symbolic language is proper to the subject matter because God remains hidden" (Funk 154). Bultmann could not have said it better himself. We should recall that for Bultmann any theological statement which posits a rupture in the cause–effect nexus is mythological. It is not only alien to the spirit of modern science, it is theologically objectifying and, therefore, sinful. To claim that God intercedes directly in human affairs is misguided and sinful – it is the fundamental sin of liberal theology and is the cause of the contemporary crisis of faith. Theological statements can be legitimate only if they are anthropological (i.e. "God is gracious to me" instead of "God is gracious") and affirm *the hidden nature of God* (see NTM 9–10, 109–112; JCM 19). Bultmann's entire discussion of the meaning of God acting is premised around the need to keep God's actions hidden (JCM 60–85). "Faith itself demands to be freed from any world-view produced by man's thought, whether mythological or scientific . . . In our age faith has not yet . . . genuinely understood the transcendence and hiddenness of God as acting . . . The invisibility of God excludes every myth which tries to make God and His action visible; God withholds Himself from view and observation" (JCM 83–84). Or, as Funk explains, an authentic parable "shifts attention away from God and from Jesus himself, i.e., from the religious question, to a specific way of comporting oneself with reality. God and Jesus remain hidden" (Funk 197). Parable criticism is the American offspring of Bultmannian demythologizing, as the parable acts as another version of the demythologized kerygma.

World-shattering metaphors

According to Bultmann, the everyday is both the arena of divine activity (which cannot occur elsewhere lest it be mythological) and the locus of degeneration and inauthenticity. The parables, therefore, reveal that there is something fundamentally askew in the everyday. They must do so if they are to be found authentic. And since we know in advance that they are authentic, we also know that they must dismantle the conventional everydayness of "the They". It is only by demythologizing the conventional everyday world that the teachings of Jesus are able to open up the authentic world of grace. Funk attributes this violent overthrowing of the mundane, conventional world to the metaphorical nature of the parables (Funk 136–140). For Funk, metaphors are the antithesis of the mundane and conventional world of everyday conversation, of prattle (i.e. idle talk), and of technique. For Funk and those who follow him, the analysis of metaphoricity is imbued with Heideggerian–Bultmannian existentialism and only makes sense from within that context. Without the authenticity/"They" dichotomy, Funk's analysis of the function of metaphor lacks solid foundation.

The existentialist metaphor looks something like this. The conventional world employs an objectifying logic which objectifies, quantifies, dissects, manipulates, and crushes. Metaphors, on the other hand, are the major non-objectifying means of communicating. If Bultmann solves the problem of objectification through relationality, parable scholarship solves the same problem through metaphoricity, which creates and discloses meaning. If conventional logic crushes the imagination, metaphors set the imagination aflame and produce an impact on the imagination that is otherwise unavailable. Through the process of meaningful juxtaposition, an authentic metaphor "shatters the conventions of predication in the interest of a new vision" (Funk 139). This explains all of the violent language associated with parables: rupturing, shattering, fracturing the everyday world, cracking the shell of mundane temporality (especially Funk 156–162). For Funk, parables shatter the anonymous, conventional world of "the They". A parable "exposes the pretensions of the prevailing way of comporting oneself with reality. In so doing it challenges the authority of the anonymous 'they' by ridiculing it" (Funk 195). It is "linguistic aperture onto a world qualified by something other than the anonymous 'they'. This x-factor . . . shatters the old world" (Funk 196). It "delivers language from the tyranny of fossilized tradition" (Funk 141). Through the parables, "Jesus both witnesses to the dawn of the kingdom and brings it near" (Funk 197).

Funk is abundantly clear about what Jesus' parables do. They shatter the complacent and comfortable world built up by individuals who have been lulled to sleep by the banality of the everyday world of conventionality. In so doing, they challenge the hearer to take up a revitalized, authentic mode of existence. What Funk is unable to explain is *how* exactly the parables perform this task. He offers a fully developed anthropology with an underdeveloped aesthetic. As a result he is able to explain how an individual might be transformed from inauthenticity to authenticity, but is less clear on how parables assist in that transition. Most importantly, his analysis of metaphor is suggestive but unfinished. Someone who accepts his fundamental Heideggerian analysis and his enthusiasm for parables needs to come along and explain how it is that these particular poetic texts make possible an existential transformation. That someone is J.D. Crossan, in his seminal study *In Parables*. It is Crossan who renders comprehensible the claim that parables are essentially world-shattering *metaphors*. Before assessing the ideological cost of the parabolic Heidegger, it will prove helpful to turn to Crossan's aesthetics.

Poetry, language, and experience: aestheticizing existential self-understanding

This was the call of life to his soul not the dull gross voice of the world of duties and despair, not the inhuman voice that had called him to the pale service of the altar . . . His soul had arisen from the grave of boyhood, spurning her graveclothes. Yes! Yes! Yes! He would create proudly out of the freedom and power of his soul, as the great artificer whose name he bore, a living thing, new and soaring and beautiful, impalatable, imperishable.

James Joyce, *A Portrait of the Artist*

To make enigmatic what one thinks one understands by the words *proximity, immediacy, presence* . . . is my final intention in this book.

Derrida, *Of Grammatology*

While Crossan applauds the work of Wilder and Funk, he bemoans their unsophisticated approach to all things literary.

Some recent works on the parables of Jesus have insisted on the necessity of treating them as literature and placing special emphasis on their relationship to the world of poetic metaphor . . . This would seem to be a definite step in the right direction but, of course, it would not help to locate Jesus' parables in the world of poetic metaphor unless one knows more or less accurately what this latter means.

(*IP* 10).

Crossan is at his most stimulating when he seeks to define the essence of poetry, of poetic language, of metaphor, and, by extension, of parable. Fundamental to his entire argument is the problematic assumption that poetic language has an intrinsic essence, an essence which regulates poetic/metaphoric utterances and which guides the reception of poetic, metaphoric, and ultimately religious language. Since everything in his highly influential study hinges upon this analysis of the fundamental essence of poetic language, closer examination of this analysis is in order. After analyzing Crossan's (fundamentally Romantic) aesthetics, we shall be in a better position to ascertain the ideological implications of his position.[8]

Crossan posits a fundamental, and fundamentally essentialized, relationship between the artist, his/her poetry, and the creative poetic experience. Let us keep our eyes on the way that Crossan glides effortlessly from language to experience and back again. His parable scholarship is brimming with naive faith in the immediacy of experience and in the unmediated circular movement between language and experience. Crossan's fundamental claim is that poetry arises from poetic experience and that poetry brings that experience to life in words. The artist is driven primarily by his/her artistic experience, which guides the production of his/her poetry. "At the heart of poetry is the poetic experience itself and it is the poet's vocation so to articulate this event metaphorically that the referent of the experience is contained and incarnated in it" (*IP* 17). Unbreakable is the bond between poetry, experience, and linguistic expression. "Poetic experience terminates only with its metaphoric expression . . . The experience and the expression have a profound intrinsic unity in the depths of the event itself' (*IP* 22).

Poetic language is not only the articulation of particular human experiences, it is the articulation of exceptional experiences. The artist-genius, driven by his/her inner muse, is a unique and fundamentally singular figure. "A great poet or a great artist is one who establishes in and by and through his work new criteria for artistic or poetic greatness by establishing a new world in which it *is* such

. . . On the day we have prior criteria for genius, be it artistic, poetic, philosophical or religious, we shall no longer need either forever" (*IP* 18). This great artist flaunts social or literary conventions, pre-established criteria, and rules of every sort. The language produced is as extraordinary, exceptional, and unconventional as the experience embodied therein. Poetic experience is fundamentally opposed to the atrophied world of everyday living, and poetic language is fundamentally opposed to the fossilized, impoverished world of literal language (*IP* 15). The poetic is fundamentally opposed to the conventional.

Not only does poetic language emerge from a profoundly poetic experience, it also produces a radically new experience on the part of the hearer. "A true metaphor is one whose power creates the participation whereby its truth is experienced" (*IP* 18). The hearer participates in the poetry and, thereby, participates in the poetic experience. He/she who properly listens to poetry, develops a new *consciousness*. "The thesis is that metaphor can also articulate a referent so new or so alien to consciousness that this referent can only be grasped within the metaphor itself. The metaphor here contains a new possibility of world and of language so that any information one might obtain from it can only be received *after* one has participated through the metaphor in its new and alien referential world" (*IP* 13). It is only upon entering this new world, upon participating in the poetic experience, that the hearer is able to partake of the poetic experience from the inside (*IP* 13). Art and poetry create worlds that are antithetical to this tired old world and, by calling the hearer out of the old and into the new, poetry transforms the hearer's consciousness (*IP* 15–16). This sense that the hearer participates in the poetic experience is essential to Crossan's analysis. Without it, Jesus' experience, as made visible in his language, would remain inaccessible. This sense of hearing/participation requires faith on Crossan's part in the immediacy of language and experience, in the unmediated access to another's experience, and in the unlimited potency of (essentialized) poetic language.

For Crossan there exists an intrinsic unity between poetic experience, poetic articulation, and poetic reception. The poet and the hearer are united in the articulation/reception of the poetic experience. At the core of this theory is poetic experience, which is unconventional, singular, profound, and mysterious. For Crossan, this poetic experience is structurally similar to religious experience. "There is no intention in this book of confusing poetry and religion. It is clear, for example, that the world for which and to which Jesus is speaking is the world of religious experience. Yet it is becoming increasingly clear that the specific language of religion, that which is closest to its heart, is the language of poetic metaphor in all its varied extension. There is apparently some peculiar appropriateness or even necessity for poetic expression and religious experience to walk so often hand in hand" (*IP* 18). If the core religious experience is the Wholly Other, that experience can only be articulated indirectly and metaphorically (*IP* 18–19). Symbols and metaphors, then, become the link between the poetic and the religious experiences. Metaphor will help define the poetic essence of religious experience and religious language, and religious experience and language will help define the essence of the metaphoric. Both poetic and religious language emerge out of similar kinds of experiences. They both are capable of articulating this experience properly only in symbols or metaphors. They are both averse to the conventional, normal world of the pious, the literal. They are both diametrically opposed to Heidegger's "the They".

This general theory on poetic/religious experience forms one essential element of Crossan's interpretation of the parables. Before turning to the parables themselves, it might be helpful to examine this theory critically. Two sets of issues immediately present themselves. The first involves the intellectual heritage and ideological implications of this particular aesthetics. Where does it come from? What ideological commitments does it assume? The second set of issues involves the degree to which this theory does, and does not, lead him away from Heidegger. Is there anything in his particular aesthetics that challenges the discipline's historic commitment to Heidegger? When he turns to Heidegger's temporality, does his embrace of Romantic aesthetic lead him to a nonanthropocentric, nonBultmannian Heidegger?

Romanticism, aestheticism, and ideology

Beautiful art is only possible as a product of genius.
Kant *Critique of Judgment*

Each time that a rhetoric defines metaphor, not only is *a* philosophy implied, but also each conceptual network in which philosophy *itself* has been constituted.
Derrida, "White Mythology"

What we call ideology is precisely the confusion of linguistic with natural reality, of reference with phenomenalism.
Paul de Man, *Resistance to Theory*

Crossan's understanding of metaphor is rooted in Romanticism. This is more than a case of a fondness for certain Romantic poets (i.e. Goethe, Coleridge, *IP* 8–10). Crossan has assumed a particular view of poetry, language, and experience which has its roots in the philosophical and aesthetic Romanticism of the late eighteenth and early nineteenth centuries. It is this philosophical system, rather than anything inherent in the essence of poetry itself, which gives force to many of Crossan's central assumptions about the immediacy of poetic experience and about the dichotomy between the ordinary and the literary. As Paul de Man argues:

> it can be shown however that, in all cases, this success (in separating literary language from ordinary language) depends on the power of a system (philosophical, religious or ideological) that may well remain implicit but that determines an *a priori* conception of what is "literary" by starting out from the premises of a system rather than from the literary thing itself – if such a "thing" indeed exists.
>
> (de Man 1986: 5)

As Romanticism faded away, other literary and philosophical movements appropriated some of its central tenets about creativity, figurative language, metaphor, and the artist. Hegel's idealism, Gadamer's hermeneutics, T.S. Eliot's symbolism, the New Critic's definition of the poem – they all have their roots in a Romanticism which they also struggle against (see Norris 1988: 28–38). Long before Crossan came along, central tenets of Romanticism had been dislodged from the philosophical system and historical situation which had supported them and given them meaning. These tenets were transformed into universal truths about the nature of creativity and art, truths that were so widely disseminated and accepted that it was difficult to recognize them as propositions at all. They had become so thoroughly naturalized and normalized that they became synonymous with the very word art. Crossan's universalizing and naturalizing of these categories follow in a long and honorable tradition. It is my position that we should reverse the process and begin to recognize the historical, philosophical, and ideological assumptions buried in the seemingly natural category of "metaphor". It is my position that we should examine critically the discourse that gives coherence to metaphor.

I have already discussed the post-Enlightenment (i.e. Romantic) aesthetic ideology that helped nurture and give shape to much nineteenth-century nationalism.[9] Since this ideology plays an important role in Crossan's aesthetic, it might be helpful to summarize briefly my earlier analysis before turning to Crossan's analysis of the parables. Many intellectuals in the early part of the nineteenth century (particularly in Germany) argued that society was afflicted by a variety of social problems – ranging from atomism and alienation to Napoleonic imperial conquests. For many of these intellectuals, these social problems were rooted in, and were the inevitable result of, the inherent flaws in Enlightenment rationality. These intellectuals sought to overcome these problems by turning away from Enlightenment rationality and towards the realm of the aesthetic. Genuine art alone was capable of elevating human consciousness and reestablishing the severed relation between the self, others, and the world. Art makes possible an *organic* relationship between self and language, self and others, self and world. As the self is reunited with the world, genuine art and a genuine and properly rooted culture can bring social cohesion, organicity, and harmony. The result will be, or certainly should be, an organically cohesive, rooted, primordial people (*Volk*) that provides the foundation for a harmonious and authentic society. From the beginning, this aesthetic ideology will be racialized – as the rooted and primordial *Volk* provides the inspiration for a rooted culture and an authentic, primordial, national literature. Within this ideology, art elides seamlessly into creativity, which elides into organicity and social harmony.

As Henry Sussman convincingly argues, this process of elevating art and the artist is central to the intellectual organization of what he describes as "the broader modernity". The artist is central to this process of secularization and reappropriation (Sussman 4, 34–39, 134–162; see also Eagleton; Norris 1988: 28–64). Sussman demonstrates that modern systems of thought from Luther through Nietzsche have invested the artist with extraordinary powers. "The artist is distinguished by intuition, sensibility, perspicacity, and social exemplary as well as by the presence and immediacy that Derrida notes" (Sussman 136). These intuitive powers, which are rooted in that which Derrida calls "logocentrism", enable the artist to mediate between the transcendental and the human, making the art "the official religion in a secular, philosophy-oriented world. Artists, creative individuals, and thinkers will be the priests in this new religion" (Sussman 150). It is no wonder that biblical scholarship eventually got around to reversing the process. If artists, in the modern era, took the place of religious leaders and even of Jesus (see

Sussman 151), then it is only appropriate that Jesus be reconfigured as an artist. There is no need to modernize and secularize Jesus, because, buried deep within the earliest strata of the gospel tradition, is a Jesus who is already an artist (i.e. modern, secular, and thoroughly European).

Crossan's turn to Romanticism, while not without substantial ideological and philosophical concerns, could have led to a serious confrontation with Heideggerian phenomenology. Most strikingly, the two philosophical systems have radically different views of the place of the human subject. Romanticism is fundamentally concerned with the development of higher consciousness, while, at least in theory, Heidegger rejects such a quest as illusory, anthropocentric and subject-centered. While later Heidegger does also seek refuge in works of art, his aesthetics is radically different from, and in many ways a direct challenge to, the aesthetics of Romanticism. In his essays on Hölderlin and in "On the Origin of the Work of Art", Heidegger seeks to redefine art away from the creative, imaginative subject. "The art work opens up in its own way the Being of beings . . . Art is truth setting itself to work" (Heidegger 1977a: 166). Whatever that murky sentence means, it does suggest that Heidegger's post-metaphysical aesthetic (in which art clears a space for Being) differs from the anthropocentric aesthetic of Romanticism (which sees art as elevating consciousness).

I have already discussed the troublesome ideological implications of Heidegger's emphasis on organicity, which played a particularly important role in the development of racialized antiSemitism, *völkisch* nationalism, and (eventually) National Socialism. Romanticism shares many of the same ideological commitments: a fondness for metaphors of rootedness and soil; an unappetizing attraction to the aesthetic ideology of the *Volk*; a call for racialized national cultures as a source of regenerating a decadent society; and a tendency to identify degeneration with Jewification. This is not to suggest that Crossan explicitly takes up any of Romanticism's inherently *völkisch* strains. It does mean, however, that Romanticism will not provide Crossan with the resources to challenge the racialized and aestheticized ideology of organicity – the ideology that helped Heidegger's thought turn itself towards National Socialism.

If Funk's definition of parable is informed by Bultmannian-Heideggerian existentialism, then Crossan's exists at the crossroads between Heidegger and the Romantic aesthetic ideology. This aesthetic ideology is structured around a series of related antitheses: literal/figural, alienated consciousness/unalienated consciousness, inorganicity/organicity, sign/symbol. This theory of literary production (and of social criticism) brings with it a series of aesthetic and political judgments. Mediocre art, which is barely worthy of the name art, aligns itself with the first terms of the dichotomies (literal, alienated, inorganic, sign) while authentic art aligns itself with the latter terms (figural, unalienated, organic, symbol). Authentic art, then, is by definition immediate, natural, infinitely suggestive, creative, original, and unique. It elevates the consciousness by attacking one's sense of complacency and helps to liberate a decaying West. Inauthentic art, on the other hand, is necessarily mediated, unnatural, decorative, dryly rational, illustrative, derivative, and didactic. It confirms the decadent, corrupt, Jewified social order and leaves the hearer's degraded consciousness unchallenged. In the former, there exists an organic relationship between the work of art and the subject broached by the work. In the latter, this relationship is arbitrary and inorganic, as the same point could be better made in another way.

Creative freedom: parable versus allegory

> To live, to err, to fall, to triumph, to recreate life out of life!
> ... His soul was swooning into some new world, fantastic,
> dim, uncertain as under sea, traversed by cloudy shapes and
> beings.
>
> Joyce, *A Portrait of the Artist*

This aesthetic dichotomy (the immediate, natural, and creative versus the unnatural, decorative, and didactic) should sound familiar to most biblical critics. It indispensable to the very definition of parable. If Heideggerian existentialism (i.e. the antithesis between authenticity and "the They") informs the scholarly argument as to the effect of the parable, Romantic aesthetic judgments inform the construction of the parable/allegory antithesis. We have already described how Wilder's description of Jesus' language is laced with aesthetic judgments, judgments which can only be described as Romantic. Crossan takes the nascent Romanticism that has been underlying earlier scholarly discussion of parable/allegory and brings it to the center of his analysis. Dissatisfied with the "totally inadequate conceptualization" that has dominated the discussion, he seeks to "reopen the entire discussion on a more profound level" (*IP* 9). The solution is found in "some of our greatest poets" who have stressed "the tremendous difference between allegory and symbol"

(*IP* 9). He turns to four poets: Goethe, Coleridge, Yeats, and T.S. Eliot (*IP* 9–10). The first two are explicitly connected with the Romantic school, and the latter both appropriate the Romantic view of symbol (see Norris 1988: 22, 29, 35–36, 83–85). In each case, the interpretation of allegory is infused in the sort of aesthetic judgments identified above. Symbol is infinitely active, translucent, and artistic. Allegory is abstract, illustrative, intellectual, and moralistic. If symbol participates organically in the reality it evokes, allegory's relation to its subject matter is artificial and unnatural. If symbol expresses what can only be expressed metaphorically, thereby bringing the hearer to experience the reality evoked, allegory expresses what can better be expressed in other ways and is irrelevant to the reader's experience. We have before us two types of story. One is organic, immediate, natural, effective, and powerful, while the other is inorganic, arbitrary, disposable, and impotent. It is not difficult to imagine which one biblical scholars will apply to Jesus and which one scholars will apply to Jesus' Jewish opponents.[10]

Crossan claims that he has no desire to denigrate allegory and allegorization as literary forms. "In this book there is no presumption that the term 'allegory' has a pejorative connotation or that allegory is a bad or inferior literary form" (*IP* 10). Despite this disclaimer, his actual description of parable and allegory betrays familiar aesthetic judgments (*IP* 10–22). Allegory falls away like a useless garment and is didactic, pedagogical, dogmatic, illustrative and expendable. Parables, on the other hand, are irreplaceable, irreducible, and indispensable. A good parable is "linguistic art at its most profound and indispensable moment" (*IP* 16). "Jesus' parables are radically constitutive of his own distinctive historicity and all else is located in them. Parable is the house of God" (*IP* 33). It is hard to see how claims such as this do anything but elevate parable at the expense of allegory.[11] His intention, to appreciate allegory, is no match for the full weight of his intellectual resources, which are pulling him in the opposite direction.

The ideology of parables: Funk, Crossan, and the myth of origins

Crossan, Funk, and the existential morality tale

Bultmannian existentialism brings with it theological and ideological commitments. The theological commitments, identified above, involve the hiddenness of God, the paradoxical nature of God's

activity, and the banality of the everyday. The ideological commitments are found primarily in the contours of the existentialist
morality tale around which Bultmann weaves his theological history
of early Christianity. As I argued above, this existential morality tale
is structured around three moments: habitual inauthenticity, existential encounter producing exhilarating moments of authenticity,
slothful fall back into convention. There is something inevitable and
irrevocable about the movement between these three moments. They
are assumed to reflect the very structure of human existence and to
be the only three human moments of lasting significance. Human
nature itself demands that the individual will fluctuate in this way
– that most will wallow in inauthenticity and that those who escape
will constantly struggle with the lure of inauthenticity.

When this structure is historicized, these three moments become
embodied in specific historical groups and texts. This process of
historicizing the existential structure of existence also tends to
racialize this structure. Certain peoples are taken to be more capable
of authenticity and certain texts more reflective of authenticity as
well. So, for Bultmann, inauthenticity is embodied in Oriental,
legalistic Judaism; the existential encounter is embodied in the
Western, Hellenistic, Pauline kerygma; and the fall back into
convention is embodied in early Catholicism, which is associated
both in Hegel–Tübingen and in later Heidegger with Latin
Romanism. The movement is religious-racial: from the Jewish East,
to a moment of pure, Greco-Germanic freedom, before the fall back
into the tepid compromise of Roman Catholicism. Funk and Crossan
follow the general structure of this morality tale but shift the locus
of his originary moment from the Pauline kerygma to the teachings
of Jesus. Thus the structure of their narrative of Christian origins
remains the same, but the existential moments are embodied in
different peoples and in different texts. Judaism remains the embodiment of inauthenticity, but Jesus' parables replace the Pauline
kerygma as the primal, originary moment. It is the early Church
which earns a description echoing that of early Catholicism, even
if that derogatory term is reserved for later, more fallen, stages in
early church history. In the final section of this chapter we shall
analyze the Heideggerian myth of origins, the Heideggerian
morality tale, and see how it influences the conclusions of Funk and
Crossan.

The problem of ideological commitment in parable scholarship
is complicated by a cultural shift that occurred in the six years
between the publication of *Language, Hermeneutic and Word of God*

and *In Parables*. The intervening years witnessed the flowering and disintegration of the civil rights movement, the second wave of feminism, the beginnings of the gay liberation movement, the escalation of the anti-war movement, and the increase in Jewish–Christian dialogue. Funk's *Language, Hermeneutic and Word of God* employs the sort of antiJudaism that was typical of the scholarship of his day. Crossan's *In Parables*, on the other hand, seeks to break free from the prison house of ethnocentrism and religious chauvinism.

Escape from chauvinism is, of course, easier to claim than to achieve. In Crossan's case his intentions prove to be at odds with his intellectual resources. He desires to escape traditional antiJudaism yet remains committed to the (structurally antiJewish and Orientalist) Heideggerian myth of origin/fall. There is no doubting his genuine opposition to religious, racial, ethnic, or gendered chauvinism. Unlike earlier scholars, there is no overt antiJudaism or sexism in his writings and plenty of critique of religious, gender, or racial hierarchies. At the same time, I will demonstrate that Crossan, throughout *In Parables*, has recourse to Heideggerian categories and a Heideggerian thought structure, as well as the (Romantic) aesthetic ideology of organicity. There is, in short, a conflict between his intellectual resources (which are committed to social inequality and which inscribe that commitment in their very categories) and his personal beliefs (which hold antithetical commitments). Are these good intentions strong enough to overcome the disturbing ideological commitments buried deep in Crossan's intellectual resources? It is this question which renders *In Parables* such a fruitful object of ideological analysis.

Crossan and demythology

Singular, poetic experience comes to be articulated in the extraordinary poetic language of metaphor. Since Jesus' language is fundamentally poetic, we can move from his parables to his own experience of God as reflected in the parables.

> The fact that Jesus' experience is articulated in metaphorical parables, and not in some other linguistic types, means that these expressions are part of that experience itself . . . There is an intrinsic and inalienable bond between Jesus' experience and Jesus' parables. A sensitivity to the metaphorical language of religious and poetic experience and an empathy with the profound and mysterious linkage of such

> experience and such expression may help us to understand
> what is most important about Jesus: his experience of God.
>
> (*IP* 22)

After all his aesthetic speculation and historical reconstruction, Crossan ends up at the same place as the New Hermeneutic: with Jesus' experience of God and the implication of that experience for the faith of contemporary Christians. Jesus' unsurpassed experience of God is articulated in his profound parabolic words – this should all sound distressingly familiar. Crossan's parable scholarship, like Funk's before him, is an act of demythologizing. As such, it inevitably returns to Heidegger, who has been standing silently in the background, beckoning us to remain faithful. After all, is there any other way to talk honestly about God? More so even than Funk, Crossan succeeds in importing Heideggerian categories into the very heart of his analysis of Jesus' parables.

While the fusing together of Romanticism and Heidegger does not work philosophically, Crossan's own artistic skill ensures that *In Parables* works rhetorically. Many biblical scholars have turned to Heidegger since Bultmann first began appropriating his categories and thought-structure in the 1920s. The vast majority of them have done so in explicitly Bultmannian terms, even as they may have tried to move beyond him on key points. Crossan's appropriation of Heidegger is the most imaginative and highly original since Bultmann's demythology essays. It also wears its Heidegger lightly, avoiding existentialist jargon and slogans. Those who find it difficult to slog through the turgid prose of the New Hermeneutic can delight in Crossan's rhetorical skills, his charming prose, and his engaging style. Crossan and the New Hermeneuts may end up at roughly similar destinations, but the trip there is far more pleasant with Crossan at the helm. It is for this reason that we shall dwell extensively on Crossan's existentializing of the parables of Jesus. We shall return to Funk when we take up the question of those forces that are opposed to the parables.

Crossan turns to Heidegger for his understanding of temporality. "It is against this understanding of temporality and historicity that the parables of Jesus will be interpreted in this book. They express and contain the temporality of Jesus' experience of God; they proclaim and they establish the historicity of Jesus' response" (*IP* 32). The parables of Jesus reflect, and are structured around, the Heideggerian modes of existence. Thus Heideggerian temporality, which is one of the most important and most disturbing categories of *Being and Time*, proves to be absolutely essential to *In Parables*. "The understanding of time in this book is based on the constant probing of ontological time in the thought of Martin Heidegger, from *Being and Time* in 1927 to 'Time and Being' in 1962" (*IP* 31). Even though much of the preparatory analysis of *In Parables* has been Romantic, Heidegger reappears in the actual structure of the book and in the textual details. Despite the lengthy foray into Romanticism at the opening of *In Parables*, the majority of the book is structured around Heideggerian temporality.

To understand Crossan's analysis of the parables of Jesus, we must travel back to the Heideggerian categories of temporality and historicity and, most especially, to the care-structure of *Being and Time*.

> Human time and human history arise from response to Being which comes always out of the unexpected and the unforeseen, which destroys one's planned projections of a *future* by asserting in its place the *advent* of Being. Its advent discloses a very different *past* from that which was taken for granted as objectively given before this advent. It may well involve the radical reappraisal and even *reversal* of that past. But it is this advent and this reversal which constitutes the force and power of a *present* which is now really and truly an *action*. Instead of the objective and surface succession of three moments in past–present–future, one now receives a deeper and more ontological simultaneity of three modes in advent–reversal–action.
>
> (*IP* 31–32)

These three Heideggerian modes of existence turn out to be far more important for Crossan's overall argument than they first appear. These three ontological modes of existence provide the fundamental categories into which Crossan groups the parables.[12] The three ontological modes of existence announce the "three modes of the Kingdom's temporality" (*IP* 36). They reveal the fundamental structure of Jesus' anthropology, an anthropology that makes it clear that Jesus, helped along by *Being and Time*'s existential morality tale, will set out to revitalize the West.

Advent: the existential moment

Of the three existential moments articulated by the three parable groupings, advent comes first. "In the triple but simultaneous modality of the Kingdom . . . ontological primacy belonged to the *advent* . . . It was from this that all else flowed and it was this that determined new time and new history for the discoverer" (*IP* 37–38, his italics). We have often seen that authenticity begins with the existential encounter (i.e. the existential moment). For Bultmann and his heirs this means the sudden revelation of the radical insecurity at the heart of human existence, a revelation which brought the realization that life is a gift which can be neither secured nor controlled. The advent parables are Crossan's existential encounter. While these parables, which are primarily about the natural world, may seem to foreground themes of natural growth, they actually underscore the importance of gift and miracle. The nature imagery highlights

> the graciousness and the surprise of the ordinary, the advent of bountiful harvest despite the losses of sowing, the large shade despite the small seed. It is like this that the Kingdom is in advent. It is surprise and it is gift.
>
> (*IP* 51)

For Crossan, like for Bultmann before him, it is all about grace. The crucial existential moment, which is ontologically primary, is the revelation of grace.

As we have already seen in Funk, grace and the everyday necessarily have an ambiguous relationship with each other. Funk often values the everyday positively as the locus of grace. This occurs when he opposes the everyday to the inauthentic world of piety, church structure, and heaven. As often as not, however, he values the everyday negatively, as that which is closed off to grace. This occurs when he equates the everyday with conventionality, ossification, and the world. We see this same ambiguity in Crossan. The nature themes of the advent parables reveal that everyday existence is the locus of grace. "It is, therefore, not unimportant that Jesus' parables of the Kingdom's advent are taken from the utter normalcy of actual or possible existence" (*IP* 53). Their very extravagance, however, shatters the normalcy of the conventional everyday. "One must speak of what comes beyond expectation or, even if expected, is always experienced as permanently gracious and undeserved" (*IP* 53).

Reversal: freedom from the herd

"Advent demands reversal" (*IP* 55), which explains the second major parable grouping. Crossan does not ever really explain why encounter demands reversal, but perhaps, at this point in the discipline's history, he does not need to. The narrative structure of Heideggerian existentialism, as mediated by Bultmann, demands it. The antithesis between authenticity and "the They" has become so well established within the discursive structure of Heideggerian biblical scholarship that it need no longer be articulated or defended. It has become the unspoken, yet absolutely essential, support for Crossan's parabolic theology.

The existential encounter (i.e. advent) is the first moment that challenges the ubiquitous perceptual reality of "the They". It reveals the illusory nature of human security and underlines the fundamentally ungrounded and radically insecure nature of human existence. "Jesus is proclaiming . . . the permanent presence of God as the one who challenges world and shatters its complacency repeatedly" (*IP* 26). The individual who has experienced existence as radically insecure and gracious can no longer tolerate drifting along with the herd. The entirety of conventional existence must be overthrown. The Kingdom "demand(s) the overturn of prior values, closed options, set judgments, and established conclusions" (*IP* 65). It announces "radical judgment" (*IP* 66) on the everyday world of (Oriental, Jewified) conventionality and normalcy, a judgment of "radical and absolute reversal of their closed human situation" (*IP* 73). Absolute, radical change is required. The sort of singular reversal that we find in the Hebrew Bible (e.g. Joseph's spectacular rise or Job's catastrophic fall) will hardly do. This dire situation calls out for existential reversal, for what Crossan calls "polar" reversal; reversal that shakes us down to our foundation, that shatters our preconceived illusions, that leaves us defenseless, exposed, and, ironically enough, open to God.

> (Parables) are stories which shatter the deep structure of our accepted world . . . They remove our defences and make us vulnerable to God. It is only in such experiences that God can touch us, and only in such moments does the kingdom of God arrive.
>
> (Crossan 1975: 122)

Radical, existential, polar reversal is absolutely essential to any genuine experience of God, as Jesus astutely recognizes.

The New Hermeneuts long ago argued that the parables of Jesus did more than identify the Kingdom: they actually bring the Kingdom near. Crossan concurs and develops an argument to that effect that is far more persuasive than anything that preceded him. Not only do Jesus' parables recognize the need for radical reversal, they make such an experience possible (see also *IP* 52). He demonstrates this claim with his widely admired reinterpretation of the Good Samaritan. This had long been considered an "example story",[13] as a simple story with a moral point ("go and do likewise") rather than a sharp paradox. With great originality and verve, Crossan argues against the tide. In one sense, his analysis of the Good Samaritan relies on some rather well-established principles of parable scholarship, particularly the claim, traced back to Dodd, that parables shock the imagination and produce active thought. His analysis is especially effective because he is applying these well-established principles in a new and exciting way. His reading is innovative enough to create a stir and conventional enough to win adherents. His reading is also effective in part because it is remarkably well written. It is easy to follow his soaring eloquence and to ignore the complex web of philosophical, aesthetic, ideological, and disciplinary assumptions that render his argument coherent.

For Crossan, the Good Samaritan should not be reduced to a comfortable call to moral rectitude, but is, instead, a sharply fashioned challenge capable of awakening a slumbering consciousness. "The literal point of the story challenges the hearer to put together two impossible and contradictory words for the same person: 'Samaritan' (10:33) and 'neighbor' (10:36). The whole thrust of the story demands that one say what cannot be said, what is a contradiction in terms . . . The story demands that the hearer respond by saying the contradictory, the impossible, the unspeakable" (*IP* 64). It is through our struggle with the impossible that the Kingdom of God bursts upon us. "The hearer struggling with the contradictory dualism of Good/Samaritan is actually experiencing in and through this the inbreaking of the Kingdom. Not only does it happen like this, it happens in this" (*IP* 66).

The parable, like Bultmann's kerygma on which it is loosely modeled, brings about authentic self-understanding on the part of the hearer. Like the Bultmannian kerygma, the parables of reversal are the absolute antithesis to the Jewish sins of self-security and boasting. "When the north pole becomes the south pole, and the south the north, a world is reversed and overturned and we find ourselves standing firmly on utter uncertainty. The parables of reversal intend to do precisely this to our security because such is the advent of the Kingdom of God. Or, as Paul might have put it, see if you can boast from the middle of an earthquake" (*IP* 55). With the (Eastern, Jewish, despotic) spirit expelled by means of the parable of reversal, Jesus' audience can become open to the Western spirit of freedom. The parable is the gospel demythologized.

Action: living authentically

The existential moment (advent) calls us out of the everyday world of inauthenticity (reversal). In an exhilarating moment of absolute freedom we throw off the shackles of conventionality and embrace the radical insecurity of existence. Humbled, vulnerable, and shaken, we are truly open to God. In that moment of radical insecurity and absolute openness, we may be faced with a decision. At this moment of decision, we can either act resolutely, grounded in the moment, or we can refuse to act, and turn a blind eye to the advent of the Kingdom. Such is the theme of the final grouping of parables, the parables of action. "These parables portray crucial or critical situations which demand firm and resolute action, prompt and energetic decision" (IP 84). So, for example, the parable of the Wicked Husbandmen (IP 86–96) is about "some people who recognized their situation, saw their opportunity, and acted resolutely upon it" (IP 96). The parable highlights their resolute action in the face of a crisis, rather than the morality or immorality of their crime of murder.[14]

Authentic decision must be grounded in the existential moment. From advent to reversal to action – that is the logic of parabolic authenticity. Any break in that chain can open space for the reintroduction of inauthenticity. Advent produces exhilarating moments of existential clarity, when the insecurity of human existence is illuminated. The existential moment, however, will eventually pass and the radiant clarity that comes with it will eventually dissipate. We cannot live forever in a state of authenticity, and we eventually return to the everyday world of convention, normalcy, programs, and security.

> The parables of Jesus seek to draw one into the Kingdom, and they challenge us to act and to live from the gift which is experienced therein. But we do not want parables. We want precepts and we want programs. We want *good* precepts and we want *sensible* programs . . . We want them to tell us exactly what to do and they refuse to answer. They make us face the problem of the grounding of ethics and we want only to discuss the logic of ethics.
>
> (IP 82)[15]

"Falling" is built into the structure of Heidegger's anthropology. Even the authentic can fall prey to the lure of objectification and security, can temper the scorching existential moment with tepid moralizing, can fall from the heights of originality and authenticity to the mediocrity of compromise and conventionality.

This is not to suggest that ethics are unimportant. The problem arises when they are turned into absolutes, into idols, into self-satisfied means for evading the existential reality.

> Our ethical principles and our moral systems are absolutely necessary and so also is their inevitable shattering as part and parcel of the shattering of world. We walk a knife-edge between absolutism on the one hand and indifference on the other. All of which is rather frightening and makes one wish for just one little absolute, even one pale, frail, anemic one to hang onto for security. But the only absolute we keep glimpsing is the Kingdom snapping our absolutes like dried twigs.
>
> (*IP* 82)

We are to live ethically, but are not to smugly boast of our own virtue or to transform our ethics into self-security. We are justified by parable alone, not by the works of moralizing allegory. The initial overcoming of inauthenticity and "the They" is necessarily followed by the perpetual struggle between, and movement between, authenticity and inauthenticity. The servant parables, a subgroup of the action parables, are designed to address just this problem of post-reversal falling. Crossan argues that the servant parables can be divided into two types: one (A) where the good are rewarded and the wicked punished in an orderly and conventional manner; followed by a second (B) where this theme is questioned, probed, and contradicted. The servant parables introduce a very disturbing note into Jesus' teaching. We should be ready, like a wise and prudent servant, to respond to the demands of the Kingdom; "but, unfortunately, the eschatological advent of God will always be precisely that for which wise and prudent readiness is impossible because it shatters also our wisdom and prudence" (*IP* 120). The parables of reversal challenge us to reorder our entire misguided world, while the servant parables challenge us to continually reorder our world lest we fall into complacency and convention. The servant parables demand perpetual reversal because they recognize the eternal movement between falling and recovery.

The myth of the fall: the rabbis, the early Church, and allegory

For those with ears to hear, Jesus' originary parables shatter false consciousness and bring about new and better self-understanding. Unfortunately, according to Funk and Crossan, not everyone has ears to hear, as the Church's misappropriation of the parables revealed. Terrified by the radical freedom and primordial power of the parables, the early Church tamed and domesticated them by transforming them into edifying, theological, or moralizing allegories. The original parables are barely recognizable in their allegorized, Gospel form. According to Funk, "once a metaphor has passed into language it may become ossified and subsequently adapted to lexicons and logic, with the consequent loss of its hermeneutical potential" (Funk 139). This is exactly what Funk sees as happening to the original parables of Jesus. The early Church attached inappropriate applications, which closed off the open-ended nature of the parables. This inappropriate and unchallenging domestication of the parables came about because the Church, dazzled by the existential lure of security, sought "firm anchorage" (Funk 12). As parable gave way to allegory, the originary moment gave way to the loss of hermeneutical potential, to the slackening of the originary power, and to the betrayal of the scandal of the cross. In so doing, the Church hardened, domesticated, and tamed the dynamic teachings of Jesus (see Funk 134–135, 179). This loss of hermeneutical potential ensured a lower level of consciousness/ self-understanding on the part of organized Christianity. The parables may still maintain their power but they are buried under two millennia of misinterpretation, misunderstanding, and dead weight. It is up to the critic to bring the original parables to the light of day and to stand back as their originary power is unleashed.

Such is the view of early Christian history, as revealed in the parable scholarship of both Crossan and Funk. As this description makes clear, both assume the entirety of the Heideggerian myth of origins. This Heideggerian narrative of origins–fall–recovery has been repeated in Bultmann and in the New Hermeneutic. The details change, but the structure of the grand narrative remains remarkably similar. I have argued that these earlier versions of the myth of origins brought with them explicit and disturbing ideological commitments. The movement of breaking free, origin, fall has often been racialized: breaking from Orient, Judaism; originary freedom as Western, Hellenistic, Christian; fall as reJudaizing and

Catholicizing (i.e. Latinizing) the gospel. Funk accepts this narrative without question, and, by virtue of his commitment to the myth of origins, Crossan's thought is pulled in the same direction. On the other hand, by virtue of his own personal belief system, which is at odds with any form of racialization, Crossan questions the ideological conclusions implicit in this narrative. The discourse which informs Crossan's work ensures that, contrary to his own intention, his own analysis will become racialized.

Funk's Palestinian Judaism: inauthenticity

Had belonging to such a religion as Judaism, which is alleged to inculcate unremitting severity, deprived the Pharisees of all semblance of humanity?

E.P. Sanders, *Jesus and Judaism*

I have been arguing, with the help of Heschel, that, under the influence of historical criticism, theological antiJudaism escalated within the discourse of biblical scholarship (see Heschel 1998: 9–13, 63–68, 226–228). Modern biblical scholarship insisted upon the spiritual and existential uniqueness of Jesus (and Paul), and could only do so by thoroughly denigrating first-century Judaism. As I have argued, both Baur and Bultmann systematically denigrated "late Judaism" in order to sharpen the contrast between degenerate Judaism and authentic Christianity. Bultmann's Judaism, for example, was primarily defined by the absence of God, by legalism, and by boastful justification by works. Much of this finds its ways into Funk as well. This should not surprise us. The New Hermeneutic has been constructed, at least by Fuchs, around the grace/works dichotomy. According to Robinson, Fuchs "hears Heidegger's lament about inauthentic language as an indirect witness to true language, somewhat as the law is related to the gospel" (Robinson 1964: 49). Funk, following along in this direction, draws the following emphatic conclusion to his discussion of Jesus.

(Jesus) does not allow the law to dominate love as God's drawing near. Rather, Jesus proclaims the law in a context qualified by the event of divine love . . . For Jesus the law labored under severe handicaps. It has been confined to a field in which God was ostensibly present but from which he was actually remote. The scribes and Pharisees sought to relate it to everyday existence in countless ways, but it grew

less relevant with each step. Rabbinic interpretation of the
law sought to engage the Jew, but ended by disengaging
him from reality. Jesus attempted nothing less than to
shatter the whole tradition that had obscured the Law. To
put it in a way that is still enigmatic, but in the way parable
suggests, Jesus had to interpret the law in parable.

(Funk 221–222)

The parables are constructed around the grace/Law antithesis.

Bultmannian legalism is not, however, the only religiously flawed
attribute of Jesus' Jewish opponents. Funk, like his contemporary
Norman Perrin, was indebted to Jeremias's description of Palestinian
Judaism (see especially Perrin 1967: 94–103). Funk's Jewish opponents of Jesus are most striking for their obstinate and malicious
contempt for the poor, the sinners, the swineherd, the tax collect-
ors, and the outcasts. According to this view, taken from Jeremias,
salvation was unavailable to the outcasts and, therefore, the Pharisees
held them in contempt. Jesus' association with the poor and sinners
is, in this view, a direct challenge to the core of a bankrupt Judaism.
This claim is essential to Funk's argument, even if it is taken as
historically established rather than argued.[16] Like Bultmann's charge
of legalism, this position has hardly stood the test of time and has
been authoritatively refuted by Sanders (1985: 174–211). This
charge brings together a millennium of antiJudaism (which saw
Judaism as incapable of offering genuine forgiveness of sins),
centuries of Orientalism (which saw Easterners as clannish, unfor-
giving, obsessed with honor, and incapable of true love), and
Heideggerian existentialism (which developed authenticity and its
parallels in dialogue with both antiJudaism and Orientalism). The
only thing missing was serious engagement with the appropriate
Jewish texts and Jewish thinkers or a modicum of sympathy and
open-mindedness.

If Jeremias (and his student Perrin) sought to demonstrate
contemptuous arrogance of Jesus' Jewish opponents, Funk has something more elaborate up his sleeve. His major criticism of Jeremias
is that he is too literal-minded in his reading of Jesus' opponents.
Funk certainly accepts that the Pharisees were the historical Jesus'
concrete opponents, and accepts Jeremias's description of their
reasons for opposing Jesus. He wants to go beyond that, however,
and to transform "Pharisaic intransigence" (Funk 12) into a universal
human trait. He takes over a fundamentally antiJewish prejudice
about a historical group and *inscribes it into his definition of parable.*

The parable is an offense to the religiously disposed ("the Pharisee"), but a joyous surprise to the religiously disinherited ("the tax-collectors and sinners"). The parable, like the comportment of Jesus (he eats with tax-collectors and sinners), is an affront to the "logic" of piety, but good news to the dispossessed because they have no basis for a claim on God. The latter but not the former can accept the "logic" of grace (both understand it, the former only too well).

(Funk 197)

Rather than rejecting the antiJudaism of the Bultmannians, Funk aestheticizes it. As Käsemann warned us about the danger of the Jew within, so Funk implicitly warns us about the Pharisee within. If the Jew within encouraged merit and boasting, the Pharisee within blinds us to the meaning of the parables. The Pharisees (or the Pharisee within) represent the pious rejection of grace, the desire to master the text rather than to be interpreted by it, and the tyranny of conventionality. The Pharisees signify the triumph of the anonymous, inauthentic, urban "They" which must be escaped in the name of authenticity. Heidegger took up and secularized popular racial and religious hostility to Jews to construct the category of "the They". By incorporating the categories of *Being and Time*, Heideggerian biblical scholars have taken over this ideologically troublesome category ("the They") and applied it to the Jews of Jesus' day. The circle is once again closed. For the modern West to be revitalized, the parable must shatter the Eastern, Jewish, Pharisaic world. This world must be shattered in the name of freedom, in the name of authenticity, in the name of grace, and in the name of love.

Crossan's Pharisees

At one point Crossan had sought to rethink the figural/literal divide and the negative valuation of allegory. In the end, however, the force of his commitment to his own particular version of Romantic existentialism pulled him back towards affirming that which he had sought to reject. In the same way, he also seeks to rethink the traditional denigration of the Jew as a way of elevating Jesus. Will his ideologically tinged sources also pull him away from the full implications of this rejection of antiJudaism? I have argued that Crossan is a direct descendant of the New Hermeneutic. We have already seen how Funk's (New Hermeneutical) construction of the Pharisees is deeply indebted to the language and intellectual world of modern antiJudaism. His Pharisees are boastful, legalistic, ritualistic, and contemptuous of the poor and the sinners. This negative view of the Pharisees as radically opposed to divine grace is inscribed by Funk into his very definition of parable. Parable reveals the essence of God's graciousness to sinners, and, as such, it is rejected or trivialized by those opposed to divine grace. This has the effect of making the Pharisees Jesus' eternal enemies, as archetypes of smug justification by works, of piety, of normalcy, and of conventionality. The New Hermeneutical Pharisees embody resistance to the gospel as told in parables, as surely as the Bultmannian Pharisees had embodied resistance to the gospel as preached in kerygma.

One of the few substantial differences between Crossan and the New Hermeneutic occurs at this very point. Writing in the wake of the civil rights movement and the emergence of the Jewish–Christian dialogue, Crossan has no place in his thought for the casual denigration of the Pharisees and of Judaism. He makes this point repeatedly. He claims no desire to elevate Jesus' stories at the expense of the rabbinic narratives and completely rejects the picture of Pharisees as uncaring, legalistic hypocrites of the later Christian traditions (*IP* 52, 55, 80–83). The Pharisees and Jesus have different existential and spiritual stances which produce different aesthetic experiences. We should be content to celebrate these differences without translating them into rigid hierarchies. The Pharisees are venerable religious leaders who communicate their own profound spiritual and ethical insights through their own distinguished texts and practices.

As we shall see, however, it is more difficult than it first appears to put aside the deeply entrenched, racialized ideology of modern biblical scholarship. This ideology is deeply ingrained in the discourse of Heideggerian biblical scholarship and permeates the categories, methods, aesthetics and theologies assumed by Crossan. As such it is perfectly capable of reasserting itself in the course of Crossan's critical analysis. We see this in the aesthetic claims made on behalf of parable, and in the theological claims rooted in Bultmannian existentialism. Let us take a closer look at his initial claim that he does not wish to elevate Jesus at the expense of the rabbis.

> This is not an attempt to exalt Jesus above the rabbis as an exercise in Christian chauvinism. It is to insist that they are doing completely different things. Their stories are didactic

figures, those of Jesus are poetic metaphors; theirs are subservient to the teaching situations, those of Jesus are
subservient only to the experienced revelation which seeks
to articulate its presence in, by, and through them. It is
neither necessary nor advisable to turn difference into hierarchical order.

(*IP* 20–21)

In this very revealing passage we can quite literally see Crossan being
pulled in two very different directions. On the one hand, we see the
positive evaluation of Judaism described above. On the other hand,
the seeming neutrality of the passage is overwhelmed by the social
values implied in the clearly articulated aesthetic judgments. Even
a cursory reading of *In Parables* reveals that, for Crossan, rabbinical
didacticism is inferior to Jesus' articulation of immediate poetic
experiences. In case that point is missed, Crossan asserts that the
Pharisees are merely able to communicate conclusions drawn from
their own (admittedly profound) spiritual experiences, while Jesus'
parables are able to help others experience the Kingdom themselves
(*IP* 52).

This pattern is repeated elsewhere. Let us take as an example the
contrast between parables and allegories. Despite his disclaimers to
the contrary, parables are clearly positive and allegories are equally
clearly held in contempt. Parables are positive, dynamic, immediate,
and poetic while allegories are illustrative, didactic, rational, mediated, unnecessary, and literal. He also makes it clear that Jesus
speaks in parables while the rabbis employ allegories (see *IP* 54–55).
This is immediately followed by the hollow claim that this is not
intended as a slap at the rabbis. "In no way is this intended to denigrate the rabbinical story in favor of that of Jesus. It is simply to
insist that they are doing radically different things: one illustrates
a rather obvious text which would be quite clear even without it;
the other incarnates the mystery of the Advent" (*IP* 54–55). Given
the consistent aesthetic values attached to parable/allegory throughout the course of *In Parables*, it is difficult to take seriously the claim
of descriptive neutrality. Add to that the very diction of the
antithesis (the incarnation of the mystery of the Advent versus
useless and obvious illustration), and the ranking of the two types
of teaching moves from the explicit to the implicit. To top it off,
this analysis concludes with Bultmannian-styled attacks on insecurity and boasting – two categories that had long been associated
with the inadequacy of Judaism. Crossan is not disingenuous in his

desire to avoid denigrating the rabbis, but he is not persuasive either. Appalled by Christian chauvinism, he is unable to escape from its grasp.

Crossan's analysis of the Pharisees is even fuzzier. He is careful to avoid explicit insults and is equally careful to praise them as fine spiritual guides and moral teachers. This praise is tempered, however, by a Bultmannian antipathy towards "Pharisaic righteousness" (*IP* 27). The Pharisees may be fine moral teachers, but moral teaching is itself suspect. "In fact, the Pharisees were superb moral guides. But there precisely lay the problem which Jesus and Paul saw so clearly" (*IP* 80). The problem stems from a fundamental flaw in the Pharisaic perspective, which mistakenly thought that obedience led to God. They had it backwards: it is the gift of God's presence, the advent of the Kingdom, that makes possible authenticity. The rhetoric is certainly kinder than anything we have seen so far, but the implicit conclusions are not structurally different from those of Funk, Bultmann, Baur, or Hegel: the Pharisees represent justification by works, while Jesus and Paul represent justification by grace. The Pharisees represent Eastern despotism, security, piety, conventionality, and normalcy, the very ideas that the parables set out to overturn. Crossan's Pharisees may be fine moral teachers, but they are aesthetically challenged, they misunderstand the nature of grace, they prefer security to authenticity, and they teach in a didactic manner which is not conducive to recognizing that life is a gift. At least implicitly, they are part of an (Eastern) world that needs to be overturned, reversed, and shattered, in the name of (Western) divine grace.

It is important to recognize, however, how divided Crossan's work is at this point. It is not the case that he is simply or disingenuously antiJewish. His early parable scholarship represents a relatively early stage in the attempt to purge New Testament scholarship of its unfortunate history and language of antiJudaism. As such, there is much that is praiseworthy here. His positive rhetoric about Judaism is refreshing when compared with the hostility freely expressed by mainstream scholarship less than a decade earlier. We should also keep in mind that both Funk and Crossan have published extensively and that these books represent early stages in long, varied, and productive careers. Crossan in particular has been relentless in his desire to identify and attack the roots of Christian antiSemitism and goes a long way towards completing the process begun with *In Parables*. His *Who Killed Jesus?* is to be commended for putting Auschwitz and Christian antiSemitism at the center of its analysis (see especially ix–xii, 31–38, 147–159, 218–221) – asking provocatively whether "those stories of ours send certain people out to kill" (32). In terms of Crossan's overall career, *In Parables* represents a partially successful attempt at scholarship that is free from the taint of antiJudaism. In terms of Jesus scholarship, *In Parables* represents a transitional text, caught between the demands of post-Auschwitz morality and traditional antiJudaism.

At the same time, however, it is also important to recognize that *Language, Hermeneutic and the Word of God* and *In Parables* are major milestones in contemporary biblical scholarship. Both scholars have moved on to new topics and have incorporated into their scholarship revised views of the Pharisees and first-century Judaism. Crossan in particular has played an important role in challenging biblical scholars, myself included, to take seriously the question of Christian antiJudaism. This docs not change the fact that these two extremely influential works continue to be definitive examples of parable scholarship. All current research on the parables must take them into account and much recent literary criticism, especially of the Gospel of Mark, has been deeply influenced by the parable scholarship of Funk and Crossan (see especially Donahue; Fowler; Kelber 91–93, 121–129, 217; Perrin 1972: 363–372; 1977: 34–38, 57, 64–65). Because *Language, Hermeneutic and the Word of God* and *In Parables* continue to remain influential, in both parable scholarship and literary criticism, attention must be paid to the ways that racialization and antiJudaism find their way into these texts. Despite Crossan's later writings, it is important, therefore, to recognize that the still widely read and extremely influential *In Parables* is unable to fully escape the weight of two centuries of scholarly slogans about Judaism. This realization will lead me to ask, in the Conclusion to this book, whether escape from racialization and antiJudaism is possible at all.

Conclusion

The Heideggerianized parable scholarship of Funk and Crossan is a direct descendant of the Heideggerianized New Testament criticism of Bultmann and his students. Funk and Crossan read Heidegger through Bultmann's eyes, which means that their work contains many of the same problems that can be found in Bultmann's Heideggerianized program of demythology. Funk and Crossan inherit from Bultmann the assumption that Heidegger developed an existentialist anthropology that revolves around the categories of temporality, the care-structure and authenticity. These assumptions (about authenticity, inauthenticity, temporality, the care-structure,) led Bultmann's demythologizing program in unfortunate directions and they do the same for parable scholarship.

Bultmann's problematic reading of Heidegger comes together in what I have called the existential morality tale. It is this existentialist morality tale that allows Bultmann to bring together various Heideggerian themes which, when combined with the Hegelian–Tübingen narrative of world history, meld into a powerful mythology about the origins of Christianity. In this tale, authenticity comes about by overcoming the pervasive inauthenticity that occurs when one is lost in "the They". Once authenticity has been achieved, the individual slides back and forth between authenticity and habitual inauthenticity. When applied to earliest Christianity, this tale, helped along by the Hegelian–Tübingen narrative of world history, takes on an explicitly racialized structure. "The They" becomes equated with Eastern Judaism; primordial encounter becomes equated with the Western, Hellenistic gospel of Paul; and the post-encounter slide back to inauthenticity becomes equated with the tepid compromise of early Catholicism. Funk and Crossan take over this existential morality tale wholesale and translate it to the parabolic teachings of Jesus. In the update of the tale, Eastern, Palestinian, and Pharisaic Judaism remain the embodiment of "the They"; the parables of Jesus take over the role of the Western, Hellenistic, primordial encounter; and the allegories of the primitive Church take over the role of tepid, Catholic compromise. Their mutual commitment to Heidegger (and to a particular reading of Heidegger) encourages Bultmann and Funk/Crossan to construct remarkably similar versions of the rise and corruption of earliest Christianity. While their narratives have different turning points, they both maintain a fundamentally similar, and fundamentally racialized, structure. In this narrative, authenticity means breaking free from the servile and Jewish east. Authenticity belongs to the West, and can only be maintained by those pure, Hellenistic Westerners who refuse to compromise with the spirits of the East or of Rome.

At the same time, Funk and Crossan do seek to distance themselves from Bultmann, particularly on the question of language. This turn to the later Heidegger could have brought about enormous shifts, both positive and negative, within the discipline. After all, it is the later Heidegger that thoroughly rejects the anthropocentrism implicit in the early Heidegger – the very anthropocentrism that is essential to Bultmann's existentialist anthropology. Attention to the later Heidegger could have had the salutary effect of directly challenging the excessive anthropocentrism in modern biblical scholarship, an anthropocentrism that has aligned itself with a variety of forms of racialization. Turning to later Heidegger could have led to a radical rethinking and reconfiguration of Bultmann's project. At the same time, the later Heidegger also explicitly embraces National Socialism and works strenuously to inscribe his own, idiosyncratic version of *völkisch* nationalism into the heart of his thought. He does so most explicitly in his analysis of language and of poetry, the very ideas which most concern the New Hermeneutic and parable scholarship. Turning to the later Heidegger could have produced the very negative effect of further miring New Testament scholarship in the swamp of racialized thinking.

In the end, the turn to the later Heidegger was far less significant than it could have been. It brought about neither a radical rethinking of Bultmannian existentialism, nor a further racializing of the discipline. Rather than rethinking the excessive anthropocentrism of modern thought (as Heidegger tries to), Funk and Crossan continue to construct their reading of the parable around Bultmann's existentialist anthropology. At the same time, neither Funk nor Crossan escape the influence of Heidegger's Greco-Germanic, racialized aesthetic, an aesthetic which leaves limited traces on the way that the parables are read. Even as Funk and Crossan challenge Bultmann's view of language, they do so in a way that remains within Bultmann's anthropocentric and existentialist orbit. As a result, the turn to later Heidegger does little to change the racialized dynamic of modern, Bultmannian New Testament scholarship, although it does play a significant role in further spreading (some of) Heidegger's racialized ideas throughout the discipline. What had once been limited, primarily, to Pauline and Lukan scholarship, now found its way into the center of the thought of two scholars who have done much to shape current historical Jesus research.

The parable scholarship of Funk and Crossan inherits its views on the creation and reception of art from Romanticism rather than from the later Heidegger. While the parabolic debt to Romanticism goes back (at least) to Dodd, it is Crossan who is decisive in turning here for inspiration. The debt to Romanticism can be seen in the assumptions made about creativity and originality, and in the aesthetic values that permeate parable scholarship (i.e. direct, immediate, vibrant, dynamic, natural, versus arbitrary, static, impotent, disposable, formulaic). These values, when combined with Bultmann's existentialist anthropology, are essential in defining crucial aspects of the seminal parable scholarship of Funk and Crossan. They determine how parable and allegory are defined, what parables are supposed to reveal about Jesus, how parables are thought to work, how parables are thought to be received, and even how they are categorized (at least by Crossan, whose threefold categorization reflects Heidegger's threefold temporal care-structure). It is my contention that, far from disclosing the natural essence of language and literature, these values have a troubled history and gain their force from being part of an ideological system. These aesthetic values, which are inherent in the Romantic view of creativity, reflect the racialized ideology of organicity, an ideology which has been continually linked with racialization and with *völkisch* nationalism. These aesthetic values ensure that the racialized aesthetic of organicity, which is so important to both Romanticism and Heideggerianism, will remain an essential part of the scholarly discourse on parables – at least to the extent that that discourse is defined by Funk and Crossan.

7

CONCLUSION

Our narrative of racialization in the discourse of modern biblical scholarship has culminated in a moment of impasse. On the one hand, Crossan the individual sought to free himself and his work of chauvinism, ethnocentrism, and antiJudaism. On the other hand, Crossan the Heideggerian and heir of parable scholarship was unable to accomplish what he set out to do. I wish to be careful here. It is not the case that Crossan's intentions are in any way disingenuous, deficient, or inadequate. His long career, most notably in his *Who Killed Jesus?*, makes it abundantly clear that he is genuine in his commitment to equality and in his repudiation of fascism or totalitarianism. The problem resides at the level of discourse rather than intention. Crossan may want to construct an interpretation of the parables that is free from chauvinism, but his philosophical, aesthetic, and disciplinary resources pull his thought in the opposite direction. He is (rightly) critical of traditional biblical scholarship for its casual denigration of rabbinical and Pharisaic Judaism, but his indebtedness to Romanticism and Heideggerian existentialism prevents him from thinking differently about these topics. Such is the impasse identified in the lengthy historical analysis offered throughout the course of this book. The discourse within which biblical scholarship finds itself imbedded (i.e. Hegelianism, Heideggerianism, Romanticism) is, to a significant degree, racialized. That discourse ensures that biblical scholarship will remain racialized, despite the best intentions of individual biblical scholars, who have no personal commitment to racism.

My basic thesis is that modern biblical scholarship is trapped in a racialized discourse. I certainly doubt that there are very many current scholars who consciously commit themselves to the principles of white supremacy and radical antiSemitism. On the other hand, mainstream scholarship has inherited some deeply troubling categories and perspectives, as well as deeply racialized narratives of history. This study has demonstrated the ways that these categories, perspectives, and narratives are, to varying degrees, caught up in the process of racialization. Some are idiosyncratic to biblical scholarship and can be pushed aside, while others are essential to the critical study of the Bible and can be reconfigured differently. I will begin this conclusion by distinguishing between those concepts, goals, themes, and perspectives that can plausibly be abandoned and those concepts, goals, themes, and perspectives that should be reconfigured differently. In short, I propose that some inherited critical practices must be discarded while others can profitably be redefined. We will then be in a position to ask if these two gestures (i.e. discarding and redefining) are enough to solve the problem of racialized biblical scholarship.

Discarded

One of Derrida's most compelling insights is that the destructive discourses of later modernity (Freud, Nietzsche, Heidegger, Lévi-Strauss) are also caught up in that which they seek to destroy. That does not mean, however, that everything that is said within modernity is equally profound, equally compelling, equally challenging, and equally caught up in an ambiguous and ambidextrous discourse. Some of what is produced in modernity is merely not well thought through and can be criticized rather than rigorously deconstructed. In other words, some of what has been identified in this book as problematic can be rejected, discarded, and pushed aside.

To begin with, biblical scholarship would be wise to do without the most important categories drawn from Heideggerian existentialism: authenticity, primordiality, fallenness, "the They", and temporality (i.e. the care-structure). I have tried to show that these categories have been widely applied to the New Testament since Bultmann began doing so in the 1920s. They have been essential to Bultmann's demythologizing program, to the consensus position on Paul and Luke–Acts put forth by Bultmann's students, to the New Hermeneutic, and to parable scholarship. It is an open question, to be taken up another time, as to the degree to which newer trends in scholarship have put these categories aside.

Much current biblical scholarship explicitly seeks a healthy dialogue with Judaism and explicitly embraces a post-civil rights, egalitarian ethos on questions of gender and race. I have argued, throughout the second half of this book, that these Heideggerian categories reflect the racial anxieties of the Weimar Republic and that they implicitly yet forcefully endorse the racialized politics of post-First World War German fascism. They are, in short, anachronistic, structurally racialized, and quietly antiSemitic. They necessarily pull the discourse of biblical scholarship in an ignoble direction, and they do so despite the genuinely benign intentions of current scholarship. Much current biblical scholarship wants to free itself from its chauvinistic past. It is my contention that the discipline will remain unable to succeed in doing so as long as it continues within the orbit of Heideggerian existentialism.

In practical terms, putting aside these categories means several things.

1. I have demonstrated how the existentialist morality tale (i.e. habitual inauthenticity, existential encounter, slothful fall back into conventionality) has become essential to the project of existentializing modern scholarship. It is able to tie together a number of disparate Heideggerian ideas (i.e. temporality, primordiality, fallenness) into a coherent whole. It has provided the framework for a variety of diverse forms of historical reconstructions of the biblical era. This is especially true of the Bultmannian reconstructions (where late Judaism represents inauthenticity, Paul the existential encounter, and Luke–Acts and early Catholicism the great fall) and of the parable scholarship of Funk and Crossan (which substitues the parables for Paul and the allegories and written Gospels for Luke–Acts). In both instances, the structure of the history is remarkably similar: a great moment of Western, individualized, primordial, originary authenticity quickly gives way to Eastern, fallen, institutionalized inauthenticity.

This existentialist framework bequeaths to current scholarship an important but thoroughly problematic fundamental goal. Under this framework, it is the job of the scholar to identify the single moment when early Christianity defined itself in its purest form, when Jesus (or Paul or Q or Mark) uttered the words that revealed the pristine essence of salvation or of authenticity. It is then the job of the scholar to identify the ensuing moment that this pristine essence was fundamentally betrayed, distorted, and concealed. A scholar working out of this framework seeks to find these two moments (primordial essence versus inauthentic fall) so as to bring about the possibility of encounter with the primordial. There is something noble about the goal, which seeks to create a form of scholarship that is liberating and fundamentally free. Unfortunately, as I have argued, the primordial/inauthentic antithesis is thoroughly racialized. The inauthentic is necessarily Eastern, Jewish, and servile, while the authentic is necessarily Western, Greek, and free. The logic of the existentialist morality tale pulls scholarship in this direction, irrespective of the intentions of the practitioners. The purging of the inauthentic to make possible authenticity, which has structured much of the twentieth-century's most respected biblical scholarship, necessarily means identifying and shattering the forces of Jewification to better create a racially pure West.

If the morality tale is itself problematic, then the many historical reconstructions that explicitly or implicitly flow from it are also potentially problematic. It is one of my unfinished tasks to follow this process into more recent scholarship. If my argument is correct, then it may be necessary to reconceive how it is that the discipline reconstructs the origins of Christianity. The question would be this: is it possible to rediscover the historical Jesus without indulging in the racialized myth of origins? Is it possible to reconstruct the *origins* of Christianity without implicitly employing the Heideggerian category of *originary*?

2.   The Heideggerian category of "the They" has become equally essential to the project of existentializing modern scholarship. It has proven itself to be an essential part of many of the same momentous figures identified above (Bultmann, the New Hermeneutic, Funk, and Crossan). As I explained above, "the They" represents, for Heidegger, a particularly aggressive and particularly corrupt form of inauthenticity. It represents the ossified, trite, degenerate form of public discourse ("idle talk") that overwhelms, seduces, and consumes inauthentic *Dasein*. It represents a form of absorption that is so total and so thorough that it completely wipes out all traces of individuality. For Heidegger the greatest danger is that we shall lose ourselves in the shallow and rootless discourse of the public. The "idle talk" of "the They" is that which makes it impossible for the individual to ever achieve authenticity or freedom. For those who accept Heidegger's analysis, the "idle talk" of "the They" is the mortal enemy which must be mercilessly unmasked and completely overcome.

I have identified the thoroughly problematic nature of these two categories ("idle talk" and "the They"). They are problematic philosophically in that they prevent Heidegger from successfully decentering the subject and from successfully reconceiving the relationship between the self and the world. In other words, these categories prevent Heidegger from doing what he wants to do (i.e. reconceive the self–world relationship), and encourage him to do what he does not want to do (i.e. reinforce the foundational role of the subject). More importantly for our project are the ways that these categories inscribe Heidegger's radically rightist politics (his fascism and his radical antiSemitism) into his philosophical categories. As I demonstrated above, these categories reflect *völkisch* stereotypes, a loathing for the city, a deep longing for aestheticized racial and Germanic purity, a fear of racial mixing, and a fear of Jewification. Heidegger may oppose the "idle talk" of "the They" in the name of authenticity and freedom, but he is assuming views of authenticity and freedom that are, presumably, abhorrent to the vast majority of current biblical scholars.

"The They" plays a crucial role in the economy of the thought of those biblical scholars, identified above, who are under the sway of Heidegger. This does not mean, however, that each thinker identifies "the They" in the same way or with the same categories. For Bultmann and his exegetical heirs (Bornkamm, Conzelmann, Käsemann), "the They" is identified with theological objectification. For the New Hermeneutic, Funk, and Crossan, however, "the They" becomes synonymous with moribund conventionality as ossified and objectified language becomes the embodiment of "idle talk". It is this particular spin on Heidegger which renders inseparable the concepts of authenticity, freedom, and unconventionality.

There is within recent, experimental criticism a foregrounding of the unconventional (see, for example, Fowler; Moore 1992). If the Heideggerianized version of unconventionality is problematic, then this recent criticism might also prove to be problematic. It is another of my unfinished tasks to follow the way that the ideal of unconventionality functions within current scholarship. If my argument is correct, then it may be necessary for experimental critics, myself included, to reconceive how it is that the discipline relates the conventional to the unconventional. The question would be this: How is it possible to carry out experimental criticism without implicitly employing a Heideggerianized, and therefore racialized, view of unconventionality?

Redefined

Discarding Heideggerian existentialism (as mediated by Bultmann) will go a long way towards opening up alternative forms of biblical scholarship. This in and of itself, however, will not be enough to entirely deliver biblical discourse from racialization. Some of the crucial concepts and themes discussed in this book can be profitably reconceived and redefined rather than rejected. There is nothing inherently wrong with the categories of art, creativity, metaphor/symbol/allegory, freedom/tyranny, Hebrew/Hellene. The categories are, for the most part, essential in the analysis of the biblical text and must be employed in one form or another. It is difficult to read the New Testament without recognizing an often hostile Greco-Roman presence in Palestine. In the same way it is difficult to think about what are primarily literary texts without making assumptions about the nature of art and creativity. It is equally difficult to analyze literary texts without identifying and coming to terms with the textual metaphors and symbols found therein. Serious analysis of the New Testament, from whatever perspective one chooses to employ, will necessarily bump up against these concepts. Biblical scholars can decide against Heideggerian existentialism, but cannot decide against these categories.

The question becomes, then, how are these categories to be conceived? Within what theoretical framework are they to be defined? It has been my contention that much modern biblical scholarship, influenced by German philosophy (especially by Herder, Hegel, and Heidegger), has functioned within the orbit of *völkisch* Romanticism, which is a form of aestheticized and racialized nationalism. In other words, much biblical scholarship has implicitly fallen under the sway of the Romantic aesthetic ideology of organicity that the later Paul de Man deconstructed with such care. Under the influence of Romanticism, authentic art and all that went with it (i.e. creativity, metaphor) was perceived as capable of elevating consciousness which had been alienated through the forces of instrumental reason, consumerism, and race mixing. By elevating consciousness, authentic art would bring about an organic relationship between the self and the world. This, in turn, would make possible a properly rooted, harmonious, and organic society, a society free from the disruptive forces of degeneration. *Völkisch* Romanticism, like Heideggerian existentialism, is no longer able to withstand philosophical scrutiny and, more importantly for our study, *völkisch* Romanticism brings with it some rather unsavory political and racial commitments. Within this framework, degeneration easily elides into racial impurity and Jewification, while organicity becomes the driving metaphor behind an aestheticized and racialized nationalism.

Völkisch Romanticism has bequeathed two thoroughly problematic assumptions to the discipline of biblical scholarship. The first is a series of troubling aesthetic values and the second is an unpalatable narrative of the natural flow of world history. Let us first turn to the former before taking up the latter.

It is Romanticism, particularly *völkisch* Romanticism, which has given shape and meaning to the concepts of creativity and metaphor/allegory/symbol. Romanticism has also helped existentialism shape the meaning of the concept of freedom. As I have argued throughout this study, these crucial concepts and categories, which have been, and continue to be, so influential to modern biblical scholarship, have gained their power and force from the system they are part of, rather than from anything inherent in the biblical text (see Derrida 1982b: 230). The question becomes, Do current biblical scholars want to continue importing this particular system and this particular conceptual network into biblical scholarship? If not, how else could these categories be grounded? It is one thing to be suspicious of *völkisch* thinking and to doubt the immediate relationship between the artist and his *Volk*; it is quite another to reject the idea that poetic language embodies the profundity of poetic experience put to language. Is it not obviously the case that the authentic artist rips his/her language from the depths of his/her soul and produces a work that is unique, fundamentally singular, and untainted by the ossified world of conventionality? Is it possible to think of creativity differently? The very force of these questions reveals the degree to which the aesthetic assumptions of Romanticism have been naturalized and universalized. Unless biblical scholars are able to come up with a new ground for aesthetic categories like creativity, the ghost of Romanticism, and the politics of racialized nationalism, will continue to haunt even the finest work the discipline is able to produce.[1]

The Romantic aesthetic ideology has also played an important role in the construction and dissemenation of a distinctive narrative of world history that has held sway since the beginning of the nineteenth century. The narrative takes the following form: civilization and culture originated in Greece, and moved through the increasingly oppressive and uncivilized worlds of Rome and the Middle Ages, before resting in modern Europe, which was able to revive itself by returning to its Greek roots. This book, particularly in the analysis of Hegel and Tübingen, has carefully analyzed this narrative and its ideological underpinnings. The Romantic aesthetic ideology, with its commitment to linguistic and racial purity, helps shape the construction of this potent and alluring narrative. This ideology helps establish this narrative's boundaries and its inner workings. Central to this ideologically driven narrative is the myth of the autonomous, self-creating, organic, and harmonious Greeks. This narrative, with its emphasis on the foundational role of the Greeks, is fundamentally racialized and helps sustain the Euro-American sense of its own distinctive superiority. The emphasis on self-creation and autonomy helps to identify those parts of the world that are to be excluded from the realm of philosophy, high culture, and rationality. The Greeks, originators of philosophy of freedom and of the West, were untainted by the degenerate and despotic worlds of the Orient or Africa. Instead, rationality and philosophy began when the Greeks decisively broke from the Orient and, in the process, heroically invented the West. As a result, rationality belongs to the West and those outside of the West are incapable of that which rationality produces: freedom, culture, autonomy. Furthermore, the emphasis on organicity and harmony helps construct Europe around racialized lines. If the organic and untainted Greeks represent the highpoint of authentic culture, then modern European peoples can revive themselves by creating cultures that are equally organic, equally pure, equally rooted, and equally untainted by foreign contamination.

This narrative calls for the exclusion of the seemingly inferior races and the establishment of rigorous and impenetrable cultural and linguistic barriers. It feeds the aestheticization of political categories like freedom and autonomy, and furthers the racialization of the worlds of culture, art, history, and literature. While biblical scholars from Tübingen through the New Hermeneutic worked comfortably within the confines of this narrative, more recent scholarship has begun to challenge some of its central tenets. In particular, the sharp line drawn between the Greeks and the Jews has started to come undone. A new narrative of world history, or at least of antiquity, should further unsettle this troublesome narrative. This new narrative should highlight the permeable nature of cultural borders and the degree to which people, both ancient and modern, borrow from their neighbors. Most especially, it is important that we remind ourselves of the ways in which our views of antiquity often reflect modern dreams and modern desires. Even if it is difficult to avoid anachronistic projections upon antiquity, it is possible to challenge the ideological underpinnings of these particular projections. In this case, the dream is one of racial and ethnic purity. It is built by radically excluding the nonEuropean from world history and by maintaining strict linguistic and cultural boundaries within Europe itself. Alluring as this dreamy narrative of world history may be, it would behoove biblical scholarship to renounce it in favor of something whose costs will not keep us awake at night.

The illusion of a fresh start: deconstruction and escaping racialization

> It is precisely the force and the efficiency of the system that regularly change transgressions into "false exits".
>
> Derrida, "The Ends of Man"

This book is hardly the first to criticize the Tübingen school or Bultmannian existentialism. Much recent scholarship has been dedicated to challenging the methodology, historiography, aesthetics, and ideology of these formative figures. If the 1960s witnessed the Germanization of American scholarship, the last two decades have witnessed an explosion of scholarly innovation. There has been an onslaught of new methods (narrative, semiotic, poststructural criticisms), new forms of ideological critique (African-American, feminist, Jewish, postcolonial), and new approaches to the first-century world (historical revisions, sociological, anthropological criticisms). They have found a home at scholarly conferences, are taught in graduate schools, and are published in elite journals and by respected publishing houses. The current world of biblical scholarship is substantially different from the world that produced the New Hermeneutic. While none of the new methods and perspectives are without their detractors, major changes are clearly afoot within the discipline. Writing from the perspective of the new millennium, a scholarly revolution seems to be taking place.

Are these new methodologies and new perspectives able to solve the problems posed by this book? Will they provide critical scholarship with the intellectual resources to avoid the lure of racialized discourse? It would certainly be premature to answer this question in the affirmative without submitting these new methodologies and perspectives to analysis and rigorous critique, which is a task for another day. It is certainly the case, however, that they offer a more promising starting point than anything that can be found either in Heideggerian existentialism or in the traditional scholarly methods of source and form criticism. This rich mixture of new and innovative scholarship provides biblical scholarship with a series of potent critical tools and insightful critical perspectives. It is these new methods and perspectives that will allow the discipline of biblical scholarship to begin to inch away from its racialized past.

At the same time, wisdom dictates that we proceed with caution. As scholars from Appiah to Said are able to demonstrate, racialized discourse is both crafty and resilient. Escape from its clutches is far easier to claim than to achieve. I have been arguing that biblical scholarship has been trapped in a racialized discourse and further have been arguing that racialization itself is imbedded in the very fabric of modernity. If this is the case, addressing the ways that biblical scholarship itself has employed racialized categories will only do so much. It is always possible that, in replacing the inherited categories with new ones, scholarship will be trading one form of racialized discourse for another. Heideggerian existentialism, Romanticism, and Hegelian historiography are not the only ways that racialization intersects with modernity's critical methods and modes of rationality. Turning to a new set of aesthetic categories, developing a new methodology, proposing a new historical framework, uncovering ideological distortions in the text and the critical tradition – these moves are simultaneously essential and fraught with danger.[2] Without such moves, biblical scholarship will remained trapped in the racialized framework identified in this book, but such moves do not and cannot guarantee that the category of race will be fully and finally relegated to the ash heap of history. If we acknowledge that race has infused itself into many of modernity's essential categories and modes of rationality, and acknowledge that we are very much heirs to those categories and modes of rationality, then we must also acknowledge that, whether we like it or not, it is entirely possible that race will continue to haunt twenty-first-century biblical scholarship. Perhaps I can, with the help of Jacques Derrida, sharpen the problem a little further.

No one has spent more time pondering the question of escaping metaphysics than Derrida.[3] Derrida's carefully nuanced and double-handed readings demonstrate the way that metaphysics continues to operate in the thought of those setting out to destroy it. He draws some general conclusions on the problem in "Structure, Sign and Play in the Discourse of the Human Sciences".

> But all of these destructive discourses (i.e. Nietzsche, Freud, Heidegger) and all their analogues are trapped in a kind of circle. This circle is unique. It describes the form of the relation between the history of metaphysics and the destruction of the history of metaphysics. There is no sense in doing without the concepts of metaphysics in order to shake metaphysics. We have no language – no syntax and no lexicon

– which is foreign to this history. We can pronounce no single destructive proposition which has not already had to slip into the form, the logic, and the implicit postulations of precisely what it seeks to contest.

(Derrida 1978: 280–281)

This gesture of employing the categories of metaphysics to destroy it ensures that philosophy continues to exert an influence long after the victory over metaphysics has been declared. "Since these concepts (of metaphysics) are not elements or atoms, and since they are taken from a syntax and a system, every particular borrowing brings with it the whole of metaphysics" (ibid.). There is no surer way to ensure the perpetuation of metaphysics than to declare victory over it.

This does not mean that Derrida is advocating that one passively accept the inevitability of the dominance of metaphysics and the systematic exclusions inscribed therein. "It goes without saying that these effects do not suffice to annul the necessity for a 'change in terrain'. It also goes without saying that the choice between these two forms of deconstruction cannot be simple and unique. A new writing must weave and interlace these two motifs of deconstruction. Which amounts to saying that one must speak several languages and produce several texts at once" (Derrida 1982b: 135). As Simon Critchley explains, this practice of double-reading is the "double refusal both of remaining within the limits of the tradition and of the possibility of transgressing that limit" (Critchley 1999a: 20). This double-reading ceaselessly moves between metaphysics and its other, between what philosophy says and what it excludes (Critchley 1999a: 20–31).[4]

We can take from Derrida a sharpened definition of the problem of the enduring power of racialization and the realization that there is no pure perspective or thinker (including deconstruction and Derrida himself, as he would readily acknowledge) who is not part of the racialized discourse of modernity. Racialization, like modernity itself, has a nasty habit of reasserting itself in the most unlikely of places – even in the work of those who are self-consciously opposed to racism and its effects (see, for example, Appiah 2–46; Gilroy 19–36). It seems that we are unlikely to come across any pure critical stance, any untainted thinkers to embrace and follow, or any pristine method of reading the biblical text. This does not mean that we can only throw up our hands in despair, but it does mean that caution and rigor are required before we can claim anything resembling freedom from, or escape from, racialized modernity. All critical perspectives, within both *modern* biblical scholarship and *modern* (and postmodern) secular criticism, are part of the same discursive world,[5] a world infused with the category of race.

The only solution to the problem of racialization, if it can indeed be called a solution, is to turn ourselves back towards that which we (or at least I) would very much like to spurn: racialized modernity. While this need not entail returning to, say, Heideggerian existentialism or Hegelian historiography, it does entail returning towards the tainted figures of modernity (including Heidegger and Hegel).[6] Rather than trying to reject that which will not go away, we need to find a way to situate ourselves in relationship to modernity's tainted figures and racialized modes of rationality.

The challenge, then, would be to find a way to carry out a series of double-readings – double-readings of the (racialized) heritage of modernity and double-readings of the biblical text itself. This is no small task and cannot be accomplished, or even adequately defined, in the space remaining. Fortunately, however, biblical scholarship is not left to its own devices as it contemplates the problem of resituating itself critically and ethically towards a tainted modernity. There are a number of scholars, inside and outside of biblical scholarship as well as inside and outside of deconstruction, who are taking up this challenge. I would like to wrap things up by focusing on one area of critical inquiry that, I suspect, will prove most helpful in further framing the issues that have been raised throughout the course of this book.

Postcolonialism, race, and literature

> We will never be finished with the reading or rereading of Hegel.
>
> Derrida, *Positions*

My graduate training was in literary criticism, and I continue to align myself, at least in some important ways, with the narrative-critical analysis of the Gospels. At the same time, I have become increasingly aware of the many ways in which recent literary criticism, including recent postmodernist or poststructuralist criticism, appropriates a variety of modern methodological and aesthetic assumptions. It could not be otherwise. It would be a lengthy, arduous process to identify the various racialized assumptions that have found their way into competing literary-critical readings of the gospels. While such an analysis cannot be carried out here, it may be helpful to conclude this book by reflecting briefly on the difficulty of defining the term "literature".

I have argued that many European (and by extension American) ideas about literature have proven to be rooted in *völkisch* nationalism. As a result, one of the most urgent tasks facing current narrative critics would involve reconceiving the idea of "literature". Given the tainted history of much recent, Western views of literature, one might be tempted to turn instead to sources outside of the West. The analysis of Derrida, given above, warns against being overly naive about the efficacy of such a move, by implying that escape of this sort is difficult to achieve. Recent postmodernist studies of race in African and African-American culture confirm Derrida's insight. Appiah and Gilroy, for example, have demonstrated the ways that Romanticism, *völkisch* nationalism, and racialized essentialism found their way into the Pan-African movement and its black nationalist and postcolonial heirs (see Appiah 2–46; Gilroy 19–36). While their complex and rigorous arguments cannot be traced here, their conclusions are worth considering. According to Appiah, "in his later writings, (W.E.B.) Du Bois . . . was unable to escape the notion of race he explicitly rejected. I shall show in later essays that this curious conjunction of a reliance on and a repudiation of race recurs in recent African theorizing" (Appiah 46). This conclusion should not be as surprising as it first appears. As Appiah explains, "literature", "race", and "nation" belong together because "from the start they were made for each other. Once the concept of literature was taken up by African intellectuals, the African debate about literary nationalism was inevitable" (Appiah 59). Many of the leading intellectuals of the Third World were educated in the West or by Westerners, were working within a world dominated by Western imperialism, and were enlisting the categories of high European culture in their own struggle against public claims of their racial inferiority. It is not surprising, therefore, that Western ideas on race have reverberated beyond the confines of Europe.

The solution, then, will not come from finding a starting point for redefining "literature" that has been untainted by European, racialized thought. No such starting point exists. The solution, then, comes from engaging the work of sophisticated literary and cultural theorists. This will allow biblical scholars to produce a double-reading of the sort proposed by Derrida. Following Appiah, I would suggest that we can move in that direction by defamiliarizing the term itself (see Appiah 59). We can start this process by disrupting the discourse of race and tribal difference, in the same way that Derrida proposed disrupting the smooth flow of logocentrism (see Appiah 179). This disruption can be accomplished, in part, by tracing the history of the term "literature" and the ideological baggage that it brings with it. This genealogical reconstruction can help remind biblical scholars that the term "literature" is neither natural nor neutral, that it has a history and that it brings with it certain contested and problematic values. I have tried to carry out aspects of such a genealogy throughout the course of the study.

According to Appiah and Gilroy, disrupting the racialized discourse on race, nation, identity, and literature should help clear the way for the emergence of more productive ways of looking at the categories of literature and identity. They want to find new ways of conceiving of literature, ways that are not explicitly dependent upon racialized and essentialized views of identity, human collectivity, and creativity. This is a long and arduous task, which has figured in the work of recent literary critics, philosophers, and cultural critics. These thinkers have ensured that biblical scholars are not without resources in their quest to redefine the problematic of literature.

Another important step is being taken by the critical movement of postcolonialism, which is starting to make its presence felt within the discipline of biblical scholarship (as can be seen with the new Society of Biblical Literature program unit "New Testament Studies and Postcolonial Studies"). As I have argued, literature has been problematically associated with the categories of authenticity, purity, rootedness, and origins. As long as literature is conceived around these categories, race and racialization will continue to lurk in the background. Postcolonial critics make the persuasive case that one way out of the trap of racialization involves reconceiving literature and cultural productions around the values of mutation, hybridity, intermixture, and rootlessness (see, for example, Gilroy 198–200, 223). Hybridity was a staple of the nineteenth-century racist right before being reclaimed and redefined by Bakhtin and by Homi Bhabha (R. Young 1995: 6–26). The postcolonial emphasis on hybridity manages to acknowledge the reality and power of racialized discourse and to contest that discourse from within. It also helps highlight the contested, fluid, constantly changing nature both of identity and of textuality. It provides critics with a way of talking about literature, texts, culture, history, and identity, without falling prey to the alluring and seductive language of purity, authenticity, and rootedness. It confirms and incorporates a Derridean perspective and employs Derrida's double-handed reading strategies, but does so in the more readily comprehensible world of cultural analysis. It also helps flesh out Derrida's rather nebulous and a-political ideas about alterity.[7] For these reasons, the postcolonial turn from rootedness to hybridity will go a long way towards helping biblical scholars put aside the fundamentally racialized quest for purity.

Throughout the course of this book, I have argued that racialization entered into biblical scholarship by means of the intellectual resources employed by those scholars who helped form the discipline. I also argued that, as long as scholarship continues to remain indebted to these same intellectual resources, it will continue to remain trapped in a discourse that is fundamentally racialized. The problem facing current scholarship, I wish to reiterate, is one of objectionable intellectual resources rather than of flawed intentions. Current scholarship remains racialized because its intellectual resources pull it in that direction, not because its practitioners necessarily want to affirm white supremacy.

If the problem is one of resources rather than intention, then the solution comes by turning elsewhere for intellectual sustenance. It is long past time that biblical scholarship turn away from its commitments to Romanticism, to Hegelianism, and especially to Heideggerian existentialism. Deconstruction, postmodernism, and postcolonialism will provide biblical scholarship with more innovative, more contemporary, more vibrant, and more egalitarian conversation partners. These perspectives, when put in conversation with the refreshing methodological innovations already occurring within recent biblical scholarship, will help in the creation of a form of biblical scholarship that is no longer captive to the misguided and oppressive category of race.

NOTES

1 RACIALIZED DISCOURSE

1 For a critique of literary deconstruction, see Frank Lentricchia (1980; 1983). For a defense of de Man in particular, see Norris 1988.

2 This is not to suggest that Said is immune to critique. For a summary of the debate about Said, see R. Young 1990: 119–156. His later work (*Culture and Imperialism*) addresses many of these problems.

3 For a more extensive discussion along these lines, see Kelley 213–216.

4 Jews represented the most problematic of racial categories. Their non-European languages, their non-Christian culture, and their non-Christian religious habits (i.e. kosher, Jewish holy days) seem to render them essentially Oriental. Longstanding Christian denigration of the Jewish religion and the Jewish people further fed the sense that they must be racially alien. Their continuing presence inside the heart of Europe was, therefore, difficult to understand and accept. European intellectuals, particularly in Germany, came up with a variety of ways of solving the "problem" of continued Jewish existence inside Europe. These solutions ranged from the traditional Christian view that the Jews faced divine wrath for the crime of genocide, to the liberal hope that Jews would renounce Judaism and fully assimilate, to the radical antiSemitic hope that the Jews would be exterminated (see Tal, for an analysis of the nineteenth-century German responses to the "Jewish Question").

2 THE HEGELIAN SYNTHESIS

1 On the viability of using the lecture courses as a source, see Walsh 181 n. 1.

2 As Schlomo Avineri shows, the use of the English word "Germanic" can lead to misunderstanding of Hegel's intention, particularly given the Nazi atrocities committed in the name of German supremacy. Hegel uses *germanische*, which signifies Germanic, or even European, culture rather than *deutsche*, which signifies the German political world (see Avineri 128–130). Thus Avineri and Gillespie effectively refute the charge that he was a proto-Nazi or a fanatical nationalist (Avineri 109–112, 122–126; see also Gillespie 110–111, 187–188 n. 57). Unfortunately, the debate has not been satisfactorily framed (for those accusing Hegel, see Avineri 134 nn. 13–15).

The horrors of the Holocaust should not blind us to other forms of racialized assumptions. Hegel is certainly not a rabid nationalist or a Nazi, but he does clearly place Europe at the culmination of world history and he also clearly assumes that Europe has surpassed Africa and the Orient in every way (see Walsh 189–191). Certainly that belief is also worthy of critical examination.

3 What follows is indebted to Derrida (1990: 207–211), Gilman (1982: 93–102), and Walsh (183–187).

4 This does not make him an antiSemite, particularly by the frenzied standards of his contemporaries. He opposed the simple antiJudaism of traditional Christianity, even as he secularized some of its key elements. He opposed Fichte's rabidly antiSemitic revolutionary nationalism (see Rose 117–132; Sluga 29–41), Fries's Romantic nationalism, and Schlegel's Aryanism (Avineri 109–111). He supported the granting of Jewish civil rights and he influenced his students to open their *Burschenschaften* to Jewish students (Rose 114). His narrative of world history simply found them to have outlived their usefulness. It is this narrative of world history, rather than his support of Jewish civil rights, that will find its way into emerging biblical scholarship.

3 JESUS AND THE MYTH OF THE WEST

1 I am slightly modifying Menzies' translation, here. See *Paul* I. 50, which uses "nation" for my "people" and "passion" for my "characteristic".

2 This translation slightly modifies that of Menzies. See *CH* I. 3, which uses "countries" for my "peoples".

3 We should also note, following Tal, that this debate was occurring alongside the redefinition of German identity that occurred in the wake of Napoleon's conquest. For the vast majority of Germans, this new identity was to be constructed around Christianity and German nationalism. By retaining their Jewishness, Jews were seen as rejecting both Christianity and Germanness. Jews were seen as standing in the way of the creation of a new German identity (see especially Tal 291–294).

4 The remaining quotes for the next two paragraphs are found in *Paul* I. 48–50 (*Paulus* I. 55–57).

5 This translation slightly modifies that of Menzies, who uses "materialism" for my "the sensuous".

6 Hill shows how this position, which has remained, until recently, the dominant one, rests on extremely shaky exegetical foundations. See Hill 19–101.

7 As Kümmel shows, even those critics who objected to the absolute nature of Baur's Pauline/Petrine antithesis (Bernhard Weiss, Adolf Jülicher) agreed on the fundamental significance of that antithesis (Kümmel 1972: 173–176).

4 AESTHETIC FASCISM

1 Heidegger is not the only intellectual whose wartime activities have provoked controversy. It was discovered that Paul de Man, the preeminent literary critic and deconstructionist, was a journalist and cultural critic who had collaborated with the Nazis during the occupation of Belgium. This

has led to a heated debate about the relationship between fascist journalism and his later scholarship. It has also become a central issue in the contentious debate about the politics of deconstruction. For de Man's writings, see Hamacher *et al.* eds. 1988. For the ensuing debate, see Carroll 248–261; Derrida 1988; Hamacher *et al.* eds. 1989; Norris 1988: 177–198.

2 After the war, Heidegger claimed that he reluctantly accepted the post of rector because the faculty thought he might be able to prevent the complete politicization of the university. According to his post-war account, he resigned when he recognized the impossibility of his situation and transformed himself into a potent critic of the regime, eventually putting his own life in peril. According to Ott, however, Heidegger actively sought the post of rector so that he could bring the university in line with all of the goals of National Socialism, including its racial goals. Once in office, he gave a series of lectures in support of the regime, lectures far more horrifying than his elegant Rector's Address. He seemed to see himself as the philosopher-king of the revolution, as the man who would bring to light the deeper meaning of the movement. The regime needed no help from an erudite philosopher in developing its "solution" to the spiritual crisis of the day and, as a result, Heidegger resigned from his post. Despite resigning as rector, however, he remained an active party member in good standing and a vocal supporter of Hitler and the war. Like countless other faithful followers of Hitler, he criticized other Nazis when he felt that they were not true to the principles of the movement. It is quite simply not the case that these criticisms made him expendable, or even anti-Nazi. Who can say whether the oft-repeated claim of expendability, so important to his rehabilitation, was a conscious lie or a necessary illusion.

3 The dramatic shift in the position of American Heideggerians most clearly reveals the impact made by Ott and Farias. Compare especially Krell 1977: 27–28 with Krell 1992: 135–214; and Zimmerman 1986: 169–197 with Zimmerman 1990.

4 Even those most eager to convict Heidegger are critical of Farias's book. Wolin, for example, argues that Farias overstates his case, draws unwarranted conclusions, employs the technique of guilt by association, and offers an unconvincing reading of Heidegger's text (see Wolin 1993c: 276–280).

5 For a sustained critique of Wolin, see J. Young. Young is more effective in refuting Wolin than in exonerating Heidegger, partly because he does not pay sufficient attention to the more subtle rereadings put forth by lifelong Heideggerians (Caputo, Krell, Zimmerman).

6 The bad blood between Derrida and Wolin was further exacerbated by a conflict over the publishing rights to an interview with Derrida entitled "Philosopher's Hell". The interview was originally published in French in *Le Nouvel Observateur* (6–12 November 1987). Wolin obtained the rights from the journal, translated it, and published it in the first edition of his volume *The Heidegger Controversy: A Critical Reader*. Derrida objected to the fact that Wolin never asked him for permission to publish the essay and further objected to the quality of the translation. Wolin defended the quality of the translation and implied that there was something hypocritical about Derrida, relentless critic of traditional notions of authorship, defending his authorial rights with the help of a lawsuit (see Wolin 1993b: x). The interview was removed from the second edition and the volume was

republished with a new press (MIT University Press instead of Columbia University Press), along with an introductory note blasting Derrida's decision to remove the interview and his reading of Heidegger, implying bad faith on Derrida's part (Wolin 1993b: ix–xx). The issue was taken up by Thomas Sheehan in his review of the volume in *The New York Review of Books* (see Sheehan 1993), which led to a series of nasty exchanges between Derrida, Sheehan and Wolin (see *NYRB*, 11 February 1993: 44–45; 4 March 1993: 57; 25 March 1993: 68–69). For Derrida's response to Wolin's charges, see Derrida 1995: 422–454.

7 Heidegger asks etymology to carry a heavy argumentative burden. Authenticity and phenomenology are only two terms he defines etymologically. His defense of this practice is worthy of closer examination. "We must avoid uninhibited word-mysticism. Nevertheless, the ultimate business of philosophy is to preserve the *force of the most elemental words* in which Dasein expresses itself, and to keep the common understanding from levelling them off" (*BT* 262, his emphasis). Etymology is part of the deconstruction of the decayed traditions of the West, and is, therefore, a way of restoring language to its original vibrancy. This mystical quest for the original vitality of language abruptly, and without reflection, becomes a quest for the original vitality of the *German* language. He searches for the vitality of German by positing a unique relationship between German and Greek. There are traces of this move in *Being and Time* and in his early lectures on Aristotle, but it becomes definitive for his thought as he turns to fascism, and it remains definitive throughout the rest of his career. This move is an indispensable element of his philosophical racism and fascism (see Adorno 42; Caputo 1993: 21–33, 82–90; Derrida 1989: 4–6, 31–46, 66–72; Lacoue-Labarthe 51–76; Norris 1990: 243–244), and it provides his Rector's Address with its fundamental structure (see Heidegger 1993a).

8 AntiJudaism permeates most of his sources, which should not surprise us since it permeated almost all pre-Holocaust (and much post-Holocaust) Christianity. Heidegger's lectures on religion (as reconstructed by Kisiel and van Buren) incorporate the structure of oppositions that reside at the heart of antiJudaism (law versus grace, fear versus love, ritual versus authentic worship). As his thought develops, he will continue to hold on to these values and will aestheticize them. Even as his writings become less influenced by theology, they will continue to contain strong traces of the antiJudaism of his early career. At the same time, he will become increasingly influenced by the aesthetic ideology of organicity, the ideology which is so important to racialized antiSemitism and to *völkisch* nationalism. By the mid-1920s, his traditional antiJudaism will become complemented by the more radical, racist antiSemitism and nationalism that erupts with such force during the last years of the Weimar Republic and which comes to dominate the Nazi era.

9 For the historical connection between organicity, fascism, and anti-Semitism, see Carroll *passim*; Herf 18–48; Rose *passim*. For a philosophical exploration of similar themes, see Caputo 1993: 1–8; Derrida 1978: 152–3; Lacoue-Labarthe 61–104; Lacoue-Labarthe and Nancy; Lyotard 3–48; Norris 1988: 28–64.

10 This is a further example of the ambiguous place of Dasein in *Being and Time*. On the one hand, Heidegger is attempting to reject the modern claim

that the intentional subject is the locus of meaning (and thus attempting to escape the problem of subjectivity). On the other hand, the further he drifts from theology and into secularized philosophy the more he asks of Dasein. Throughout *Being and Time*, the possibility of meaning is dependent upon the transcendental structure of Dasein as revealed in the birth, life, and death of Dasein. This certainly *seems* to return the conscious subject back to center stage and certainly encourages the sort of anthropocentric, voluntaristic reading of *Being and Time* that we find in Bultmann and his heirs.

11 Besides those critics whom I have already cited, see especially Dreyfus and Rubin, "Kierkegaard, Division II and Later Heidegger" in Dreyfus 283–340.

12 One need not go all the way with Daniel Goldhagen's assertions about ubiquitous German antiSemitism, unrivaled anywhere in the world, to recognize the deep historical and cultural roots of German antiSemitism. See, for example, Gilman 1991; Goldhagen 49–128; Rose; Weiss.

13. He wrote this letter as part of a grant application for his pupil Eduard Baumgarten. By 1933 he was no longer convinced that Baumgarten was capable of fighting off Jewification. In a report to the League of National Socialist University Lecturers, Heidegger concluded that Baumgarten had become untrustworthy because of his recent association with liberal-democratic intellectuals, particularly "the Jew Fraenkel". He concluded that "a decent probationary period needs to elapse before he can be permitted to join any organization of the National Socialist Party" (quoted in Ott 190). It was Jasper's discovery of this letter that led to his final break with Heidegger. Baumgarten himself always felt that Heidegger's objections to him were personal rather than ideological, and that he was using whatever tools were available to block his career (see Lang 101–111).

14 The most thorough and thoughtful analysis of Heidegger's antiSemitism appears in Lang 61–82.

15 Contra J. Young (35–38), who insists on limiting the notion of racism to biological racism. For a response to the general position taken by Young, see Lang 25–26, 61–82.

16 The connection between cities, disease, corruption, and Jews was a staple of the *völkisch* movement which was passed down to most German fascists, becoming one of the organizing principles of Hitler's *Mein Kampf* (see the chapter entitled "Causes of the Collapse"). For analysis of the inner logic of this position, see Gilman 1991: 31–33, 38–52, 96–99; Herf 55–59, 133–151.

17 We should note the verbal connections between send (*schicken*, as in sending the heritage) and fate (*Schicksal*); as well as between collective destiny (*Geschick*), history (*Geschichte*) and historizing (*Geschehen*). Historizing (*Geschehen*) Dasein is the ground for history (*Geschichte*), which produces our collective destiny (*Geschick*). Historizing Dasein also produces heritage, which is sent (*schicken*) to us giving us our fate (*Schicksal*). See Heidegger 1929: 383–385; *BT* 436 n. 1.

18 Following Fritsche's, my translation modifies the translation of Macquarrie and Robinson. They have "historizing of a community of a people" rather than of "the people". See Fritsche 1999: 238–239 n. 17.

19 The *Gemeinschaft/Gesellschaft* opposition has deep roots in German nationalism and Romanticism (see Schama 113–120) and was formalized in 1887

with Ferdinand Tönnies's tome *Gemeinschaft und Gesellschaft*. Reprinted in 1912, it became a bestseller in Germany and strongly influenced both traditional conservatives and fascists. Spengler, who helped usher in the radical right and who strongly influenced Heidegger, was particularly influenced by Tönnies's ideas (see Beistegui 20–21; Safranski 168).

20 The wide currency of these ideas leads Fritsche to conclude that Heidegger's use of them is hardly as inexplicable as may first appear. He argues that American scholars find Heidegger's embrace of these categories inexplicable and Heidegger's explanation of these terms unsatisfactory because American scholars project particularly American views of the self-made man onto Heidegger's text (see Fritsche 1999: xiv, 207–213). To combat this problem, Fritsche opens his study with an extended discussion of Heidegger's language in this section (Fritsche 1–67, see also the endnotes for this section, pp. 229–268), demonstrating that much of Heidegger's philosophical terminology (i.e. *vorlaufen* ("anticipate"), *Entschlossen in den Tod vorlaufen* ("anticipation of death"), *Entschlossenheit* ("resoluteness"), *vorlaufende Entschlossenheit* ("anticipatory resoluteness"), *Erwidert* ("reciprocative rejoinder"), *Schicksal* ("fate"), *Erbe* ("heritage"), *Geschick* ("destiny"), *Überlieferung* ("tradition"), *ursprünglisch* ("primordial")) deliberately echoes the language of political fascism.

21 Lang has listed a series of examples (see pp. 40–42). One could also point to his many glowing allusions to farmers (Heidegger 1977a: 242) and oak trees (Fritsche 1995: 152), which were seen, by German nationalists, as the symbolic abode of the authentic Germanic gods (see Schama 101–109). We could also point to his reliance upon oppositions like simple/busy (Heidegger 1977a: 222–223), primordial/cosmopolitan (1977a: 219) and native/alien (1977a: 159, 167). Most glaringly, we have his interpretation of a van Gogh painting which is the centerpiece to "The Origin of the Work of Art" (1977a: 162–164; see also Derrida 1991: 277–309). The painting is of a pair of shoes. Even though there is no textual or extra-textual information about the owner of the shoes, Heidegger spins his "naive, impulsive, precritical" (Derrida 1991: 304) interpretation around the life world of the *peasant* woman, who wore them as she worked the *soil*.

22 We should note that, at this point, Heidegger is inventing another Greece, one that is at odds with, and more primordial than, the Greece of conventional philosophical historiography. The quest for a primordial Greece emerges out of the longstanding problems of German identity and German nationhood (see Lacoue-Labarthe and Nancy 300–301).

23 These recently unearthed quotes have been much commented upon and much analyzed. See especially Beistegui 146–157; Caputo 1993: 118–147; Fritsche 1995: 128–129, 136–142; Lacoue-Labarthe 34–37, 116–117; Lang 16–21; Lyotard 84–89, 94; Sluga 242–246; Wolin 1990: 168–169; J. Young 171–188, 204–205. All except Young find Heidegger's comments here woefully, scandalously inadequate.

5 IN THE SHADOW OF HEIDEGGER

1 The first quote is found in a letter from Heidegger to Jaspers (quoted in Ott 125) and the second is found in a letter from Heidegger to Blochmann (quoted in van Buren 156).

2 Eskola's analysis here is quite helpful in understanding Bultmann's use of Heidegger's philosophy. Eskola argues that, despite Bultmann's turn to existentialism, he remained deeply influenced by neo-Kantianism, a philosophical position that was at odds with Heidegger's ontology. This commitment to neo-Kantianism goes a long way towards explaining why Bultmann, despite his enthusiasm for existentialism, was so uninterested in Heidegger's philosophical phenomenology. See Eskola 334–337.

3 These joint seminars are often mentioned by both philosophers and New Testament scholars (see Johnson 21; Kisiel 1995: 111, 218, 282 n. 20, 558–559; Mörchen 557ff.; Ott 5, 125; Perrin 1969: 19–20; Robinson 1971: 3; van Buren 156; Zimmerman 1986: 16).

4 Barth's aversion to historical criticism, his increasing neo-orthodoxy, his concern with dogmatics, and his aversion to Heidegger, prevented the two from ever forging a unified theological position. A great deal has been written on the complex relationship between Bultmann, dialectical theology, liberal theology, and historical criticism. See Harvey 127–163; Johnson 10–17; Ogden 13–17; Perrin 1969: 16–19; Robinson 1959: 9–12; 1964: 1–39.

5 See especially the following essays, all of which can be found in *Faith and Understanding*: "Liberal Theology and the Latest Theological Movement" (1924); "What Does it Mean to Speak of God?" (1925); "The Significance of 'Dialectical Theology' for the Scientific Study of the New Testament" (1928). See also "Karl Barth's *Epistle to the Romans* in its Second Edition" (1922), which can be found in *Rudolf Bultmann: Interpreting Faith for the Modern Era*.

6 We lack the space to detail Bultmann's views on Jesus and his relationship to Paul and Hellenism. He takes this question up most explicitly in "The Significance of the Historical Jesus for the Theology of Paul" (in *F&U*) and in the first volume of *Theology of the New Testament*. See also Perrin 1969: 56–60; Robinson 1959: 12–22.

7 As Ogden argues, Bultmann's argument that authenticity is only available in faith sits uneasily with his Heideggerian view that authenticity is universally available. His simultaneous enthusiasm for Heidegger's ontology and for Luther's Christocentrism creates the contradiction that is highlighted by critics on his left (who urge him to purge the Christocentrism in favor of universal authenticity) and on his right (who urge him to purge the existentialism in favor of Christian exclusivity). For a detailed analysis see Ogden 95–126.

8 It is worth reiterating that this reading of Paul and of late Judaism problematically repeats the standard tenets of Christian antiJudaism (see especially E.P. Sanders 1977: 147–182).

9 Several texts helped create the controversy: Philip Vielhauer's "On the Paulinism of Acts" (1951); the posthumous publication of previously written essays by Martin Dibelius (*Studies in the Acts of the Apostles*, in 1951); Hans Conzelmann's 1954 *Die Mitte der Zeit* (whose title should be translated *The Middle of Time* rather than as *The Theology of Saint Luke*); the first edition of Ernst Haenchen's commentary on Acts (1955); and Ernst Käsemann's 1953 essay "The Problem of the Historical Jesus". Bultmann's *Theology* also appeared in the middle of this flurry of publications. For a critique of the exegetical presuppositions, see Gasque 213–214, 225–234,

240–243, 287–291, 294–296; Talbert 202–207; van Unnik 28; Wilckens 65–67.

10 The reference is to a fine article by W.C. van Unnik ("Luke–Acts, a Storm Center in Contemporary Scholarship") analyzing the debate that raged in the wake of the Bultmannian assault on Luke. There were also several other equally insightful reviews of this era of Lukan scholarship. See also Kümmel (1975), Talbert, Wilckens, and Gasque.

11 The majority of the book (Parts II–IV) takes up the question of Lukan temporality. Part II focuses on Luke's eschatology, Part III on salvation history (*Gott und die Heilsgeschichte*), Part IV on Jesus as the Middle of Time (*Die Mitte der Geschichte*), and Part V on salvation.

12 See "The Task of Theology in the Present Situation" (2 May 1933) (translated from "Die Augfabe der Theologie in der gegenwärtigen Situation") and "Autobiographical Reflections" (1956). Both are in *Existence and Faith*. See also "Forms of Human Community" and "The Significance of the Idea of Freedom for Western Civilization", two previously unpublished tracts included in 1955's *Essays*. See also Bultmann 1966.

13 Ogden translates *Volk* as nation and *Volkstum* as nationality. See especially *EF* 158–159 and Bultmann 1933: 161–162.

14 It was not uncommon in the Confessing Church to claim that the Nazis or the German Christians, who were attacking or usurping the Church, were infused with the spirit of Jewification. See Baranowski 103.

15 There is much debate among Holocaust scholars and historians about the dating of the beginnings of the final solution. For a helpful discussion of the issues involved, see Breitman; Cesarani ed.

16 This contention is confirmed by his own claim that during the Nazi era he worked to ensure that "free scientific work retained its proper place in the face of reactionary tendencies" (*EF* 288).

6 PORTRAIT OF THE ARTIST AS A YOUNG MESSIAH

1 The Second World War and its immediate aftermath were significant in other ways for the civil rights movement as well. African-American soldiers who had fought for freedom in Europe were particularly impatient with segregation on the homefront. The disconnect between the war experience and the postwar socio-political environment was particularly acute for those who had served as officers during the war but whose postwar options were decidedly more limited. Truman's postwar desegration of the military further fueled the demand for widespread social change, as did the wartime migration of Southern sharecroppers to Northern and Western cities.

2 For a helpful and readable introduction to the New Hermeneutic, see Achtemeier 1969.

3 As Eskola shows, the New Hermeneutic also brings some of Bultmann's neo-Kantianism to their reading of the later Heidegger. See Eskola 338–339.

4 Funk is more typical in this regard. He traces the evolution of Heidegger's career in purely philosophical terms, without any mention of his political engagement and subsequent disappointment with National Socialism (Funk 44–46). Funk's Heidegger moved from engaged existentialist to

poetic recluse out of inner necessity and was, apparently, uninfluenced by merely historical events (i.e. his turn to Hitler, his disillusionment with the regime, his humiliation at the hands of the French denazification hearings, his fevered attempts at rehabilitation).

5 Historians dispute the claim that the churches were systematically persecuted (see Baranowski 106–109; Friedländer 44–49, 59–60; Eriksen and Heschel eds. 9–10). Historians also dispute the claim that the regime terrified the German people (Kershaw 1999: 435–437). Even the Confessing Church did not directly challenge the legitimacy or the policies of the Nazi regime (see Baranowski 102). Individual Germans (including many Christians) were persecuted, but usually if they were leftists or were active in opposing the regime (see Friedländer 17–18; Kershaw 1999: 454–462). There were periodic outbursts against the churches, which would have reached the level of persecution had the regime won the war. These outbursts were limited by the need to maintain Christian support for the war effort (see Kershaw 2000: 424–429). Far from being terrorized, the general public, enthusiastic about the advent of the national renewal, generally supported the regime and its assaults on communism and on the Jews.

6 Funk's analysis of the language of Jesus assumes and incorporates a great deal of important scholarship written in the decade following Bultmann's *Theology of the New Testament*. The central texts which made possible this shift include Jeremias's work on the parables and Käsemann's 1953 lecture ("The Problem of the Historical Jesus" (see Käsemann 1964: 15–47)), which helped reopen the quest from a Bultmannian perspective. The New Hermeneutic, Robinson's *A New Quest of the Historical Jesus*, and Perrin's *Rediscovering the Teachings of Jesus* are some of the important documents which followed in the wake of Jeremias and Käsemann. While I would welcome a careful ideological critique of these texts, such an analysis is well beyond the scope of this study. For an interesting beginning to raising such questions about the quest, see Marsch.

7 The literature on the parables is voluminous. The central documents are Jeremias's *The Parables of Jesus*, Dodd's *The Parables of the Kingdom*, and Wilder's *Early Christian Rhetoric*. Perrin's *Rediscovering the Teachings of Jesus*, which is published around the same time as Funk's *Language*, also devotes substantial space to the parables (see 82–159) and contains an annotated bibliography on parable research (257–258).

8 We can actually trace the scholarly indebtedness back further – to Dodd's original definition of parable (see Dodd 13–21; see also Perrin 1967: 84–87). I am grateful to Jeff Tucker for pointing out Dodd's Romanticism.

9 See Chapter 2, especially the section "Aesthetic and Racial Nationalism".

10 It is worth remembering, at this point in the argument, the essential role that organicity played in the development of racial antiSemitism. It was organicity which helped bring Heidegger into the National Socialist sphere. I should also mention that both Eliot and Yeats had their own problems: with antiSemitism (in the case of Eliot) and aesthetic fascism (in the case of Yeats). As with Heidegger, biblical scholars should neither dismiss their ideological commitments as irrelevant to their aesthetics, nor reject them entirely in the name of political authenticity. If biblical scholarship is going to ground analysis in their work, then biblical scholarship needs to take into account their troublesome ideological commitments, commit-

ments which were often carried out in the name of organicity and aesthetic purity. At the same time, they need to do so without reducing these often profound thinkers to their ideological commitments. I will discuss this problem of a double-reading of Heidegger *et al.* in the Conclusion.

For an interesting analysis of these questions in the case of Eliot, see Louis Menand, "Eliot and the Jews", *New York Review of Books*, 6 June 1996: 34–41. Menand's article is an extended review of *T.S. Eliot, Anti-Semitism, and Literary Form* by Anthony Julius (Cambridge University Press).

11 In the writings that follow *In Parables*, Crossan does attempt to rehabilitate allegory and does seek to distance himself from the Romantic assumptions that dominate *In Parables*. In *Cliffs of Fall* he challenges the antithesis between figurative and literal language (Crossan 1980: 5–11), yet ultimately reasserts the dichotomy by arguing for the universality of the figurative (i.e. "the primordial metaphoricity of language", p. 8). Similarly, he reconsiders the nature of allegory in *Raids on the Articulate* (Crossan 1976: 115–131). He argues that allegory contains many positive virtues, and is careful to describe, in considerable detail, allegory's many diverse and affir mative literary functions. He concludes that there is only one type of allegory that deserves the sort of censure that has traditionally fallen upon all allegories: the example allegory. Unfortunately, these are the very sort of allegories favored by the primitive Church and by the Gospel writers. We are left, once again, with paradoxical parables which are domesticated by the early Church. This suggests that there are firm limits on how far Crossan is willing and able to go in rethinking his commitment to Romanticism. He is willing to expand on the place allotted to the figural-parable-metaphor by making many allegories paradoxical and by making much that is literal figurative. He is unwilling, however, to question the legitimacy of the dichotomy itself, the philosophical and ideological system that gives shape to the dichotomy, or the categories that flow from that dichotomy. Despite his best intentions, and despite his limited forays into theoretical positions that could lead to a more direct challenge to Romanticism (i.e. structuralism, Foucault, Derrida), his parable scholarship never leaves Romanticism behind. For an appreciative yet critical response to Crossan's dabbling in postmodernism, see Moore 1989: 137–150.

12 They are also the categories around which he structures the book: Advent–future, Chapter 2; Reversal–past, Chapter 3; Action–present, Chapter 4.

13 For a critique of the antithesis between parable and example story, see Tucker 164–274.

14 Heidegger's fondness for resolute decision has long been offered as an explanation for his fascism (see Wolin 1990: 22–53; Zimmerman 1986: 170–179). The argument is that if authenticity means resolute action in the face of a crisis, then it is difficult to discern criteria by which one could criticize the resolutely violent action of the Storm Troopers. While the charge of "empty decisionism" grows out of a misreading of Heidegger (see J. Young 79–84; Fritsche 1999: 207–215), it does seem to apply to this aspect of Crossan's thought.

15 Crossan is working from Heidegger's "Letter On Humanism" (see Heidegger 1977a: 193–242), where he seeks a ground for the human that is more originary and profound than humanism or ethics. The Letter,

written in 1947, played an important role in rehabiliting his tarnished reputation.

16 See for instance, Funk 175–182, 197–198, 213 n. 63. On Jeremias's view of Jesus' opponents, see Jeremias 11, 38, 61–63, 124–146, 160.

CONCLUSION

1 Paul de Man, in the final years of his life, was in the process of rigorously deconstructing this ideology. He did not have the opportunity (and perhaps not the inclination) to develop alternative means of reading that avoided the lure of this racialized ideology. Henry Sussman continues the process of deconstructing the ideology, but, with "the aesthetic contract" has begun the process of redefining creativity without relying upon the categories of intuition, immediacy, and inspiration (see especially Sussman 4, 165–169).

2 For a helpful analysis of this general problem as it applies to feminism, see Armour. She explores the inability of feminist theory and theology to address adequately, despite its best intention, the reality of racial difference and argues that this failure stems from feminism's reliance upon certain metaphysical categories (especially the category "man").

3 This problematic is taken up in most of Derrida's writings. I have found "Structure, Sign and Play in the Discourse of the Human Sciences" to be the most accessible introduction to the question and "The Ends of Man" to be a difficult yet essential explication of the problem.

4 This double-reading is designed to open up a series of possibilities: the possibility of identifying and challenging the exclusions (including the racial exclusions) of Western metaphysics, the possibility of rendering the (newly configured) human subject genuinely open to alterity and difference. Critchley argues that this openness to alterity, which emerges from Derrida's engagement with Levinas, is essential to deconstruction and forms deconstruction's central ethical imperative (see Critchley 1999a; 1999b). The claim that deconstruction functions primarily out of an ethical horizon certainly contradicts the mistaken yet widely held view that deconstruction rejects all traditional forms of thought, including ethics (for further analysis of the problematic of postmodernism and ethics, see Bauman 1993). Critchley's position has not influenced, for example, Stephen Moore's deconstructive writings. It has, however, started to influence other biblical postmodernists, especially Gary Phillips. See especially Eskanazi and Phillips eds.; Fewell and Phillips eds.; Phillips 1994.

5 The relationship between modernity and postmodernism is a complicated one, although it seems to me to be a mistake to see postmodernism as having broken free from and stepped beyond modernity. For helpful introductions to postmodernism, see Adam ed.; The Bible and Culture Collective.

6 For examples of this, in relationship to Heidegger, see Caputo 1993; Krell 1992; van Buren 363–393.

7 For an evaluation of Derrida's politics, see Critchley 1999a: 188–200; 1999b: 143–182. For a discussion of the relationship between deconstruction and postcolonialism, see Critchley 1999b: 122–142.

BIBLIOGRAPHY

Achtemeier, P. (1969) *An Introduction to the New Hermeneutic*, Philadelphia: Westminster Press.

Adam, A.K.M. (1995) *What is Postmodern Biblical Criticism?*, Minneapolis: Fortress Press.

Adam, A.K.M., ed. (2000) *Handbook of Postmodern Biblical Interpretation*, St. Louis: Chalice Press.

Adorno, T. (1973) *The Jargon of Authenticity*, trans. K. Tarnowski and F. Will, Evanston, Ill.: Northwestern University Press.

Anderson, V. (1995) *Beyond Ontological Blackness: An Essay on African-American Religious and Cultural Criticism*, New York: Continuum.

Appiah, K.A. (1992) *In My Father's House: Africa in the Philosophy of Culture*, New York: Oxford University Press.

Armour, E. (1999) *Deconstruction, Feminist Theology, and the Problem of Difference: Subverting the Race/Gender Divide*, Chicago: University of Chicago Press.

Arnott, P.D. (1967) *An Introduction to the Greek World*, London: St. Martin's Press.

Ashcraft, M. (1972) *Rudolf Bultmann*, Waco, Tex.: Word Books.

Avineri, S. (1970) "Hegel and Nationalism", pp. 109–136 in *Hegel's Political Philosophy*, ed. Walter Kaufmann, New York: Atherton Press.

Bailey, R. (1991) "Beyond Identification: The Use of Africans in Old Testament Poetry and Narratives", pp. 165–184 in Felder ed.

—— (1995) " 'Is That Any Name for a Nice Hebrew Boy?' Exodus 2:1–10: The De-Africanization of an Israelite Hero", pp. 25–36 in Bailey and Grant eds.

Bailey, R., and J. Grant, eds. (1995) *The Recovery of Black Presence: An Interdisciplinary Exploration*, Nashville: Abingdon Press.

Baird, W. (1992) *History of New Testament Research: From Deism to Tübingen*, vol. i, Minneapolis: Fortress Press.

Baranowski, S. (1999) "The Confessing Church and Antisemitism: Protestant Identity, German Nationhood, and the Exclusion of the Jews", pp. 90–109 in Ericksen and Heschel eds.

Barkan, E. (1992) *The Retreat of Scientific Racism: Changing Concepts of Race in Britain and the United States Between the World Wars*, Cambridge: Cambridge University Press.

Barnes, K.C. (1999) "Dietrich Bonhoeffer and Hitler's Persecution of the Jews", pp. 110–128 in Ericksen and Heschel eds.

Barnett, V. (1992) *For the Soul of the People: Protestant Protest Against Hitler*, New York: Oxford University Press.

Bauer, B. (1958) *The Jewish Problem*, trans. H. Lederer, Cincinnati, Ohio: Hebrew Union College (Readings in Modern Jewish History, ed. E. Rivkin).

Bauman, Z. (1989) *Modernity and the Holocaust*, Ithaca: Cornell University Press.

—— (1992) *Intimations of Postmodernity*, London: Routledge.

—— (1993) *Postmodern Ethics*, Oxford: Blackwell.

Baur, F.C. (1831) "Die Christuspartei in der korinthischen Gemeinder, der Gegensatz des petrinischen und paulinischen Christenthums in der ältesten Kirche, der Apostel Petrus in Rom", *Tübinger Zeitschrift für Theologie* 5 (1831): 61–206.

—— (1860) *Das Christenthum und die christliche Kirche der drei ersten Jarhhunderte*, 2nd edn, Tübingen: Fues.

—— (1866–7) *Paulus, der Apostel Jesu Christi: Sein Leben und Wirken, seine Breife und seine Lehre*, 2nd edn, 2 vols, Leipzig: Fues.

—— (1876) *Paul, the Apostle of Jesus Christ, His Life and Work, and His Epistles and His Doctrine: A Contribution to a Critical History of Primitive Christianity*, 2 vols, trans. A. Menzies, London: Williams and Norgate.

—— (1878) *The Church History of the First Three Centuries*, 3 vols, trans. A. Menzies, London: Williams and Norgate.

—— (1968a) *Ferdinand Christian Baur on the Writing of Church History*, ed. and trans. P. Hodgson, New York: Oxford University Press (Library of Protestant Thought).

—— (1968b) "Introduction to Lectures on the History of Christian Dogma", trans. P. Hodgson in Baur 1968a.

Beiser, F. (1987) *The Fate of Reason: German Philosophy from Kant to Fichte*, Cambridge, Mass.: Harvard University Press.

—— (1992) *Enlightenment, Revolution, and Romanticism: The Genesis of Modern German Political Thought, 1790–1800*, Cambridge, Mass.: Harvard University Press.

—— (1993a) "Introduction: Hegel and the Problem of Metaphysics", pp. 1–24 in Beiser ed.

—— (1993b) "Hegel's Historicism", pp. 270–300 in Beiser ed.

Beiser, F. ed. (1993) *The Cambridge Companion to Hegel*, Cambridge: Cambridge University Press.

Beistegui, M.D. (1998) *Heidegger and the Political: Thinking the Political*, London: Routledge.

Bergen, D. (1996) *Twisted Cross: The German Christian Movement in the Third Reich*, Chapel Hill: University of North Carolina Press.

—— (1999) "Storm Troopers for Christ: The German Christian Movement and the Ecclesiastical Final Solution", pp. 40–67 in Ericksen and Heschel eds.

Berghahn, K. (1988) "From Classicist to Classical Literary Criticism, 1730–1806", pp. 13–98 in Hohendahl ed.

Bernal, M. (1987) *Black Athena: The Afroasiatic Roots of Classical Civilization, The Fabrication of Ancient Greece 1785–1985*, New Brunswick: Rutgers University Press.

Bernasconi, R. (1995a) "Heidegger and the Invention of the Western Philosophical Tradition", *Journal of the British Society for Phenomenology* 26/3 (1995): 240–254.

—— (1995b) "On Heidegger's Other Sins of Omission: His Exclusion of Asian Thought from the Origin of Occidental Metaphysics and His Denial of the Possibility of Christian Philosophy", *American Catholic Philosophical Quarterly* 69/2 (1995): 333–349.

Bible and Culture Collective (1995) *The Postmodern Bible*, New Haven: Yale University Press.

Bornkamm, G. "The Missionary Stance of Paul in I Corinthians 9 and Acts", pp. 194–207 in Keck and Martyn eds.

Bourdieu, P. (1991) *The Political Ontology of Martin Heidegger*, trans. P. Collier, Stanford, Calif.: Stanford University Press.

Boyarin, D. (1994) *A Radical Jew: Paul and the Politics of Identity*, Berkeley: University of California Press.

Breitman, R. (1991) *The Architect of Genocide: Himmler and the Final Solution*, New York: Knopf.

Brent, L. (aka Hariet Jacobs) (1987) *Incidents in the Life of a Slave Girl*, pp. 333–515 in Gates ed.

Brown, R. (1994) *The Death of the Messiah: From Gethsemane to the Grave. A Commentary on the Passion Narratives in the Four Gospels*, 2 vols with continuous pagination, Anchor Bible Reference Library, New York: Doubleday.

Brumlik, M. (1999) "Post-Holocaust Theology: German Theological Responses since 1945", pp. 169–188 in Ericksen and Heschel eds.

Bultmann, R. (1933) "Die Aufgabe der Theologie in der gegenwärtigen Situation", *Theologische Blätter* 12 (June 1933): 161–166.

—— (1948) *Theologie des Neuen Testaments*, Tübingen: Mohr.

—— (1951a) "Neues Testament und Mythologie", in *Kerygma und Mythos* i, 2nd edn, ed. H.W. Bartsch, Hamburg: Herb Reich-Evangelischer Verlag.

—— (1951b) *Theology of the New Testament*, vol. i, trans. K. Grobel, New York: Charles Scribner's Sons.

—— (1955a) *Essays: Philosophical and Theological*, trans. J.C.N. Greig, London: SCM Press.

—— (1955b) *Theology of the New Testament*, vol. ii, trans. K. Grobel, New York: Charles Scribner's Sons.

—— (1956) *Primitive Christianity in its Contemporary Setting*, trans. R.H. Fuller, New York: Meridian Books.

—— (1957) *History and Eschatology: The Presence of Eternity*, New York: Harper and Row.

—— (1958) *Jesus Christ and Mythology*, New York: Charles Scribner's Sons.

—— (1960) *Existence and Faith: Shorter Writings of Rudolf Bultmann*, trans. and ed. S. Ogden, New York: Meridian Books.

—— (1966) "Der Arier-Paragraph im Raum der Kirche", in W. Fürst ed., *"Dialektische Theologie" in Scheidung und Bewährung 1933–1936: Aufsätze, Gutachten und Erklärungen*, Munich: Chr. Kaiser.

—— (1969) *Faith and Understanding*, trans. L.P. Smith, New York: Harper and Row.

—— (1984) *New Testament and Mythology and Other Basic Writings*, trans. and ed. S. Ogden, Philadelphia: Fortress Press.

—— (1991) *Rudolf Bultmann: Interpreting Faith for the Modern Era*, ed R.A. Johnson, The Making of Modern Theology, 2, Minneapolis: Fortress Press.

Caputo, J. (1993) *Demythologizing Heidegger*, Bloomington: Indiana University Press.

—— (1997) *The Prayers and Tears of Jacques Derrida: Religion Without Religion*, Bloomington and Indianapolis: Indiana University Press.

Carmichael, J. (1992) *The Satanizing of the Jews: Origin and Development of Mystical Anti-Semitism*, New York: Fromm International.

Carroll, D. (1995) *French Literary Fascism: Nationalism, Anti-Semitism and the Ideology of Culture*, Princeton, N.J.: Princeton University Press.

Cesarani, D., ed. (1996) *The Final Solution: Origins and Implementation*, London: Routledge.

Conzelmann, H. (1954) *Die Mitte Der Zeit: Studien zur Theologie des Lukas*, Tübingen: Mohr (Paul Siebeck).

—— (1961) *The Theology of St. Luke*, trans. Geoffrey Buswell, New York: Harper and Row.

Copelston, F. (1960) *A History of Philosophy*, vol. vi: *Modern Philosophy II: Kant*, New York: Image Books.

Copher, C. (1991) "The Black Presence in the Old Testament", pp. 146–164 in Felder ed.

Critchley, S. (1999a) *The Ethics of Deconstruction: Derrida and Levinas*, 2nd edn, West Lafayette, Ind.: Purdue University Press.

—— (1999b) *Ethics–Politics–Subjectivity: Essays on Derrida, Levinas and Contemporary French Thought*, London: Verso.

Crossan, J.D. (1973) *In Parables: The Challenge of the Historical Jesus*, New York: Harper and Row.

—— (1975) *The Dark Interval: Towards a Theology of Story*, Allen, Tex.: Argus Communication.

—— (1976) *Raids on the Articulate: Comic Eschatology in Jesus and Borges*, New York: Harper and Row.

—— (1980) *Cliffs of Fall: Paradox and Polyvalence in the Parables of Jesus*, New York: Seabury.

—— (1995) *Who Killed Jesus?: Exposing the Roots of Anti-Semitism in the Gospel Story of the Death of Jesus*, San Francisco: HarperSanFrancisco.

Dallmayr, F. (1993) *The Other Heidegger*, Ithaca: Cornell University Press.

de Man, P. (1982) "Sign and Symbol in Hegel's *Aesthetics*", *Critical Inquiry* 8/4 (1982): 761–775.

—— (1983a) "Hegel on the Sublime", pp. 139–153 in M. Krupnick, ed., *Displacement: Derrida and After*, Bloomington: Indiana University Press.

—— (1983b) "The Rhetoric of Temporality", pp. 187–208 in *Blindness and Insight: Essays in the Rhetoric of Contemporary Criticism*, 2nd edn, London: Methuen.

—— (1984) "Phenomenality and Materiality in Kant", pp. 121–144 in G. Shapiro and A. Sica, eds., *Hermeneutics: Questions and Prospects*, Amherst: University of Massachusetts Press.

—— (1986) *Resistance to Theory*, Minneapolis: University of Minnesota Press.

Derrida, J. (1978) *Writing and Difference*, trans. A. Bass, Chicago: University of Chicago Press.

—— (1982a) *Positions*, trans. A. Bass, Chicago: University of Chicago Press.

—— (1982b) *Margins of Philosophy*, trans. A. Bass, Chicago: University of Chicago Press.

—— (1988) "Like the Sound of the Sea Deep Within a Shell: Paul de Man's War", *Critical Inquiry* 14 (1998): 590–652.

—— (1989) *Of Spirit: Heidegger and the Question*, trans. G. Bennington and R. Bowlby, Chicago: University of Chicago Press.

—— (1990) *Glas*, trans. J.P. Leavey Jr. and R. Rand, Lincoln, Neb.: University of Nebraska Press.

—— (1991) *Between the Blinds: A Derrida Reader*, ed. P. Kamuf, New York: Columbia University Press.

—— (1995) *Points . . . Interviews, 1974–1994*, ed. E. Weber, Stanford, Calif,: Stanford University Press.

Diamond, J. (1994) "Race Without Color", pp. 83–89 in Hoffman ed.

Dodd, C.H. (1961) *The Parables of the Kingdom*, rev. edn, New York: Scribner.

Donahue, J. SJ (1981) "Jesus as the Parable of God in the Gospel of Mark", pp. 148–167 in J.L. Mays, ed., *Interpreting the Gospels,* Philadelphia: Fortress Press.

Douglass, F. (1987) *Narrative of the Life of Frederick Douglass, An African Slave*, pp. 243–331 in Gates ed.

—— (1993) "What to the Slave is the Fourth of July?", pp. 157–160 in *Crossing the Danger Water: Four Hundred Years of African-American Writing*, ed. Deirdre Mullane, New York: Anchor Books.

Dreyfus, H.L. (1994) *Being-in-the-World: A Commentary on Heidegger's Being and Time, Division I*, Cambridge, Mass.: MIT Press.

DuBois, W.E.B. (1990) *The Souls of Black Folk*, New York: First Vintage Books (Library of America Editions).

Eagleton, T. (1990) *The Ideology of the Aesthetic*, Oxford: Blackwell.

Ebeling, G. (1964) "Word of God and Hermeneutic", trans. J. Leitch, pp. 78–110 in Robinson and Cobb eds. 1964.

Ericksen, R.P. (1985) *Theologians Under Hitler: Gerhard Kittel, Paul Althaus and Emmaneul Hirsh*, New Haven: Yale University Press.

—— (1999) "Assessing the Heritage: German Protestant Theologians, Nazis, and 'the Jewish Question' ", pp. 22–29 in Eriksen and Heschel eds.

Ericksen, R. and S. Heschel, eds. (1999) *Betrayal: German Churches and the Holocaust*, Minneapolis: Fortress Press.

Eskenazi, T., and G. Phillips (forthcoming) *Levinas and Biblical Studies*, Semeia.

Eskola, T. (1996) "An Era of Apologetical Hermeneutics: Detecting a NeoKantian Paradigm of Biblical Interpretation", *Evangelical Quarterly* 68/3 (1996): 329–344.

Ettinger, E. (1995) *Hannah Arendt/Martin Heidegger*, New Haven: Yale University Press.

Farias, V. (1989) *Heidegger and Nazism*, ed. and trans. J. Margolis and T. Rockmore, Philadelphia: Temple University Press.

Felder, C.H. (1993) *Troubling Biblical Waters: Race, Class, and Family*, New York: Orbis Books.

Felder, C.H., ed. (1991) *Stony the Road We Trod: African American Biblical Interpretation*, Minneapolis: Fortress Press.

Ferry, L., and A. Renaut (1990) *Heidegger and Modernity*, trans. Franklin Philip, Chicago: University of Chicago Press.

Fewell, D.N., and G. Phillips (1997) "Drawn to Excess, or Reading Beyond Betrothal", pp. 23–58 in Fewell and Phillips eds.

Fewell, D.N., and G. Phillips, eds. (1997) *Bible and Ethics of Reading*, Semeia 77.

Fischer, K. (1995) *Nazi Germany: A New History*, New York: Continuum.

Fogel, R. (1989) *Without Consent or Contract: The Rise and Fall of American Slavery*, New York: Norton.

Forster, M. (1993) "Hegel's Dialectical Method", pp. 130–170 in Beiser ed.

Foti, V. (1991) *Heidegger and the Poets: Poesis, Sophia, Techne*, New Jersey: Humanities Press.

Foucault, M. (1972) *The Archaeology of Knowledge and the Discourse on Language*, trans. A. Sheridan Smith, New York: Pantheon Books.

—— (1973) *The Order of Things: An Archaeology of the Human Sciences*, New York: Vintage Books.

—— (1979) *Discipline and Punish: The Birth of the Prison*, trans. A. Sheridan, New York: Vintage.

Fowler, R. (1991) *Let the Reader Understand: Reader-Response Criticism and the Gospel of Mark*, Minneapolis: Fortress Press.

Fredrickson, G. (1987) *The Black Image in the White Mind: The Debate on Afro-American Character and Destiny, 1817–1914*, Hanover: Wesleyan University Press.

—— (1988) *The Arrogance of Race: Historical Perspectives on Slavery, Racism and Social Inequality*, Middletown: Wesleyan University Press.

Friedländer, S. (1998) *Nazi Germany and the Jews, vol. i: The Years of Persecution, 1933–1939*, New York: HarperPerennial.

Fritsche, J. (1995) "On Brinks and Bridges in Heidegger", *Graduate Philosophy Journal* 18/1 (1995): 111–186.

—— (1999) *Historical Destiny and National Socialism in Heidegger's Being and Time*, Berkeley: University of California Press.

Fuchs, E. (1964a) "The New Testament and the Hermeneutical Problem", pp. 111–145 in Robinson and Cobb eds. 1964.

—— (1964b) *Studies of the Historical Jesus*, trans. Andrew Scobie, Naperville, Ill. Allenson.

Funk, R. (1966) *Language, Hermeneutic and Word of God*, New York: Harper and Row.

Gasché, R. (1994) *Inventions of Difference: On Jacques Derrida*, Cambridge, Mass.: Harvard University Press.

Gasque, W.W. (1989) *A History of the Interpretation of the Acts of the Apostles*, Peabody, Mass.: Hendrickson.

Gates, H.L. Jr. (1985) "Writing 'Race' and the Difference it Makes", pp. 1–20 in Gates ed.

Gates, H.L., Jr., ed. (1985) *"Race", Writing, and Difference*, Chicago: University of Chicago Press.

—— (1987) *The Classic Slave Narratives*, New York: Mentor Books.

Gay, P. (1967) *The Enlightenment: An Interpretation. The Rise of Modern Paganism*, New York: Knopf.

Gibbon, E. (1910) *Decline and Fall of the Roman Empire*, vol. i, London: Dent.

Gillespie, M.A. (1984) *Hegel, Heidegger, and the Ground of History*, Chicago: University of Chicago Press.

Gilman, S. (1982) *On Blackness Without Blacks: Essays on the Image of the Black in Germany*, Boston: Hall.

—— (1991) *The Jew's Body*, New York: Routledge.

—— (1993) *Freud, Race, and Gender*, Princeton, N.J.: Princeton University Press.

Gilroy, P. (1993) *The Black Atlantic: Modernity and Double Consciousness*, Cambridge. Mass.: Harvard University Press.

Goldberg, D.T. (1993) *Racist Culture: Philosophy and the Politics of Meaning*, Cambridge, Mass.: Blackwell.

Goldhagen, D.J. (1996) *Hitler's Willing Executioners: Ordinary Germans and the Holocaust*, New York: Knopf.

Gould, S.J. (1981) *The Mismeasure of Man*, New York: Norton.

—— (1994) "The Geometer of Race", pp. 65–69 in Hoffman ed.

Guyer, P. (1993) "Thought and Being: Hegel's Critique of Kant's Theoretical Philosophy", pp. 171–210 in Beiser ed.

Haenchen, E. (1971) *The Acts of the Apostles: A Commentary*, trans. B. Noble and G. Shinn, Philadelphia: Westminster Press.

Hamacher, W., N. Hertz and T. Keenan, eds. (1988) *Wartime Journalism, 1939–1943*, Lincoln, Nebr.: University of Nebraska Press.

—— (1989) *Responses: On Paul de Man's Wartime Journalism*, Lincoln, Nebr.: University of Nebraska Press.

Harris, H. (1975) *The Tübingen School*, Oxford: Clarendon.

Harvey, V.A. (1969) *The Historian and the Believer: The Morality of Historical Knowledge and Christian Belief*, New York: Macmillan.

Hegel, G.W.F. (1833) *Georg Wilhelm Friedrich Hegel's Werke XIII, Geschichte der Philosophie*. Berlin: Duncker und Humblot.

—— (1837) *Georg Wilhelm Friedrich Hegel's Werke IX, Philosophie der Geschichte*, Berlin: Duncker und Humblot.

—— (1953a) *Reason in History: A General Introduction to the Philosophy of History*, trans. R.S. Hartman, Indianapolis and New York: Bobbs-Merrill.

—— (1953b) *The Philosophy of Hegel*, ed. C.J. Friedrich, Modern Library College Editions, New York: Random House.

—— (1953c) *Lectures on Aesthetics*, trans. B. Bosanquet and W.M. Bryant, pp. 333–395 in Hegel 1953b.

—— (1953d) *The Philosophy of History*, trans. C.J. and P.W. Friedrich, pp. 1–158 in Hegel 1953b.

—— (1963) *Lectures on the History of Philosophy*, vol. i, trans. E.S. Haldane, London: Routledge and Kegan Paul.

—— (1977) *The Phenomology of Mind*, 2nd edn, trans. J.B. Baille, New York: Humanities Press.

Heidegger, M. (1929) *Sein und Zeit*, 2nd edn, Tübingen: Max Niemeyer.

—— (1959) *An Introduction to Metaphysics*, trans. R. Manheim, New Haven: Yale University Press.

—— (1962) *Being and Time*, trans. J. Macquarrie and E. Robinson, New York: Harper and Row.

—— (1977a) *Basic Writings*, ed. D.F. Krell, New York: Harper and Row.

—— (1977b) *The Question Concerning Technology, and Other Essays*, trans. W. Lovitt, New York: Harper and Row.

—— (1981) "Why Do I Stay in the Provinces?", trans. T. Sheehan, pp. 122–125 in *Heidegger: The Man and The Thinker*, ed. T. Sheehan, Chicago: Precedent.

—— (1993a) "The Self-Assertion of the German University", trans. W.S. Lewis, pp. 29–39 in Wolin ed.

—— (1993b) "Political Texts, 1933–1934", trans. W.S. Lewis, pp. 40 60 in Wolin ed.

—— (1993c) "Letter to the Rector of Freiburg University", trans. R. Wolin, pp. 61–66 in Wolin ed.

—— (1993d) "Only a God Can Save Us", trans. M. Alter and J. Caputo, pp. 91–116 in Wolin ed.

—— (1995) *The Fundamental Concepts of Metaphysics: World, Finitude, Solitude*, in *Studies in Continental Thought*, trans. W. McNeill and N. Walker, Bloomington: Indiana University Press.

Heiman, G. (1971) "The Sources and Significance of Hegel's Corporate Doctrine", pp. 111–135 in Pelczynski ed.

Herder, J.G. von (1968) *Reflections on the Philosophy of the History of Mankind*, trans. T.O. Churchill, Classic European Historians, Chicago: University of Chicago Press.

—— (1989) *Ideen zur Philosophie der Geschichte der Menschheit*, Frankfurt: Deutscher Klassiker Verlag.

Herf, J. (1986) *Reactionary Modernism: Technology, Culture, and Politics in Weimar and the Third Reich*, Cambridge: Cambridge University Press.

Heschel, S. (1998) *Abraham Geiger and the Jewish Jesus*, Chicago: University of Chicago Press.

—— (1999) "When Jesus was an Aryan: The Protestant Church and Anti-Semitic Propaganda", pp. 68–89 in Ericksen and Heschel eds.

Hewitt, A. (1993) *Fascist Modernism: Aesthetics, Politics, and the Avant-Garde*, Stanford: Stanford University Press.

Hilberg, R. (1985) *The Destruction of the European Jews*, 3 vols, New York: Holmes and Meyer.

Hill, C. (1992) *Hellenists and Hebrews: Reappraising Division Within the Earliest Church*, Minneapolis: Fortress Press.

Hodgson, P. (1966) *The Formation of Historical Theology: A Study of Ferdinand Christian Baur*, New York: Harper and Row.

—— (1968) "General Introduction", pp. 3–40 in Baur 1968a.

Hoffman, P. ed. (1994) "Special Issue: The Science of Race", *Discover* 15/1 (November 1994).

Hohendahl, P.U., ed. (1988) *A History of German Literary Criticism, 1730–1980*, Lincoln, Nebr.: University of Nebraska Press.

Hood, R. (1994) *Begrimed and Black: Christian Traditions on Blacks and Blackness*, Minneapolis: Fortress Press.

Iggers, G. (1983) *The German Conception of History: The National Tradition of Historical Thought from Herder to the Present*, rev. edn, Hanover: Wesleyan University Press.

Inwood, M. (1993) *A Hegel Dictionary*, Oxford: Blackwell.

Jaspers, K. (1993) "Letter to the Freiburg University Denazification Committee", trans. R. Wolin, pp. 147–151 in Wolin ed.

Jeremias, J. (1972) *The Parables of Jesus*, 2nd rev. edn, trans. S. H. Hooke, New York: Charles Scribner's Sons.

Johnson, R. (1991) "Introduction", pp. 9–43 in Bultmann 1991.

Jonas, H. (1990) "Heidegger Resoluteness and Resolve", pp. 197–203 in Neske and Kettering.

Joyce, J. (1965) *A Portrait of the Artist as a Young Man*, New York: Viking.

Käsemann, E. (1964) *Essays on New Testament Themes*, trans. W.J. Montague, London: SCM Press.

—— (1969a) *Jesus Means Freedom*, trans. F. Clark, Philadelphia: Fortress Press.

—— (1969b) *New Testament Questions for Today*, trans. W.J. Montague, Philadelphia: Fortress Press.

—— (1969c) *Paulinische Perspektiven*, Tübingen: Mohr (Paul Siebeck).

—— (1971) *Perspectives on Paul*, trans. M. Kohl, Philadelphia: Fortress Press.

Katz, S. (1992) "1918 and After: The Role of Racial Antisemitism in the Nazi Analysis of the Weimar Republic", pp. 74–104 in *Historicism, the Holocaust, and Zionism: Critical Studies in Modern Jewish Thought and History*, New York: New York University Press.

Keck, L., and J.L. Martyn, eds. (1966) *Studies in Luke–Acts*, Nashville: Abingdon Press.

Kelber, W. (1983) *The Oral and the Written Gospel: The Hermeneutics of Speaking and Writing in the Synoptic Tradition, Mark, Paul, and Q*, Philadelphia: Fortress Press.

Kelley, S. (2000) "Race", pp. 213–219 in Adam ed.

Kershaw, I. (1999) *Hitler: Hubris, 1889–1936*, New York: Norton.
—— (2000) *Hitler: Nemesis, 1936–1945*, New York: Norton.
Kisiel, T. (1992) "Heidegger's Apology: Biography as Philosophy and Ideology", pp. 11–51 in Rockmore and Margolis eds.
—— (1995) *The Genesis of Heidegger's Being and Time*, Berkeley: University of California Press.
Kisiel, T., and J. van Buren, eds. (1994) *Reading Heidegger from the Start: Essays in His Earliest Thought*, Albany: SUNY Press.
Krell, D.F. (1977) "General Introduction: 'The Question of Being'", pp. 3–35 in Heidegger 1977a.
—— (1992) *Daimon Life: Heidegger and Life-Philosophy*, Studies in Continental Thought, Bloomington: Indiana University Press.
Kümmel, W.G. (1972) *The New Testament: The History of the Investigation of its Problems*, 2nd edn, trans. S.M. Gilmour and H. C. Kee, Nashville: Abingdon.
—— (1975) "Current Theological Accusations against Luke", *Andover Newton Quarterly* 16 (1975): 131–145.
Lacoue-Labarthe, P. (1990) *Heidegger, Art and Politics: The Fiction of the Political*, trans. C. Turner, Cambridge, Mass.: Blackwell.
Lacoue-Labarthe, P. and J.-L. Nancy (1990) "The Nazi Myth", trans. Brian Holmes, *Critical Inquiry* 16 (1990): 291–312.
Lang, B. (1996) *Heidegger's Silence*, Ithaca: Cornell University Press.
Langmuir, G. (1990) *Toward a Definition of AntiSemitism*, Berkeley: University of California Press.
Lentricchia, F. (1980) *After the New Criticism*, Chicago: University of Chicago Press.
—— (1983) *Criticism and Social Change*, Chicago: University of Chicago Press.
Levinas, E. (1961) *Totality and Infinity: Essays on Exteriority*, trans. A. Lingis, Pittsburgh: Duquesne University Press.
—— (1989) "As If Consenting to Horror", trans. P. Wissing, *Critical Inquiry* 15 (1989): 485–488.
Löwith, K. (1993a) "The Political Implications of Heidegger's Existentialism", trans. R. Wolin, pp. 167–185 in Wolin ed.
—— (1993b) "My Last Meeting with Heidegger in Rome, 1936", trans. R. Wolin, pp. 140–143 in Wolin ed.
Lyotard, J.-F. (1990) *Heidegger and "The Jews"*, trans. A. Michel and M. Roberts, Minneapolis: University of Minnesota Press.
Manuel, F. (1959) *Eighteenth Century Confronts the Gods*, Cambridge, Mass.: Harvard University Press.
—— (1992) *The Broken Staff: Judaism Through Christian Eyes*, Cambridge, Mass.: Harvard University Press.
Marcuse, H., and M. Heidegger (1993) "An Exchange of Letters", pp. 160–164 in Wolin ed.
Marsch, C. (1997) "Quests of the Historical Jesus in New Historicist Perspective", *Biblical Interpretation* 5/4 (1997): 403–437.
Martin, C. (1989) "A Chamberlain's Journey", *Semeia* 47 (1989): 105–135.
Mays, J.L., ed. (1981) *Interpreting the Gospels*, Philadelphia: Fortress Press.

Moore, S. (1989) *Literary Criticism and the Gospels: The Theoretical Challenge*, New Haven: Yale University Press.

—— (1992) *Mark and Luke in Poststructuralist Perspectives: Jesus Begins to Write*, New Haven: Yale University Press.

Mörchen, H. (1981) *Adorno und Heidegger*, Stuttgart: Klett-Cotta.

Mosse, G.L. (1964) *The Crisis of German Ideology: Intellectual Origins of the Third Reich*, New York: Universal Library.

Mulhall, S. (1966) *Heidegger and Being and Time*, Routledge Philosophy Guidebooks, London: Routledge.

Müller, M. (1990) "Martin Heidegger: A Philosopher and Politics: A Conversation", pp. 175–195 in Neske and Kettering.

Nanos, M. (1996) *The Mystery of Romans: The Jewish Context of Paul's Letters*, Minneapolis: Fortress Press.

Neske, G., and E. Kettering (1990) *Martin Heidegger and National Socialism*, trans. L. Harries and J. Neugroschel, New York: Paragon House.

Norris, C. (1988) *Paul de Man: Deconstruction and the Critique of Aesthetic Ideology*, London: Routledge.

—— (1990) *What's Wrong with Postmodernism: Critical Theory and the Ends of Philosophy*, Baltimore: Johns Hopkins University Press.

Ogden, S. (1961) *Christ Without Myth: A Study Based on the Theology of Rudolf Bultmann*, New York: Harper and Row.

Ott, H. (1993) *Martin Heidegger: A Political Life*, trans. A. Blunden, New York: Basic Books.

Pelczynski, Z.A., ed. (1971) *Hegel's Political Philosophy: Problems and Perspectives*, Cambridge: Cambridge University Press.

Perrin, N. (1963) *The Kingdom of God in the Teaching of Jesus*, Philadelphia: Westminster Press.

—— (1967) *Rediscovering the Teaching of Jesus*, New York: Harper and Row.

—— (1969) *The Promise of Bultmann*, Philadelphia: Lippincott.

—— (1972) "Historical Criticism, Literary Criticism and Hermeneutics: The Interpretation of the Parables of Jesus and the Gospel of Mark Today", *Journal of Religion* 52 (1972): 361–375.

—— (1974) *A Modern Pilgrimage in New Testament Christology*, Philadelphia: Fortress Press.

—— (1977) *The Resurrection According to Matthew, Mark and Luke*, Philadelphia: Fortress Press.

Pfeiffer, R. (1976) *History of Classical Scholarship from 1300 to 1850*, Oxford: Clarendon Press.

Phillips, G. (1994) "The Ethics of Reading Deconstructively, or Speaking Face-to-Face: The Samaritan Woman Meets Derrida at the Well", pp. 283–325 in *The New Literary Criticism and the New Testament*, ed. E.S. Malbon and E. McKnight, Sheffield: Sheffield Academic Press.

Phillips, G., and D. Fewell (1997) "Ethics, Bible, Reading As If", pp. 1–21 in Fewell and Phillips eds.

Pippin, R. (1993) "You Can't Get There From Here: Transition Problems in Hegel's *Phenomenology of Spirit*", pp. 52–84 in Beiser ed.

Pöggler, O. (1987) *Martin Heidegger's Path of Thinking*, 2nd edn, trans. D. Magurshak and S. Barber, Atlantic Highlands, N.J.: Humanities Press.

—— (1990) "Heidegger, Nietzsche, and Politics", pp. 114–140 in Rockmore and Margolis eds.

—— (1993) "Heidegger's Political Self-Understanding", trans. S. Crowell, pp. 198–244 in Wolin ed.

Poliakov, L. (1974) *The Aryan Myth: A History of Racist and Nationalist Ideas in Europe*, trans. E. Howard, New York: Basic Books.

Redding, P. (1996) *Hegel's Hermeneutics*, Ithaca; Cornell University Press.

Renan, E. (1888) *History of the People of Israel Till the Time of King David*, vol. i, trans. C.B. Pitman and D. Bingham, London: Chapman and Hall.

—— (1947–61) *Histoire générale et système comparé des langues sémitiques*, in vol. viii of *Œuvres complètes*, ed. H. Psichari, Paris: Calmann-Lévy.

Ricoeur, P. (1974) "Preface to Bultmann", trans. P. McCormick, pp. 381–401 in *The Conflict of Interpretations: Essays in Hermeneutics*, ed. Don Ihde, Northwestern University Studies in Phenomenology and Existential Philosophy, Evanston: Northwestern University Press.

Robinson, J.M. (1959) *A New Quest of the Historical Jesus*, London: SCM Press.

—— (1963) "The German Discussion of the Later Heidegger", pp. 3–76 in Robinson and Cobb eds. 1963.

—— (1964) "Hermeneutics since Barth", pp. 1–77 in Robinson and Cobb eds. 1964.

—— (1971) "Introduction", pp. 1–5 in Robinson ed.

Robinson, J.M., ed. (1971) *The Future of our Religious Past: Essays in Honour of Rudolf Bultmann*, trans. C.E. Carlston and R. P. Scharlemann, New York: Harper and Row.

Robinson, J.M., and J.B. Cobb, eds. (1963) *New Frontiers in Theology*, i: *The Later Heidegger and Theology*, New York: Harper and Row.

—— (1964) *New Frontiers in Theology, ii: The New Hermeneutic*, New York: Harper and Row.

Rockmore, T. (1992) *On Heidegger's Nazism and Philosophy*, Berkeley: University of California Press.

Rockmore, T., and J. Margolis, eds. (1992) *The Heidegger Case: On Philosophy and Politics*, Philadelphia: Temple University Press.

Rose, P.L. (1990) *German Question/Jewish Question: Revolutionary AntiSemitism from Kant to Wagner*, Princeton: Princeton University Press.

Safranski, R. (1998) *Martin Heidegger: Between Good and Evil*, trans. E. Osers, Cambridge, Mass.: Harvard University Press.

Said, E. (1979) *Orientalism*, New York: Vintage.

—— (1983) *The World, the Text, and the Critic*, Cambridge, Mass.: Harvard University Press.

—— (1994) *Culture and Imperialism*, New York: Vintage.

Sanders, B. (1995) "In Search of a Face for Simon of Cyrene", pp. 51–64 in Bailey and Grant eds.

Sanders, E.P. (1977) *Paul and Palestinian Judaism: A Comparison of Patterns of Religion*, Philadelphia: Fortress Press.

—— (1985) *Jesus and Judaism*, Philadelphia: Fortress Press.

Schama, S. (1996) *Landscape and Memory*, New York: Vintage.

Schulte-Sasse, J. (1988) "The Concept of Literary Criticism in German Romanticism, 1795–1810", pp. 99–178 in Hohendahl ed.

Schweitzer, A. (1959) *The Quest of the Historical Jesus: A Critical Study of its Progress from Reimarus to Wrede*, trans. W. Montgomery, New York: Macmillan.

Sheehan, T. (1979) "Heidegger's 'Introduction to the Phenomenology of Religion', 1920–1921", *The Personalist* 60 (July 1979): 312–324.

—— (1988) "Heidegger and the Nazis", *The New York Review of Books*, 16 June, 1988: 38–47.

—— (1993) "A Normal Nazi", *The New York Review of Books*, 14 January 1993: 30–35.

Shklar, J. (1971) "Hegel's 'Phenomenology': An Elogy for Hellas", pp. 73–89 in Pelczylnski ed.

Shreeve, J. (1994) "Terms of Estrangement", pp. 57–63 in Hoffman ed.

Sluga, H. (1993) *Heidegger's Crisis: Philosophy and Politics in Nazi Germany*, Cambridge, Mass.: Harvard University Press.

Snowden, F. (1970) *Blacks in Antiquity: Ethiopians in the Greco-Roman Experience*, Cambridge, Mass.: Harvard University Press.

—— (1983) *Before Color Prejudice: The Ancient View of Blacks*, Cambridge, Mass.: Harvard University Press.

Sophocles (1908) *The Antigone of Sophocles*, trans. and commentary R.C. Jebb, abridged E.S. Shuckburgh, Cambridge: Cambridge University Press.

Stendahl, K. (1976) *Paul Among Jews and Gentiles, and Other Essays*, Philadelphia: Fortress Press.

Stepan, N. (1982) *The Idea of Race in Science: Great Britain, 1800–1960*, London: Macmillan.

Sussman, H. (1997) *The Aesthetic Contract: Statutes of Art and Intellectual Work in Modernity*, Stanford: Stanford University Press.

Tal, U. (1975) *Christians and Jews in Germany: Religion, Politics, and Ideology in the Second Reich, 1870–1914*, trans. N.J. Jacobs, Ithaca: Cornell University Press.

Talbert, C. (1981) "Shifting Sands: The Recent Study of the Gospel of Luke", pp. 197–213 in Mays ed.

Tolbert, M.A. (1979) *Perspectives on Parables: An Approach to Multiple Interpretations*, Philadelphia: Fortress Press.

Tucker, J. (1998) *Example Stories: Perspectives on Four Parables in the Gospel of Luke*, Sheffield: Sheffield Academic Press.

Turner, F. (1981) *The Greek Heritage in Victorian Britain*, New Haven: Yale University Press.

van Buren, J. (1994) *The Young Heidegger: Rumor of the Hidden King*, Studies in Continental Thought, Bloomington: Indiana University Press.

van Unnik, W.C. (1966) "Luke–Acts, as Storm Center in Contemporary Scholarship", pp. 15–32 in Keck and Martyn eds.

Vielhauer, P. (1966) "On the 'Paulinism' of Acts", pp. 33–50 in Keck and Martyn eds.

Walsh, W.H. (1971) "Principle and Prejudice in Hegel's Philosophy of History", pp. 181–198 in Pelczynski ed.

Ward, J. (1995) *Heidegger's Political Thinking*, Amherst: University of Massachusetts Press.

Waters, J. (1991) "Who Was Hagar?", pp. 187–205 in Felder ed.

Weiss, J. (1996) *Ideology of Death: Why the Holocaust Happened in Germany*, Chicago: Ivan R. Dee Press.

West, C. (1982) *Prophecy-Deliverance: An Afro-American Revolutionary Christianity*, Philadelphia: Westminster Press.

Wicks, R. (1993) "Hegel's Aesthetics: An Overview", pp. 348–377 in Beiser ed.

Wilckens, U. (1966) "Interpreting Luke–Acts in a Period of Existentialist Theology", pp. 60–83 in Keck and Martyn eds.

Wilder, A. (1971) *Early Christian Rhetoric: The Language of the Gospel*, 2nd edn, Cambridge, Mass.: Harvard University Press.

Wolin, R. (1990) *The Politics of Being: The Political Thought of Martin Heidegger, 1927–1966*, New York: Columbia University Press.

—— (1993a) "'Over the Line': Reflections on Heidegger and National Socialism", pp. 1–22 in Wolin ed.

—— (1993b) "Preface to the MIT Press Edition: Note on a Missing Text", pp. ix–xx in Wolin ed.

—— (1993c) "French Heidegger Wars", pp. 272–300 in Wolin ed.

Wolin, R., ed. (1993) *The Heidegger Controversy: A Critical Reader*, Cambridge, Mass.: MIT Press.

Wood, A. (1993) "Hegel's Ethics", pp. 211–233 in Beiser ed.

Young, J. (1997) *Heidegger, Philosophy, Nazism*, Cambridge: Cambridge University Press.

Young, R. (1990) *White Mythologies: Writing History and the West*, London: Routledge.

—— (1995) *Colonial Desire: Hybridity in Theory, Culture, and Race*, London: Routledge.

Zimmerman, M. (1986) *Eclipse of the Self: The Development of Heidegger's Concept of Authenticity*, rev. edn, Athens: Ohio University Press.

—— (1990) *Heidegger's Confrontation with Modernity: Technology, Politics, Art*, Indiana Series in the Philosophy of Technology, Bloomington: Indiana University Press.

INDEX